P9-BZL-205

NATIONALISM, DEMOCRACY AND DEVELOPMENT

NATIONALISM, DEMOCRACY AND DEVELOPMENT
State and Politics in India

Edited by

SUGATA BOSE
AYESHA JALAL

OXFORD
UNIVERSITY PRESS

OXFORD
UNIVERSITY PRESS

YMCA Library Building, Jai Singh Road, New Delhi 110 001

Oxford University Press is a department of the University of Oxford. It furthers the
University's objective of excellence in research, scholarship, and education
by publishing worldwide in

Oxford   New York

Auckland   Cape Town   Dar es Salaam   Hong Kong   Karachi   Kuala Lumpur
Madrid   Melbourne   Mexico City   Nairobi   New Delhi   Shanghai   Taipei   Toronto

With offices in

Argentina   Austria   Brazil   Chile   Czech Republic   France   Greece   Guatemala
Hungary   Italy   Japan   Poland   Portugal   Singapore   South Korea   Switzerland
Thailand   Turkey   Ukraine   Vietnam

Oxford is a registered trademark of Oxford University Press
in the UK and in certain other countries

Published in India
by Oxford University Press, New Delhi

© Oxford University Press 1997

The moral rights of the author have been asserted
Database right Oxford University Press (maker)

First published 1997
Oxford India Paperbacks 1998
Seventh impression 2008

All rights reserved. No part of this publication may be reproduced,
or transmitted in any form or by any means, electronic or mechanical,
including photocopying, recording or by any information storage and
retrieval system, without permission in writing from Oxford University Press.
Enquiries concerning reproduction outside the scope of the above should be
sent to the Rights Department, Oxford University Press, at the address above

You must not circulate this book in any other binding or cover
and you must impose this same condition on any acquirer

ISBN-13: 978-0-19-564442-5
ISBN-10: 0-19-564442-5

Typeset by Excellent Laser Typesetters, Delhi 110 034
Printed in India at Pauls Press, New Delhi 110 020
Published by Oxford University Press
YMCA Library Building, Jai Singh Road, New Delhi 110 001

Contents

Contributors

Pranab Bardhan is Professor of Economics at the University of California, Berkeley, and co-chair of the MacArthur Foundation.

Sugata Bose is Gardiner Professor of Oceanic History and Affairs, South Asia at the Department of History, Harvard University.

Sumantra Bose is Reader in Comparative Politics, the London School of Economics and Politics.

Jayati Ghosh is Professor of Economics at Jawaharlal Nehru University.

Ayesha Jalal is Professor of History at Tufts University.

Anartya Sen is Lamont University Professor, Harvard University; Professor of Economics and Philosophy, Harvard University; Senior Fellow, Harvard Society of Fellows.

David Washbrook is Reader in Modern South Asian History, St Antony's College, University of Oxford.

1

Nationalism, Democracy and Development

Sugata Bose and Ayesha Jalal

Nationalism, democracy and development, variously defined, have capped the agendas of states and societies which emerged from Western colonial rule in the aftermath of World War II. In the early years of independence the ideal of democracy was unproblematically seen as the mediating link between the emotion of nationalism and the promise of development. Although chalking a democratic path to development became the concern of most post-colonial nation-states, the relationship between democracy and development has never been a simple one of means and goal. The establishment of a democratic process or its restoration after brief or lengthy spells of dictatorship has often had to be a primary political aim in the post-colonial world. Even where formal electoral exercises have regularly taken place, the absence of development in the sense of an equitable and just distribution of resources has not infrequently put a question mark on the quality and substance of such a democracy.[1] The complementary, contradictory, reciprocal and symbiotic aspects of the complex relationship between nationalism, democracy and development can be better delineated through a new and imaginative set of enquiries informed by theory and an openness to comparison that is firmly grounded in the empirical context of one of the most important countries of the developing world.

The denial of democracy as well as development had been the strongest condemnation of the colonial state voiced by the forces of anti-colonial nationalism. Yet nationalism, as a good deal of recent theoretical literature on the subject has been reiterating, is a truly Janus-faced phenomenon.[2] Its emancipatory potential was vitiated in large measure

[1] On the distinction between formal and substantive democracy see Ayesha Jalal, *Democracy and Authoritarianism in South Asia: A Comparative and Historical Perspective* (Cambridge: Cambridge University Press, 1995), Introduction.

[2] See, for instance, Benedict Anderson, *Imagined Communities: Reflections on the Origin and Spread of Nationalism* (London: Verso, 1991), Ch. 9.

by the homogenizing and hegemonizing agendas of the nation-state. Justified in terms of a liberating ideology of nationalism, these processes were sought to be sustained and promoted through barely modified institutional structures inherited from the colonial era. This institutional legacy at once qualified the democratic claims of the nation-state, even where it succeeded in setting in motion electoral processes based on universal adult franchise. While the structural continuities led the post-colonial nation-state to assert its distinctiveness through a developmentalist ideology, the strategies of development reinforced the centralizing and bureaucratic tendencies that nationalist movements had so strenuously combated in the quest for freedom and democracy. Official nationalism as articulated and practised by the post-colonial state became increasingly far removed from the ideals propagated in the anti-colonial period.

The failure to assure substantive democracy and equitable development for significant segments of civil society has resulted in the discrediting and delegitimizing of state-sponsored nationalism. Among the most dramatic manifestations of this have been conflicts along lines of class, caste and community as well as claims to distinctiveness, and at times sovereign national status, put forward by a variety of disenchanted social groups at the regional and sub-regional levels. The paradox of the inclusionary rhetoric of singular nationalism contributing to a rage of exclusionary aspirations has yet to be fully grasped by scholars and policy makers alike. Instead of acknowledging the flaws in the idioms of inclusionary nationalism, state managers have responded to exclusionary challenges by reinforcing the ideational and structural pillars of the nation-state. The disjunction between official policies and societal demands and expectations has never been more critical.

While the deepening malaise of the modern nation-state is scarcely in doubt, the diagnoses and prescriptions remain matters of considerable disagreement and debate. Some have detected the roots of the problem in the very condition of modernity as transposed and superimposed by colonialism on the subcontinent. This large critique of modernity has fostered a rejection of the very goal of development and its accompanying justificatory values of science and reason.[3] The ideal of democracy has

---

[3] For variants of the anti-modernist critique of development, see Frederique Apffel Marglin and Stephen Marglin, *Dominating Knowledge: Development, Culture and Resistance* (Oxford: Clarendon Press, 1990); Partha Chatterjee, 'Development Planning and the Indian State' in Terence J. Byres (ed.), *The State and Development Planning in India* (Delhi: Oxford University Press, 1993); Ashis Nandy (ed.), *Science, Hegemony and Violence: A Requiem for Modernity* (Tokyo:

not been tarnished in quite the same way, but its Western transplanted forms have met with their share of scepticism. Attempts to resurrect the values of 'authentic' tradition to obviate the ills of modernity may have their attractions. Yet they are grounded in many of the same ahistorical and essentialized assumptions about 'Indian tradition' for which Western orientalist scholars have been roundly castigated. There is a gaping chasm between particular critiques of development directed by the modern state and the general critique of modernity and its core values embodied in science and reason.[4]

Instead of sliding into a self-indulgent and politically disabling negativism, it seems more appropriate to take up the intellectual challenge of reevaluating nationalism, reinvigorating democracy and reconstituting development. A historical analysis of anti-colonial nationalisms in the South Asian context makes it amply clear that there were many contested visions of nationhood and alternative frameworks for its realization. Democratic norms could be subsumed under a singular conception of the allegiance of individual citizens to the nation-state only at a price. The multiple communitarian affiliations—religious, linguistic, regional, class and caste—of its people, called for a more nuanced configuration of the relationship between nationalism and democracy in the subcontinent. At the same time discrimination and exploitation based on class, caste and gender as well as inequalities along lines of community and region made it imperative to forge a conception of substantive democracy linked to equitable development. Notwithstanding the rhetoric of official ideologies, nationalism, democracy and development, more often than not, became hostage to the power of centralized post-colonial states. Simultaneously, there was a dynamic process of adaptation and appropriation of the values of democracy and development by a variety of non-state, political actors who forged solidarities along regional, communitarian, class or gender affiliations.

A reconceptualization of the webs that tie together nationalism, democracy and development needs to place the problem not in the

United Nations University, 1988) and Ashis Nandy, 'The Political Culture of the Indian State' in *Daedalus*, 118, 4 (Fall), pp. 1–25.

[4] A more elaborate statement of this argument can be found in Sugata Bose, 'Instruments and Idioms of Colonial and National Development: India's Experience in a Comparative and Historical Perspective' in Frederick Cooper and Randall Packard (eds), *International Development and the Social Sciences* (Berkeley: University of California Press, 1997).

context of the tradition versus modernity dichotomy but within the dialectic of dominance and resistance as well as in the context of the imbalances of privilege and deprivation at different levels of the society and polity. Objecting to modern constructions of nationalism, democracy and development as signs of the rude invasion of a globalizing hegemonic culture leaves most of the impediments to popular democratic development untouched. Restoring these categories within a purified indigenous cultural domain might only go a few steps further in entrenching established patterns of dominance and privilege. The celebration of the fragment in a post-modern vein against monolithic modern structures of state and economy may draw attention to the evils of the 'modern'.[5] It does not expose to the full glare of criticism the inequities concealed within the fragment. The critique of all that was wrong with colonial and post-colonial modernity misses its mark when it is launched as an undiscriminating assault on the modern and remains quite incomplete by being located within the cultural domain alone.

Anti-colonial nationalism did not occupy the moral higher ground through its claims of cultural exclusivism. While there was a fair measure of culturally rooted anti-modernism in some strands of nationalism, this did not amount to a lack of selective and creative receptivity to certain aspects of modern humanist values that strengthened projects of internal regeneration and reform. The acceptance of certain aspects of social change tended to reinforce the ability to contest Western colonial power in the domain of politics and the state. And it was a commitment to this political contestation and the willingness to reject the colonial model of the state that imbued nationalism with ethical and legitimizing authority. The particularities of the post-colonial transition in the subcontinent favoured the appropriation or imitation of the colonial state's institutional structure and ideology of monolithic sovereignty. Instead of moulding the inherited state apparatus to better reflect the emotions that had fired the nationalist movements, the imperatives of strategically placed elites in the late colonial era allowed the state to hijack the very idea of the 'nation' and become the sole repository of legitimate nationalism.

The critique of the modern nation-state has to focus on the equation between the nation and the state forged at a crucial moment in subcontinental history. India's partition along ostensibly religious lines gave added weight to notions of unity, integrity, security and stability

---

[5] See Partha Chatterjee, *The Nation and its Fragments* (Princeton, 1993) and Gyanendra Pandey, 'In Defence of the Fragment', in *Representations*, 1992 (Winter), pp. 27–55.

on both sides of the divide, making these the key ingredients of dominant nationalist ideologies. Without recovering the alternative configurations of the relationship between the nation and the state, the recent upsurge in crafting culturally sensitive, democratic development strategies may well compound the modern nation-state's crisis of legitimacy. Culture quite as much as nationalism has always been a contested site where social groupings of differential power and privilege have vied for supremacy. To treat it as the seamless web binding the 'nation' to revive faltering development agendas is to invite even greater polarization than already elicited by the state's flaunting of a singular and uncompromising nationalist ideology. This is not to say that democracy and development in South Asia, or indeed anywhere else in the world, can be wholly devoid of cultural moorings. But to present culture as the panacea for all that has gone wrong with past strategies of development is to reify it as an autonomous and undifferentiated category rather than view it as a process which is inextricably connected with the changing material domains of politics and economy. The rhetoric of cultural authenticity does not address, and in fact conveniently glosses over, the issue of persisting material deprivations that have made nonsense of the modern nation-state's developmentalist ideology. Arguments about cultural specificities may well be a useful weapon against the inexorable process of globalization. Yet they are all too frequently deployed in favour of a form of cultural relativism which, in denying the encroachments of universalisms, ends up turning specificity into a value meriting uncritical acclaim. Against a background of specific but also generalizable social injustices and economic deprivations, those entreating South Asia's policy-makers to take refuge in uncompromising cultural relativism are contriving to prolong the current developmental depression.

Far more relevant to the concerns of a democratic rejuvenation of the idea of development is the question of negotiating and accommodating the panoply of cultural differences within the nation-states. The challenge is to creatively blend individual and collective rights without reifying any particular category as the basis for collective or communitarian identity. This would have the effect of liberating culture from the homogenizing designs of the modern nation-state, turning it into one among several defining elements of democratic rights. It is precisely the inadequate institutionalization of the democratic rights of citizens which, paradoxically enough, has been encouraging the undue privileging of notions of cultural community divorced from the material domain of political economy. The quest for substantive democracy has been in large part a material struggle for social and economic security that could provide more meaningful content to culturally informed values and a sense of human dignity. Democratic development can be a worthwhile ideal only if it addresses material and cultural concerns by assuring individual and group rights at different levels of the polity.

This volume addresses a set of connected historical, political-economic and philosophical issues that are central to the problems of nationalism, democracy and development in India. The articles taken together help to sharply delineate the structural and ideological dimensions of the late colonial and post-colonial state in India. They also contribute to the larger theoretical debates on nationalism by disentangling some of the analytical confusions in the recent literature on the relationship between 'nation' and 'state'. The binary opposition between secular nationalism and religious communalism is also called into question in this book in radically new ways. While maintaining a critical stance towards the centralized post-colonial state, the contributors engage and disagree with several aspects of the recent cultural critiques of modernity, nationalism and development. Conscious of the dangers of the fragmentalist onslaught on state monoliths playing into the hands of a conservative elitism in the name of freeing the economy from statist control, this book moves towards offering alternative theories of state.

The destruction of the Babri Masjid in Ayodhya on 6 December 1992 rudely jolted scholars and intellectuals out of any residual sense of complacency they may have had in addressing the crises afflicting the state and politics in India. This volume opens with an essay by Amartya Sen which examines nationalist interpretations of India's past, the intellectual critiques of these interpretations and the contemporary political preoccupations that have given these scholarly debates their topical salience. In order to undertake this examination Sen first sifts through a number of key methodological issues. His discussion of epistemology, positional objectivity and practical reason leads him to make a case for the greater relevance of resorting to practical reason and going beyond pure epistemology and positional observations in the current debate on identities in India. He shows how a certain 'external orientation' in interpreting India's past has tended to accentuate the insistence on 'difference' with what is called the West. The substantive sections of the paper analyse the strategies devised by anti-colonial nationalism to negotiate the problem of external and internal difference and the shifts in the positional perspective on the question of national unity in the post-colonial era. Sen dissents from the now influential intellectual position which puts forward 'a programme of identification' leading from a state to a nation-state and then to a very limited view of national identity. He also notes the potential of the 'state' to play a protective role vis-à-vis inequities within the 'community'. The idea of the nation, Sen argues, cannot be reduced to a state-seeking project, particularly a state that is violent and authoritarian. Cultural critiques of the nation-state, including those undertaken from a subalternist position, failed to take account of (the lack of) material entitlements and intellectual opportunities in a context of persistent deprivations and inequalities. The real failures of the Indian nation-state lie in these domains, which would seem to call for a 'censure of governance' rather than denunciations of modernity, science and reason.

The loss of the liberating element in the idea of the nation had much to do with the structural and ideological inheritances from colonialism. David Washbrook identifies 'communalism' as one of the two legacies of the dominant British ruling tradition bequeathed to post-colonial India. This tradition held that members of civil society could only represent particular, sectional interests and privileged the state which alone was seen capable of representing the whole of society by standing above the domain of politics. The second legacy of this brand of political philosophy and practice was an inflated role for the bureaucracy in making policy. Washbrook draws a distinction between representative and democratic politics and shows how British conceptions and institutions of state and representative politics influenced and compromised post-colonial India's quest for democracy and development.

Yet, these Western modular forms of the 'state' did not go uncontested in the era of anti-colonial nationalism. The relationship between nationalist thought and colonial knowledge is re-examined by Sugata Bose. The construction of nationalist ideologies is explored in his essay along the fault lines of nation and gender, nation and class, nation and religious community, nation and linguistic region, and finally, nation and state. By recovering multiple representations of nationhood and contestations over the nature of the state, Bose calls into question the teleological readings which conflate the nation and the state before the historically decisive moment of independence and partition.

Ayesha Jalal points out the need to subject the entire notion of Muslim 'communalism' in colonial and post-colonial South Asia to probing analysis. Dissecting the dominant historical and political discourse on communalism, she shows how it essentializes the religiously informed identities, politics and conflicts it claims to be explaining and combating. Her argument draws a distinction between a religiously informed cultural identity and the politics of cultural nationalism. Contrasting the 'inevitability' of a Muslim identity, variously defined, with the 'impossibility' of a supra-regional and specifically Muslim politics in the subcontinental context, her paper demonstrates 'the largely arbitrary, derogatory and exclusionary nature of the term "communal" as it has been applied to individuals and political groupings claiming to represent the interests of Indian Muslims'. Secular and Hindu 'nationalists' have been complicitous in placing the burden of the loaded negative baggage of 'communalism' on South Asia's Muslim minority.

The ideology of Hindutva, Sumantra Bose argues in his essay, shares significant common traits with 'the monolithic, unitary conception of Indian nationalism that has increasingly served as the official ideology of the post-colonial Indian state'. Adapting theoretical formulations of Antonio Gramsci and Juan Linz, Bose delineates the roots and contours of the organic crisis of the Indian state. He shows the relationship between secularism and communalism to be dialectical, not adversarial, and characterizes 'Hindu nationalism' as the highest stage of anti-democratic state centralism. The heterogeneity of Indian society remains, however, a formidable obstacle in the path of religiously-based majoritarian nationalism. This paper also uncovers the links between shifts in political economy and the creation of a constituency for the project of cultural nationalism.

Jayati Ghosh provides a critique of much of the existing literature on development that fails to draw the theoretical and analytical connections between the state and the macroeconomy. She explains shifts in government policy in terms of the changing interaction between the state and social, economic and political processes. The absence of any genuine asset redistribution contributed in no uncertain way to the failure of the early development plans. Ghosh notices a growing convergence of increasing authoritarianism of the state with the liberalization of the economy, turning the state itself into a 'private property' of the elite.

Pranab Bardhan turns his attention to a fundamental critique of the state and its developmentalist agenda that has not been addressed by most development economists concerned with narrower debates about liberalization. He finds 'much that is persuasive and valuable' in what he terms the anarcho-communitarian critique of the modern state, but also underscores 'several problems and glaring inadequacies' in the anti-statist position, which tends to gloss over 'local oppression in communities or families'. Bardhan demystifies simplistic notions of the virtues of 'decentralized development' and puts forward a qualified defence of the state's historic role and future potential in improving people's livelihoods in a complex economy. In so doing, he rescues the normative ideal of development from the condemnation it has has suffered at the hands of the scholarly community of anarcho-communitarians whose queries have borne 'a trace of patronizing elitism'.

The denial of substantive democracy and development, this book argues, is at the root of India's economic ills and myriad social and economic conflicts. It has played an important part in the subcontinent as a whole in giving rise to a number of post-colonial 'nationalist' movements. Some of these are in defence of, and others determinedly set against, established juridical states. While a decentring of decision-making processes is crucial for the pursuit of democratic development, this should not be confused with a recipe of simple decentralization or fragmentation. The purpose of decentring would be to shift the locus of developmental initiatives from centralized state monoliths to the broad base of civil society. But it would be taking too naive a view of South Asia to ignore the anti-democratic credentials of key segments of civil society which in order to maintain their privileges would staunchly defend the centralized post-colonial state. The project of democratic development, if it is to give itself a chance of success, cannot afford to operate in the fragmentary mode. Democrats interested in sustaining development have little option but to be all-encompassing in their approach to the ultimate objective of reconstituting a decolonized state on a genuinely popular basis.

Students and scholars of South Asia face the challenge of creatively blending cultural and political-economic analysis in order to rethink outmoded notions of monolithic nation-states and sovereignty and reconfigure the relationship between the search for national self-expression and democratic development. This volume will have served its purpose if it acts as a spur to that effort.

A new understanding of the nation state

2

On Interpreting India's Past[1]

Amartya Sen

INTRODUCTION

We live in the present, but that is a tiny bit of time—it passes as we talk. The current moment, vivid as it is, does not tell us much about who we are, how we can reasonably see ourselves, and where we would place our loyalties if and when we face divisions. Our identities are strongly influenced by the past. The self-perceptions that characterize a group are associated with, and to a great extent defined by, the shared memories and recollections of the past, and by the agreed priorities and implicit allegiances that draw on those evocations.

While this applies generally to all societies, the past becomes a particularly sharp battleground when contemporary debates invoke the past to redefine a collectivity and to allege the centrality of some particular features and the unimportance of others. This is very much the situation in India today. The tentative understandings that had become intellectually dominant during the national movement (and which had provided what was claimed to be a workable basis for the polity of the newly independent and freshly separated India) are now being subjected to severe questioning. The nationalist interpretations of 'Indianness', perhaps the most influential version of which is reflected in Jawaharlal Nehru's *Discovery of India*, have been bruised fairly extensively by a variety of challenges.[2] To dismiss these challenges as

[1] An earlier version of this paper was presented as an Abha Maiti Memorial Lecture at the Asiatic Society in Calcutta. I am grateful to Akeel Bilgrami, Sugata Bose, Ayesha Jalal and Emma Rothschild for helpful comments and discussions.

[2] There were significant distinctions within these interpretations: for example, even Gandhi's own account did not entirely coincide with the Nehru version. But nevertheless there was, to a great extent, a shared national perspective, despite the differences in the understanding of the sources of that perspective. The recent challenges apply generally to the different versions.

arising out of political motivations and contingencies (such as the priorities of the newly empowered Hindu politics, or the demands of communitarian confrontation) is to minimize the force of the intellectual questioning involved in these confrontations, and to overlook the political motivation that underlies also the classical nationalist interpretation itself. In so far as some of the redefinitions that are being advanced are arbitrary and ad hoc (and governed by the immediacy of the political agenda of particular movements), these proposals might well be seen as foundationally weak. But even when this is the case, this fact would not, by itself, re-establish the intellectual standing of the classical nationalist interpretation. There is no escape from re-examining the theoretical underpinning and the cogency of the nationalist approaches, along with investigating their practical relevance and import.

The substantive purpose of this essay is to examine the nationalist interpretation of India's past and some of the challenges that have been presented to it, and to relate them to the contemporary preoccupations that are active today. I shall argue that some parts of the established nationalist conceptions survive better than others, and the vulnerabilities are not quite the ones that seem to receive the most attention. It is important to distinguish between the different aspects of the classical nationalist interpretation and to see their respective roles and congruity.

As a background to this substantive exercise, it is necessary to sort out some methodological issues involved in these interpretative programmes, and this too I shall have to attempt. The methodological issues are taken up in the next section. But before that I should make a clarificatory remark.

The limits of national identity can be compared with the identities associated respectively with (1) the *more restricted* boundaries of communities and groups within a nation, and (2) the *more inclusive* coverage of broader categories, such as the identity of being an 'Asian', or even that of belonging to the human race.[3] Critiques of 'nationalism' from the former—more restricted—perspective would tend to take quite different lines from those presented in the latter—more inclusive—contexts. Recent demands for re-examination of the classical conceptions of Indian national identity have mostly come from the former viewpoints (for

[3] Some identities can go beyond the nation and yet, within the nation, define a part of it. For example, the identity of being a woman, or a socialist, or a Muslim, is clearly not confined to the limits of a nation, and yet within a nation (such as India), there will be correspondingly circumscribed identities (such as being an Indian woman, or an Indian socialist, or an Indian Muslim).

example, emphasizing the 'fragments', as they are sometimes called, over
the 'nation'). This essay is concerned entirely with those lines of critique,
and does not consider the important challenges to nationalism coming
from *broader* identities. It is, however, worth noting that classical Indian
formulations of nationalism often did emphasize the importance of
broader concerns that go beyond national limits. In one form or another,
references to such constraints can be very clearly seen in the writings
of Gandhi, Tagore, Nehru and others. The anti-colonial nationalists often
had strong global commitments, while invoking the unity of the nation
in pursuit of demands for 'self-determination'.

POSITIONAL OBJECTIVITY, EPISTEMOLOGY AND PRACTICAL REASON

There are two methodological claims presented in this section, dealing
respectively with:

(1) the relevance of *positionality* in the objectivity of observations and
    the knowledge they yield, and
(2) the importance of *practical reason* (and decisions about actions and
    rules) in judging alternative perspectives and their respective claims
    to our attention.

I begin with the first.

I have argued elsewhere that the objectivity of an observation or an
analysis can be judged not only in uncompromisingly universalist terms
(what Thomas Nagel has called 'the view from nowhere' in his
perspicacious exploration of the demands of objectivity),[4] but also with
reference to identified 'positional' perspectives—as the view from a
specified and delineated somewhere.[5] Positionality can influence both
(i) observation of events seen from a particular position, and (ii) the
overall assessment of an event, from a particular perspective, taking note
of different observations.

To illustrate the positionality of observations with a physical example,
consider the recognition that a distant object looks smaller, or more
specifically, the contingent truth that the sun and the moon look to be
of much the same size from where we are (that is, on the earth). These
observations and their epistemic ramifications have objectivity, but that
objectivity relates to observational acts from specified positions (the sun

[4] Thomas Nagel, *The View from Nowhere* (Oxford: Clarendon Press, 1986).
[5] See my 'Positional Objectivity', *Philosophy and Public Affairs*, 1993.

and the moon may look very different in size from, say, Jupiter).

The nature of the observations and the conclusions drawn are inescapably influenced by the position of observation. These positional features need not be related to our *subjectivity*, as they may not satisfy the defining attributes of being 'subjective', such as (1) 'having its source in the mind', and (2) 'pertaining or peculiar to an individual subject or his mental operations'.[6]

Rather, they are 'positional' characteristics of actual observations and the objective interpretations of those observations. The similarity of the observed sizes of the sun and the moon from the earth does not originate in our mind (even the nature of the solar eclipse brings out the substance of positional projections). Nor are they peculiar to individual subjects, since a normal person placed in the same position, with standard eyesight, should be able to replicate similar observations. Positional objectivity is an interpersonally sharable understanding—a sharing that objectivity in any form must minimally demand.[7] But that shared understanding is specifically in terms of the view from some identified position.[8] The interpretations of history and of culture are peculiarly

---

[6] *The Shorter Oxford English Dictionary*, Vol. II (Oxford: Clarendon Press, 1975), p. 2167.

[7] There are many interesting epistemological issues raised by the positional view of objectivity, which I shall not pursue here, but on some of which see my 'Positional Objectivity' (1993). The approach was presented and developed in my Storrs Lectures at the Yale Law School in September 1990, and at some stage the revised lectures will be published as a monograph (it is in the queue behind a forthcoming monograph on Rationality).

[8] It is possible to include *among* the positional parameters some specific characteristics of the mind that influence observation or assessment. If that were done, then the resulting conclusions would be, in one sense, subjective, and yet in another sense, positionally objective *with respect to* the specified positional parameters, including the mental ones. Indeed, through parameterization, all 'subjective' influences can, in principle, be brought into the framework of positional objectivity. In some contexts, this type of 'dual interpretation' would have some advantage, but in many contexts, it would be a nuisance, since it would lead to ambiguities related to the overlapping categories of subjectivity and positional objectivity. There is, thus, some merit in imposing strict constraints on what can or cannot be included among the positional parameters. If the specially 'subjective' characteristics were excluded, then positional objectivity and subjectivity would not have any overlap. To illustrate in terms of visual observations, the physical position of the observer vis-à-vis the object could then be included among the positional parameters, but not such subjective features

mediated by the positional features of observation and interpretation. Each individual thing about the past that is observed can be understood in a particular way depending on the nature of the questions that engage and motivate the inquiry. For example, facts that are of interest for an anti-colonial national movement need not be of similar interest for a separatist programme related to the predicament of a particular community. Indeed, from the totality of the things observed, selections can be made and weights attached—most often implicitly—through the positional perspectives used in the analyses. To dismiss these positional variabilities as mere 'subjectivism' would miss out something substantial in the nature of objectivity (not all of objectivity is about 'the view from nowhere'— some relate to a specified 'somewhere'), and it would also miss the strongly *impersonal* quality of *positional* views (since different persons can occupy the same position and replicate the same observations and the implications that follow from them).[9] On the other hand, positionally objective observations cannot be taken to be position-invariant objective truths. To illustrate again with the same example, the positionally objective conclusion that the sun and the moon are of much the same size when viewed from the earth does not entail that they are of the same size in terms of all criteria of measurement. To identify the two notions of objectivity would be to miss out on the crucial role that positionality plays in the nature of these investigations. The objectivity of a particular perspective does not, by itself, establish its epistemic status beyond positional contingency.

---

as being 'overcome by fear', or 'in a state of extreme anger'. The 'dual interpretation' and the 'disjoint interpretations' are both analytically fine, and the choice between them is mainly a matter of convenience and helpfulness. Some grounds for preferring the 'disjoint' view were discussed in an earlier paper ('Positional Objectivity', 1993). The use of the idea of positional objectivity will be mainly in that line in this essay. Characteristics such as basing observations on particular records, or assessing different observations on the basis of practical priorities of importance for an anti-colonial national movement, and so on, can still be included within the body of positional objectivity, but not personal mental quirks, or for that matter, such attitudinal characteristics as an 'unwillingness to look at the facts'.

[9] The exclusion of purely mental features, or quirks of psychological attitudes, under the 'disjoint interpretation' would differentiate between subjective parameters and other positional parameters, and the former will not be included in the domain of positionally objective views and assessments.

From a variety of positionally objective understandings, we can move in three distinct directions. The first is not to move at all, and to let the matter end there—there will be no positionally independent bottom line. The second is to seek some interpositional invariance—the genuine search for 'the view from nowhere'. This second exercise is of great importance in epistemology and metaphysics, and I have tried to outline elsewhere the nature of this 'trans-positional' exercise. There are important moves we can make in seeking such position invariance, particularly in terms of the coherence of different positional views.[10] The third move, also in search of a trans-positional assessment, would be to shift the choice away from pure epistemology (and also metaphysics) to 'practical reason', and to view it in terms of their respective implications for action and to evaluate them in that light. It is this last approach, invoking *practical reason* in addition to epistemic concerns, that I shall particularly explore in this paper.

There is, of course, a role of critical reasoning in examining 'the facts of the case' in choosing between different perspectives of observation, but that reasoning cannot ultimately escape the discipline of (1) acknowledging the differences, particularly in weighting and emphasis, of distinct positional views, and (2) examining the practical consequences of adopting one perspective rather than another. Even in terms of the physical analogy invoked earlier, whether we take the virtual size of the sun and the moon to be the same or not should depend on what we wish to do with that understanding. In observational optics from the earth, for example in predicting a solar eclipse, the presumption of equi-sized—and potentially congruent—projections of the two bodies could indeed be useful. In contrast, in calculating the gravitational pull of these two objects on a spacecraft that we might send off for a planetary probe, we would be well advised to take note of differences in size, in particular the immensely larger mass of the sun vis-à-vis the moon (the equal projections from the earth being recognized as a contingent function of their respective distances).

The problem of our identities also involves both *epistemology* and *practical reason*. It is inevitably influenced by the positionally objective observations of our history and culture that can be made and the limited understandings that these positional observations provide. But the epistemology of our identities cannot come to a final stop with any given

---

[10] See my 'Positional Objectivity' (1993). See also Nagel, *The View from Nowhere* (1986), and Susan Hurley, *Natural Reasons* (Oxford: Clarendon Press, 1989).

positional observation, and there remains in particular the possibility of
reasoned choice in taking note of the implications of these understandings
for the lives we can lead and the societies we can have.[11] Indeed, I shall
argue that a good deal of the debate on identities in contemporary India
calls for more explicit reference to practical reason rather than pure
epistemology, even when armed with positionally objective visions. We
are not settling issues of pure knowledge only—important as the
positionally grounded cognitive exercises are.

EXTERNAL ORIENTATION AND EMPHASIS ON DIFFERENCE

It is not remarkable that the leadership of the Indian national movement
favoured an aggregative, cohesive, and on the whole sympathetic view
of the past of India. This is standard fare for movements of this kind.
And it is to the credit of the leadership of the movement that there was
a conscious effort to resist the temptation to make excessive use of the
rhetoric of India's 'golden ages' and 'ancient wisdoms', or to get too stuck
in the magnified image of the carefully chosen appreciations of India
entertained by people elsewhere (though such accolades were plentifully
cited by different nationalist authors in the period of the movement for
independence).

In Nehru's own writing, there is understandable pride in some of the
achievements of the civilization of the Indian subcontinent, but he also
warned against the tendency to quote foreign appreciations of India's
past, while suppressing the criticisms and censures that had also been
expressed in considerable abundance. In the *Discovery of India*, Jawaharlal
Nehru put it thus:

There is a tendency on the part of Indian writers, to which I have also partly
succumbed, to give selected extracts and quotations from the writings of

---

[11] In the context of presenting two specific case studies, Susan Bayly has drawn
attention to the general importance of understanding the far-reaching role of
'memories'—real or imagined—of 'victimhood' of members of one community
at the hands of another ('War, Victimhood, Resistance and Remembrance:
Two Case Studies from the Indian Subcontinent', mimeographed summary,
University of Cambridge, 1995). As Bayly notes, 'South Asia's political life has
been strongly influenced by 'carriers of remembrance' who see their landscape
as a giant battlefield full of sites of heroic bloodshed and unavenged crimes
against their 'communities' and their respective divine warrior-protectors' (p. 2).
The likely effects of focusing on such 'memories' well illustrates the relevance
of practical reason in the selections that are inescapably parts of understandings
of the past.

European scholars in praise of old Indian literature and philosophy. It would be equally easy, indeed much easier, to give other extracts giving an exactly opposite viewpoint.[12]

There is, however, one shared feature of the nationalist tradition, including Nehru's corrective, that deserves noting here. Much importance is attached in interpreting India's past to what people outside the country thought of it: in description, in praise, in criticism. This is to some extent true of indigenous, nationalist writings in other countries as well, and as an antidote to insularity, there is perhaps some merit in this outward alignment. But this sensitivity to foreign understanding assumed extraordinary importance in India given its colonial and dependent status in the period in which the nationalist understanding emerged.

I shall call it the *external orientation* in interpreting India's past. I shall also argue presently that this feature has had a considerable engineering impact on the ways in which Indian culture and history have been standardly characterized in the colonial and the post-colonial period. This is a diagnosis that is shared between the approach presented here and the standard post-colonial literature. However, I shall also argue that the 'external orientation' has often had the impact of making the interpretation of India's past *more inward looking*—emphasizing differences rather than similarities in cultural history. The undermining of an independent understanding of the pre-colonial past has quite often taken the form of a breathless search for *difference* from what is called 'the West'. The 'influence' of the West has sometimes taken this dialectical and largely negative form (rather than leading to a reconstruction of India's past in ways that are *similar* to a Western outlook).

The resulting *emphasis on difference* has descriptive as well as practical relevance to different interpretations of India's past. While this focus on difference is, I believe, a characteristic, inter alia, even of anti-colonial nationalist interpretation, it is often seen rather more plentifully in some of the communitarian understandings that challenge the nationalist view today. Indeed, in the effort to 'correct' the classical nationalist picture in a more indigenous direction (in searching, for example, in Partha Chatterjee's language, for '*our* modernity'),[13] the effect has been, at least,

[12] Jawaharlal Nehru, *The Discovery of India* (Calcutta: Signet Press, 1946; Centenary Edition, Delhi: Oxford University Press, 1989), p. 158.

[13] See his 'Talking about Our Modernity', mimeo, presented at the South Asian seminar at Tufts University in April 1995; see also his *The Nation and Its Fragments* (1993).

partly to *exaggerate*—rather than ameliorate—the difference-seeking distortions that had already existed in the classical nationalist picture.

CLASSICAL NATIONALISM: DIVERSITY AND NATIONAL UNITY

As far as the substance of the 'nationalist interpretations' is concerned, there was a systematic attempt to focus on unity, rather than discord, within India. This too was, to a great extent, a reaction to the colonial thesis of India's hopeless divisions, which needed an imperial hand for the establishment of peace, order and cohesion. The divisiveness that gave Britain its strongest argument for staying on in India as the ruling power—protecting each group from the marauding other—had to be denied in the classical nationalist thesis which argued for the non-necessity of any such external imperial force for safeguarding India's unity.

However, the nationalist leadership could hardly deny the existence of different religions in India, or obliterate the battles that had occurred earlier between the different communities (for example, between Hindus and Muslims, and within each of these broad groups). The argument was, rather, that despite this diversity, there was an essential unity. And that this unity was not accidental, but some reflection of the unifying tendency in Indian culture.

Mahatma Gandhi's inclination was to see in Hinduism some overarching value that transcended sectarianism and provided a cultural basis for tolerance. Search for truth might be that uniting factor, Gandhiji thought, in a passage that even Nehru found rather implausible. 'Its essential spirit seems to be to live or let live. Mahatma Gandhi has attempted to define it: "If I were asked to define the Hindu creed, I should simply say: Search after truth through non-violent means.... . Hinduism is the religion of truth. Truth is God. Denial of God we have known. Denial of truth we have not known".[14] One problem with this view—at the level of practical reason—is the usurping role that Hinduism itself is made to play here in the synthesis of the nation as a whole. The exclusionary implications of this role (for example, for the Muslims of undivided India) would impose a heavy political burden as the prospect of independence as partition approached. But no less importantly—at the level of epistemology—

[14] Jawaharlal Nehru, *The Discovery of India* (Calcutta: Signet Press, 1946; Centenary Edition, Oxford: Clarendon Press, 1989), p. 75.

one could scarcely ignore the deeply questionable nature of these claims, for example that the 'denial of truth' was, in some significant sense, unknown in Hinduism. After some critical analysis, Nehru found this Gandhian characterization to be 'no definition at all'.[15] But while Nehru was unwilling to place Hinduism in that privileged position as the source of the unitary impulses in India, he did not doubt the unitary impulses themselves. 'Whatever the word we may use, Indian or Hindi or Hindustani, for our cultural tradition, we see in the past that some inner urge towards synthesis, derived essentially from the Indian philosophic outlook, was the dominant feature of Indian cultural, and even racial, development. Each incursion of foreign elements was a challenge to this culture, but it was met successfully by a new synthesis and a process of absorption.'[16] Was this really such a special feature of India, not easily observed elsewhere? Haven't many other cultures also seen diversity, invasion and absorption?

This is a big issue and not easy to settle, and I shall not attempt here to answer that epistemological question in terms of 'trans-positional' objectivity in cross-cultural comparisons. But what is easier to see is that from the 'positionality' of a practical commitment to a national unity (and to writing and theorizing on the history of India with an overarching involvement in that commitment), many of the uniting features in the diverse history of the subcontinent would appear to be particularly important to understand and emphasize. The nationalist perspective was also much influenced dialectically by the claims made on behalf of the British Raj—convenient for the imperialists—of a hopelessly divided India, with different communities at loggerheads with each other.[17] In asking the question as to whether Indian history indicates that such internal divisiveness is inescapable in India, the point could certainly be honestly

[15] Since Mahatma Gandhi varied his emphases on different occasions, Nehru was able to quote, with greater satisfaction, Gandhiji's statement, made on a different occasion: 'Indian culture is neither Hindu, nor Islamic, nor any other, wholly. It is a fusion of all.' *The Discovery of India*, p. 363.

[16] Ibid., p. 76.

[17] Cf. 'It is necessary thus to look back on Indian history to understand the mentality of new India. This will also help us to see what truth there is in the oft-repeated charge that India has never been a nation and was always a prey to anarchy and invasion till the British came... But even in the remote past there has always been a fundamental unity of India—a unity of common faith and culture'. (*Jawaharlal Nehru: An Anthology* (ed.), Sarvepalli Gopal, Delhi: Oxford University Press, 1983, p. 8.)

made that there was no such basis for expecting perpetual hostility between different religions or diverse regions. For this it was not necessary at all to claim that a tendency towards unity and a broad synthesizing priority are very special characteristics of Indian culture—not to be much found elsewhere. If that implication seemed to enter the claims (as it certainly did), this was largely the result of the dialectics against the imperial view, which was bent on arguing exactly the opposite. The temptation to affirm uniqueness can be easily eschewed, in the perspective of today, without having to deny the elements of truth and importance in the pointers to India's historical unity, rather than its divisions.

The implicit pride in the 'special' character of India's absorptive culture played an important psychological role in 'trumping' the imperial claims of pervasive disunity of India. And politically, it fitted in well enough with the historical observation that there was indeed much unity in India despite the undoubted presence of many religions, diverse languages, and other differences on which the imperial theory had relied so heavily. So there was both an element of truth in the claim about the synthesizing tendencies of Indian culture, and much practical usefulness in focusing on—and particularly emphasizing—that particular element.

The cliché that the unity of India derives from the unifying influence of the British rule is widely repeated even now (an example was the reported invocation of this conjecture by the Chief Minister of Andhra Pradesh in a meeting of potential British investors, in London, in June 1995, to persuade the British capitalist to invest in a country of 'their creation'). That story of British construction of India has been repeated often enough to acquire some plausibility (as repeated tales often do, despite Homer's disclaimer in the *Odyssey*: 'What so tedious as a twice-told tale?'). But, surely, the concept of the Indian subcontinent as an integrated unit is not at all new, and has been implicitly invoked in many contexts over the millennia. The idea has not only influenced the conception of the natural boundaries over which an emperor (such as Chandragupta Maurya, or Ashoka, or Akbar) would seek to establish command, but has also shaped the nature and domain of various economic, cultural and social movements.

The idea of an Indian identity must not be confused with that of an Indian nationhood. For one thing, the concept of nationality is a relatively recent one, and it would be as absurd to ask what sense of Indian nationhood the Mauryan or Mughal Indian had, as it would be to seek the recognition of a Greek nationhood among the ancient Athenians or

Spartans, or a German nationhood among the Visigoths at the gate. For another, a proto-political identity can well stretch beyond contemporary national boundaries, and given a suitable opportunity, it can even be used in particular contexts to construct a supranational political unit, as is currently happening in the construction of a united Europe.[18] The form that the search for 'unity' in Indian diversity took in the classical nationalist theory was, therefore, overdemanding and overexacting. Claiming that the synthetic virtues of Indian culture were very special—almost unique—was also quite redundant. But what has to be noted are (1) the plausibility of the positional view that saw a remarkable unity in India (astonishing in a country with more diversity of languages and religions than perhaps in any other in the world), and (2) the practical urgency to focus on that unity in defending the nationalist demand that the British quit immediately (despite the oft-repeated imperial claim that the Raj was the architect of a 'united India' and the indispensable guardian of its 'wholeness').

Decades of historical work and cultural analyses in post-independent India have by now brought out the naive simplicity of the alleged overarching unity of Indian culture and history. They do require us to qualify and perhaps even to abandon the unproblematic belief in Indian unity on which anti-colonial nationalists chose to focus.[19] In presenting her illuminating studies of present-day India, what Veena Das calls 'an anthropological perspective on contemporary India', she cannot but put much more emphasis on the things that divide India, rather than what is common across the board.[20]

What we are noticing here is a shift in the positional perspective. The old classical nationalist view that tried to 'soften' the differences whenever they were visible represented a perspective that had considerable veracity

---

[18] It is also important to emphasize the non-uniqueness of identities. An Indian proto-political identity does not deny, for the same person, the forceful presence of a regional, or a religious, or a class, or a caste, or a gender identity. Nor should it be assumed that for the unity of India to have substantive content, it must be unique and thoroughly well-defined, or that a useful Indian identity has to be clear-cut and sharply delineated.

[19] As was mentioned earlier, there were different versions of this belief (even Mahatma Gandhi's form was very different from Nehru's). Nevertheless, anti-colonial nationalist beliefs—diverse as they were in some respects—still had something in common in terms of focusing on unity and on instinctive synthesis.

[20] See Veena Das, *Critical Events: An Anthropological Perspective on Contemporary India* (Delhi: Oxford University Press, 1995).

and positional relevance, and also practical value in the context of pre-independence politics (particularly, given the priority of ending British rule, with its claim of 'authorship' of a united India). Neither the contingent relevance, nor the impermanent usefulness, of this line of vision need be denied for a contemporary understanding of India, more cognizant of divisions and fragments that make up the nation.

The question that remains, however, concerns the concept of the Indian nation seen in terms of *practical reason*. I think it would be a mistake, for reasons I have already discussed, to see the nationhood of Indians as following simply from a position-independent, objective reading of Indian history. National unity as a concept is a relatively recent one anyway, and has much malleability in it, in line with the sense and practice of actual politics. The question of practical reason is, thus, central. Is the focusing on the idea of an Indian nation useful at this time, and is there enough empirical basis to make that idea plausible (without having to claim that it is inevitable)? I believe the answers are very firmly positive in the context of communal divisions, which can be both violent and brutal, as our experiences have brought out over the recent years.

To this we have to add the issue of fairness involved in the need for symmetric treatment of different religious communities, which is a political norm of some importance, and which requires the acceptance of something that unites, rather than divides, the members of different communities that make up the citizenry of India. I have argued elsewhere that the idea of secularism, which is inherently incomplete, can be best interpreted in terms of such a symmetry, rather than as something which makes the state not only neutral but also uniformly hostile to all religions.[21] In the demand for that symmetry there is the need for an overarching concept of being members of a nation (who are to be treated with symmetry).

In this sense, there is still much use for the classical nationalist concept of an Indian nation, and that concept cannot be overridden by a foundational political identity of being a member of a religious community. In our *personal and social life*, the religious identity could even be 'prior' for many people (I say this on the basis of reflective rather than experiential knowledge, since the identity of a religious community does not speak to me), but that is a separate issue from the demands of identity in the context of *political unity and entitlements*. Mahatma Gandhi was

[21] In my essay 'Secularism and Its Discontents', in Kaushik Basu and Sanjay Subramanium (eds), *Unravelling the Nation: Sectarian Conflicts and India's Secular Identity* (New Delhi: Penguin Books, 1996).

right in making a distinction between the influence of his own religion on his personal conduct and social behaviour (including holding open prayer meetings) and the political fairness of individually wanting that members of all religious communities in India be treated symmetrically (Gandhiji was shot by a Hindu activist who could not stomach the latter). Insofar as that political virtue is both important and in somewhat doubtful supply in contemporary India, there remains cogency as well as practical merit in the conception of a nation on which the classical nationalist theory had put so much emphasis. The positional perspective today is somewhat different and so are the demands of practical reason, but acknowledging these facts does not undermine the continuing relevance of that classical notion.

In the next section, some of the contemporary challenges to Indian secularism are examined, particularly in the light of the readings of India's past.

THE NATION AND THE COMMUNITIES

The classical nationalist view took the membership of the national polity to be deeper and more forceful in the *political* context than a person's religion or membership of a religious community. There was a general presumption of a separation of spheres by which religion might have a major role—for the religiously oriented—in the personal and social activities of persons, but the *political* identities of the very same persons were taken to be more oriented towards the nation, rather than being grounded in their religious creeds.

A good illustration of this framework of classical nationalist ideas is the notion of a 'nationalist Muslim' around the time of the partition of India. The term referred to Muslims in the subcontinent who gave priority to being 'Indian' in their political identity (no matter how religious they might have been in personal and social life).[22] They were thus not

---

[22] The 'nationalist' Muslims were not necessarily the less religious ones, nor were they more reformist than those who sought partition and a separate Muslim state in the form of Pakistan. In fact, often the contrary. On the different ways of classifying Muslim political leadership and the dynamics of their changing relations with each other and with other Indian politicians, see Ayesha Jalal, *The Sole Spokesman: Jinnah, the Muslim League and the Demand for Pakistan* (Cambridge: Cambridge University Press, 1985), and 'Exploding Communalism: The Politics of Muslim Identity in South Asia', (Ch. 5 of this volume).

attracted by the idea of Pakistan as a Muslim polity, and typically resisted the partition of India much more strongly than the Hindu secularist did.[23]

It is this feature of the classical nationalist view that has been subjected to the most forceful attacks in recent years. There have been at least two distinct sources of assault. First, the newly powerful forces of so-called 'Hindu nationalism', such as the Bharatiya Janata Party (BJP), the Shiv Sena, the Rashtriya Swayamsevak Sangh (RSS), the Vishva Hindu Parishad (VHP), have asserted, in one form or another, the priority of a Hindu identity. The Indian identity, when it emerges, is meant to be intermediated through that route, and 'Indianness' is, as it were, built on the religiously secure foundations of the different persons' primary religious identities.

The second line of critique, presented by communitarian intellectuals, has taken the form of arguing forcefully for the general importance of community-based identities (not just religious ones). It has stressed the immediacy, relevance and richness of belonging to a particular 'fragment', rather than to the more remote collectivity of a nation.

It is important to re-emphasize here that the challenge to the classical nationalist interpretation comes, in this line of critique, precisely in the *political* context. It is not about the general importance of religious beliefs or other community-oriented concerns in *personal* or even *social* behaviour, but the specific relevance of that identity in *political* matters (with or without involving the state). This distinction was discussed in the last section, in the narrower context of characterizing secularism.

This assertion of priority tends to come not only from religious sectarians (particularly, in recent years, the so-called 'Hindu nationalists'), but also from those who have been especially worried, often with good reason, about the over-powerful role of the state (as opposed to community), and about the violence committed by the state (on the basis of its unequal power). The idea of a 'nation' is often taken to be presupposing the discipline of a nation-state. For example, in criticizing the use of the concept of 'imagined community' by Sarvepalli Gopal and Romila Thapar, Veena Das first notes that the concept is 'applied to modern forms of religious community but not to the *nation*', and goes on to conclude: 'Thus, the claim of the *nation-state* to an eternal status, as something that goes back into the past and extends into the indefinite

---

[23] On the sense of betrayal that the secularist Muslims experienced when the Congress Party readily accepted the idea of partitioning the country, see Rafiq Zakaria, *The Struggle within Islam* (New Delhi: Viking, 1988).

future, is not subjected to critical scrutiny' (*Critical Events*, 1995, p. 46, emphasis added). That jump from the 'nation' to the 'nation-state' is a leap across a considerable conceptual divide. The concept of the 'nation', thus, is made to take on whatever abuse of power and of violence that may be attributable to the *nation-state*. Here we come into a headlong clash with the ideas underlying the classical nationalist conceptions of a 'nation' reflected in the nationalist movements. The particular communitarian conception of the 'nation', which we are discussing here, gives it immediately a forcefully 'statist' orientation, and the very idea of giving priority to political unity *across* religious communities and other social divisions, thus, acquires an inescapably harsh and austere form, with the full potentiality of authoritarian abuse. The classical nationalist conceptions did not involve this intrinsic inseparability of a nation from a nation-state.[24] Indeed, as Nehru did explicitly claim in his paper 'The Psychology of Indian Nationalism', published in 1927, what is at issue is 'the mentality of new India'.[25]

It is certainly true that in the emergence or consolidation of any national unity, the nation-state may well have an important instrumental role, but the state need not be central to the conceptual foundation of this unity, nor account for the constructive emergence of the *sense* of a national unity, and thus of 'nationhood'. The concept of a nation reflects a sense of political identity that is not split up into belonging to distinct communities, and can in principle admit anyone, irrespective of communal background, by virtue of a shared sense of political identity. The

[24] There are, as was noted earlier, distinct versions of this nationalist conception, and some versions (particularly those that became powerful in the final stages of the nationalist struggle) had a greater insistence on a 'homogeneous' concept of Indianness than had been demanded earlier. Ayesha Jalal argues in her paper, 'Exploding Communalism: The Politics of Muslim Identity in South Asia' (in this volume), that Congress moved sharply towards a narrower conception of being a 'nationalist' in the 1930s and became less tolerant of Muslim diversity. This issue, important as it is, has to be distinguished from the different—though not unrelated—question of the need for presupposing a 'nation-state' for the conceptualization of a 'nation'. That presupposition was not a part of the classical nationalist approaches, even though, as Jalal notes, the insistence on 'singularity' in some later versions much reduced the reach and capacity of Indian nationalism, as independence approached. See also her *The Sole Spokesman: Jinnah, the Muslim League and the Demand for Pakistan* (1985).

[25] Nehru, 'The Psychology of Indian Nationalism', *The Review of Nations*, Geneva, 1927; reproduced in *Jawaharlal Nehru: An Anthology*, p. 8.

non-statist conception of the nation is, thus, well captured even by Arthur Miller's somewhat whimsical witticism that 'a good newspaper, I suppose, is a nation talking to itself',[26] and this informal line of reasoning would *not* really be improved by a programme of identification whereby we (1) first identify a state, then (2) diagnose it as a 'nation-state', and then (3) derive the identity of a 'nation' from the limits of that nation-state.

To take a different type of example, it is not a category mistake to think of the 'Indian nation' prior to 1947 as encompassing the residents of the so-called 'native states' (such as Travancore), and also the non-British colonial territories (such as Goa), even though they did not 'belong to' the same *state* in any sense at all. What is crucial is the sense of political identity that cuts across communal—and even state—boundaries, and while one object of that political identity may be the determination to construct a nation-state in line with that identity, it is not necessary to begin with any conception of a state *before* having an idea of a nation. Thus, the immediate ascription of the power, authoritarianism and propensity towards violence (that are attributed to a *nation-state*) to the very concept of a *nation* is achieved somewhat arbitrarily by jumping over important conceptual divides.

There is also the further—and altogether different—issue that even the state, capable as it is of authoritarianism and violence, may sometimes have a protective role against the coercions and inequities that many traditional communities standardly impose on less privileged members (such as women, or female children, or those who belong to the lower tiers of the collectivity).[27] Classical nationalist theory did undoubtedly foresee a role of the nation-state against such injustice. While that theory was probably less forthcoming on the violence done by the nationalist state than would have been justified (and that can certainly be seen as an inadequacy of that theory), it would be no less a mistake to assume that violence and injustice cannot have its origin in the community itself.[28] The classical nationalist theory had various biases, and in the context

---

[26] *The Observer*, 26 November, 1961.

[27] In his illuminating paper, 'The State against Society: The Great Divide in Indian Social Science Discourse' in this volume, Pranab Bardhan discusses different aspects of the relation between the state and the communities.

[28] Veena Das herself raises a related concern, in a different context: 'If a commitment to cultural rights leads us similarly to empower the community against the state, how can we ensure that the individual is not totally engulfed by the community?' (*Critical Events*, 1995, p. 107).

of addressing the problems of contemporary India, it is necessary to expose and criticise those biases.[29] But it is also important not to throw away the baby with the bathwater, particularly through arbitrary ascriptions across conceptual divides. There was considerable cogency as well as practical sense in the classical nationalist conception. The confounding of the concept of the 'nation' with a characterization of the 'nation-state', tempting as it may be, is not a strong enough basis for making it impossible to think of the 'nation', without setting out, at once, the troops of an authoritarian 'nation-state' marching against dissidents. We have to take more note of the purpose and rationale of the idea of a 'nation', *with and without* the operation of a 'nation state'. Again, the central concern turns out to be practical reason, rather than pure epistemology.

DIVERSITY OF RELEVANCE

In this penultimate section, I take up the question of the changing relevance of different issues over time—a concern that relates closely to the variation of *positionality* in objective assessment. The nature of the questions that are urgent to address does shift with the change in focus of contemporary problems. The confrontations of yesterday may be archaic today. This issue has been encountered already in a limited form in trying to make sense of the classical nationalist interpretation, when the historical context of that theory had been important.

To consider a different type of problem, we may note the fact that much of the Indian history of the last two centuries seen contemporaneously

[29] Akeel Bilgrami has drawn attention to what he identifies as a major weakness of Congress's approach to 'secularism', under Nehru's leadership, in the form of the neglect of real 'negotiation' between different communities to arrive at a secular nationalism ('Two Concepts of Secularism', *Yale Journal of Criticism*, vol. 7, 1994). He argues that despite including 'nationalist Muslims' within the fold of the Congress party, 'the commitment to genuine negotiation (which alone could build the necessary bridge from the party's compositeness to a substantive secularism) was distinctly avoided by the Congress party', and the label of 'implicit' negotiation served to hide this fact (p. 222). If this criticism is accepted (Bilgrami gives considerable evidence for doing just that), then the substantive political stands taken by the Congress party would be certainly condemned. But this could not be the basis (Bilgrami does not claim that it could) of rejecting the notion of a national identity without prior intermediation of a nation *state*. There is more to politics than the forceful machinery of the state.

cannot but focus on the issue of colonialism. The nature of the colonial rule itself has been the subject of sharp differences, varying from (1) seeing colonialism as a reforming process, (2) seeing it as a system of economic subjugation, or (3) seeing it as a history of the cultural hegemony of the imperial powers established over the dominated societies.[30] There have also been differences in this context between presenting the history of resistance to British colonial rule with a concentration on elite Indian leadership (including the establishment of the Congress in 1885), and seeing it in terms of the movements of the non-elite masses (the subalterns, as they have been called).[31] Many other differences on lines of historical analysis have also emerged in the context of interpreting colonial history and seeing the present in post-colonial terms.

These issues retain their importance and will no doubt do so for a long time to come. But meanwhile new questions have arisen and become prominent for which the nature of the older classifications may not exactly fit. One of the central issues in contemporary politics in India is the relevance of science and technology (sometimes called—extremely mis-leadingly—'Western' science and technology). This has become particu-larly important in the context of a deliberately cultivated hostility to science including some use of what can only be described as obscurantism. That contrast will undoubtedly grow in importance in India, as it has in many other countries as well (sometimes accompanied by fundamentalist reli-gious politics). In that context, the hostility to what is seen as 'modernism', which has been a concomitant feature of anti-colonialism, may have the effect of confounding the lines of the present debate.

This point can be addressed only after noting the positive achieve-ments of the shift in historical tradition that has occurred. One of the

---

[30] Karl Marx's writings on India emphasized—at once—the first two interpre-tations. Recently, the focus of anti-colonial critiques, especially those related to literary theory, has moved, to a great extent, to the third; on this see particularly Edward W. Said, *Orientalism* (New York: Random House, 1978; Vintage Books, 1979), and Gayatri Chakravorty Spivak, *The Post-Colonial Critic* (New York: Routledge, 1990). For a critique of the use of literary theory in this approach, and a defence of a more classical Marxian position, see Aijaz Ahmad, *In Theory* (London: Verso, 1992).

[31] The 'subaltern school' led by Ranajit Guha has made a very substantial contribution to this shift. For a good introduction, see Ranajit Guha and Gayatri Chakravorty Spivak (eds), *Selected Subaltern Studies* (New York: Oxford University Press, 1988).

major accomplishments of recent Indian historiography has been a change in focus from an exclusively elitist view of history to one in which the masses, particularly peasant masses, are seen as central agents of change.[32] Ranajit Guha, one of the visionary historians of our times, had motivated this departure in his work by identifying a lacuna in this respect. As he put it in his introductory essay in the first volume of the *Subaltern Studies*:

The historiography of Indian nationalism has for a long time been dominated by elitism—colonialist elitism and bourgeois-nationalist elitism... Both these varieties of elitism share the prejudice that the making of the Indian nation and the development of the consciousness—nationalism—which informed this process were exclusively or predominantly elite achievements.[33]

Considerable efforts have been made in the recent years to rectify that bias and to fill the gaps through 'subaltern' history.

It is important to note that the specific problems that Ranajit Guha was addressing were the emergence of Indian nationalism, the history of the national movement, and India's confrontation with its colonial rulers. It does not slight the nature of that inquiry to suggest that the political divisions that can be observed in India today incorporate many different elements, not each of which is best addressed in terms of the dichotomy between the subaltern and the elite, even though that basic distinction will continue to figure in some of the elements that characterize our present dissensions.

One of the interesting features of the way the work inspired by the subaltern movement has tended to develop is its marriage with what is often described as 'post-modernism'. An identification of the elite as the vanguard of 'modernity' would make that alliance, in some ways, quite natural. The association of subaltern history with the rejection of modernism thus has an understandable basis, but the school of 'post-modernist literary theory' has also presented other reasons for being critical of favouring the modern over the traditional. It is not my purpose here to address that general subject, but I do want to make a comment on an associated feature of it, namely the coolness—sometimes even

[32] Gayatri Spivak puts it thus: 'The most significant outcome of this revision or shift in perspective is that the agency of change is located in the insurgent or the "subaltern"' ['Introduction', in Ranajit Guha and Gayatri Chakravorty Spivak (eds), *Selected Subaltern Studies* (New York: Oxford University Press, 1988), p. 3].

[33] Reproduced in Guha and Spivak, *Selected Subaltern Studies*, p. 37.

hostility—towards science that accompanies these literary and intellectual movements. In the context of present divisions in countries such as India, this coolness or hostility can have rather momentous consequences.

A particular line of connection here concerns the reaction to colonialism, which has had the effect of making India's reading of its past and special involvements go in a more spiritual rather than scientific direction. Partha Chatterjee discusses the origin of this attitude very well, and I quote here from his *The Nation and Its Fragments* (although I shall draw a somewhat different conclusion from this analysis than he does):

> By my reading, anti-colonial nationalism creates its own domain of sovereignty within colonial society well before its political battle with the imperial power. It does this by dividing the world of social institutions and practices into two domains—the material and the spiritual. The material is the domain of the 'outside', of the economy and of statecraft, of science and technology, a domain where the West had proved its superiority and the East had succumbed. In this domain, then, Western superiority had to be acknowledged and its accomplishments carefully studied and replicated. The spiritual, on the other hand, is an 'inner' domain bearing the 'essential' marks of cultural identity. The greater one's success in imitating Western skills in the material domain, therefore, the greater the need to preserve the distinctiveness of one's spiritual culture. This formula is, I think, a fundamental feature of anti-colonial nationalisms in Asia and Africa.[34]

To a great extent, I agree with this, and it fits in with the thesis of 'external orientation' which was discussed earlier on in this paper. I would like to see the relation between India and the West in more dialectical terms (involving a two-way relation), which I have tried to outline elsewhere,[35] but I have little quarrel with Chatterjee's diagnosis as one important clue to what happened in India (and elsewhere in the colonies). Certainly, this focus on the spiritual side aided, in some ways, the emergence and sustaining of self-confidence of a subject nation.[36] In the context of today's battles, however, that route to self-confidence extracts a heavy price, making the progress of science and technology that much more difficult and giving more force to backward-looking

---

[34] Partha Chatterjee, *The Nation and Its Fragments* (Princeton: Princeton University Press, 1993), p. 6.

[35] In 'India and the West', *The New Republic*, 7 June, 1993.

[36] There were, however, many divisions on this subject among the nationalists themselves, in the context of social reform (often requiring a rejection of the inherited beliefs and customs) and the promotion of scientific education (seeing some of India's contemporary weaknesses in that light).

politics than it could otherwise have had. The remnants of the confrontation of the colonial era partly ends up being a roadblock on the way to India's ability to make the best of what science and material knowledge can offer at this time.

If this diagnosis is right, then the question does arise as to whether it would not be appropriate, in reinterpreting India's past, to move away from this devised 'spiritual' image of Indian culture. But would it be possible? How would it fit into a historical understanding of Indian culture? Also, since science has often been pursued by the upper classes, would not such a shift in focus take us away from the masses to the elite, thereby delivering us back to old-style history of rulers and aristocracy? In answering these complex questions, I would like to make four observations.

First, as I had argued earlier, the interpretation of a culture and of tradition is not just a matter of epistemology, but also inevitably involves practical reason. If contemporary science and technology are important for the future of India, we are not shackled by any necessity to 'establish' a great scientific past to be free to focus on the role of science today.

Yet the resistance to what is seen as 'Western science' or called 'Western rationality' gives the historical interpretation a social and cultural importance that cannot be entirely ignored. This takes me to the second point. It is important to recognize that the 'spiritual' interpretation of India's speciality was itself a result of its colonial past (to which its dialectic relation with the West contributed).[37] The issue, thus, is not one of an 'invention' of a non-existent past, but looking at other parts of the past which were underemphasized through the modalities of colonial confrontation. Indeed, a significant part of what is seen as 'Western' science and technology were directly influenced by contributions from elsewhere, including Indian mathematics which reached the West through the Arabs.

Third, the role of the elite is a difficult issue in dealing with history. It is, I think, a mistake to be so 'anti-elitist' as to miss out an understanding of the role of the elite in the generation of science and knowledge that ultimately affects the lives of all—the subaltern as well as the elite. This is an issue that was well discussed by Marx himself, and certainly his rejection of what he called—in words that infuriate many post-modernists—'the idiocy of village life' relates to this general issue. Fear of elitism did

---

[37] I have presented the arguments that lead to that conclusion in 'India and the West' (1993).

not, happily, deter Joseph Needham from writing his authoritative account of the history of science and technology in China, and to dismiss that work as elitist history would be a serious neglect of China's past.[38]

Finally, the persistent deprivation of the 'subaltern' does not take the exclusive form of a denial of their *role* in the making of history. There are real deprivations of material well-being as well as denials of intellectual opportunities (including the negation of the chance, even for the most talented among the non-elite, to pursue science and technology). To do justice to the subaltern, the material circumstances and intellectual opportunities they have—*right now*—would have to expand. This task is altogether different from that of giving due recognition to the historically important role that the subalterns had played in colonial struggles and in other changes in the past. Substantive inequalities and deprivations of the present also deserve serious attention.

It can certainly be argued that the continuation of educational and social inequalities in India has been helped by the tendency of classical nationalist theory to focus on an automatic tendency towards 'unity' and to underplay differences and disparities. Despite his continuous use of the rhetoric of education for all, Nehru and the Party he led put very little emphasis in practice on universal education when they gained office. The implicit concentration on a seamless unity, which was discussed in other contexts earlier on in the paper, might well have hindered a concerted effort to remedy the deprivation of the educationally neglected.

But the eradication of this deprivation is not helped just by admiring the non-elite and their role in history, while leaving unaddressed their real deprivations that continue into the present. And in this context, a methodology that has the effect of undermining the importance of science and technology—in the guise of rejecting 'modernism'—might well be

[38] Joseph Needham, *Science and Civilization in China*, Vols. 1–5, (Cambridge: Cambridge University Press, 1954–94). A similar history of India's science and technology has not yet been attempted, though many of the elements have been well discussed in particular studies. The absence of a general study like Needham's is influenced by an attitudinal dichotomy. On the one hand, those who take a rather spiritual—even perhaps a religious—view of India's history do not have a great interest in the analytical and scientific parts of India's past, except to use it as a piece of propaganda about India's greatness (as in the bloated account of what is imaginatively called 'Vedic mathematics', missing the really creative period in Indian mathematics by many centuries). On the other hand, many who oppose religious and communal politics, are particularly suspicious of what may even look like a 'glorification' of India's past. The need for a work like Needham's has remained unmet.

deeply counterproductive. The original motivation of 'subaltern history' is not subject to this charge, since doing justice to the past need not prejudice fairness in the present. But the marriage of that historical tradition with 'anti-modernism' links the two enterprises. While the problem here arises to some extent from the befuddling notion of 'modernity' itself (and thus can be attributed to the theories of modernity that preceded post-modernism), the anti-moderns of today seem to join their hands effortlessly with modernists in seeing the concept of 'modernity' as unproblematic (the anti-modernists are against 'it', while the modernists favour 'it'). In the process the status of science—evolved in different places at different times—as an engine of social change, is deeply undermined.

When in the 11th century, the Arab-Iranian mathematician Alberuni came to India, and studied extensively Indian mathematics, astronomy, general sciences, linguistics, and history, he already spoke of the real deprivation of 'those castes who are not allowed to occupy themselves with science'.[39] That substantive deprivation remains largely untouched even today (after nearly a millennium), with half of the adult population of India (and nearly two-thirds of the adult women) still illiterate, and there is very little evidence, except in some specific regions, of a serious effort to bring education and science to the large mass of the citizens of India.[40] In the context of this overwhelming failure, to undermine the importance of science itself is to work *for* inequity and injustice, rather than *against* it. And insofar as the dereliction of policies towards general education in India is part of a failure of the state machinery, what is needed is a censure of governance, not an undermining of science.

CONCLUDING REMARKS

The interpretation of the past has importance both because of its contribution to our self-understanding, and because of its relevance in addressing contemporary problems of practical importance. The method-ological approach underlying the analysis presented here has drawn on

---

[39] *Alberuni's India*, translated by Edward C. Sachau, edited by Ainslie T. Embree (New York: Norton, 1971), Ch. 2, p. 32.

[40] On the extent of the educational backwardness and inequality in today's India, and its pervasive economic and social consequences, see Jean Drèze and Amartya Sen, *India: Economic Development and Social Opportunity* (Oxford: Clarendon Press, 1995).

two general claims (1) The relevance of practical reason (in addition to pure epistemology) in addressing issues of identity and in interpreting the past; and (2) The need to take note of positional perspectives in understanding history. Neither claim undermines the pertinence of truth and veracity, nor dismisses the demands of objectivity in knowledge and understanding. The difference lies, rather, in the discipline of selection, in particular in the construction of a coherent and cogent picture (1) based on different—and possibly diverse—positional observations, and (2) taking note of the practical implications of different criteria of selection.[41] Many things have happened in the past, and even though some claims can prove to be false in a way that others are not, there is still no escape from selection and discrimination among the class of non-false statements in 'reading' the past. In judging the relevance of particular observations, we have to place them in the context of the positionality of the observer and the analyst, and also pay attention to the cogency of different perspectives in terms of the priorities of practical choice.

The classical nationalist approaches developed in pre-independence India have to be understood and judged in terms of the tasks that were then faced, and then have to be reassessed in the light of the problems faced contemporarily. I have tried to argue that despite many lapses, which can be readily identified, there was epistemic merit as well as practical value in the classical nationalist approaches to 'Indianness', and furthermore, there are merits in some of these visions even in the context of the current challenges faced in post-independent India (particularly arising from divisiveness, sectarianism, inequality and communal tension).[42] The denial of these merits are based, in many cases, on a factual neglect of the richness of India's history, and sometimes on conceptual

---

[41] I have discussed the necessity of selection and the importance of non-arbitrary choice in 'Description as Choice', in my *Choice, Welfare and Measurement* (Oxford: Blackwell, and Cambridge, MA: MIT Press, 1982), and in 'Accounts, Actions and Values,' in C. Lloyd (ed.), *Social Theory and Political Practice* (Oxford: Clarendon Press, 1983).

[42] The limitations of 'nationalist' conceptions in the context of *international* problems are, of course, well-known and belong to a different set of concerns. Those issues—growing in importance in the strife-ridden world of today—raise other questions, which I am not addressing in this paper (as was explained in the introductory section of this essay). In fact, the move to communal diversity *within* a nation would not, in itself, do much to reduce the possibility of tension *between* nations.

confounding (for example between the concepts of a 'nation' and a 'nation-state', which are related but non-congruent).

There were also many strategic elements in Indian self-definitions that played a significant part in the confrontation with Western imperialism; they are part of what was earlier described as 'external orientation' in the reading of India's past. These features too are subject to contemporary reassessment and scrutiny, in terms both of epistemic cogency and practical reason.

For example, the brandishing of India's 'spirituality' vis-à-vis Western 'materialism' (built on very selective readings of India's intellectual past) may well have served some useful purpose in resisting Western dominance, but half a century after independence, that focus, I have tried to show, can be deeply counterproductive in contemporary India. The representative nature of this selective image was open to doubt even when this line of reasoning had proved rather effective in the assertion of India's independent standing, but that practical justification has weakened over time, without its gaining in epistemic strength through more historical evidence in that direction. The selectional priorities, despite the neglect of much contrary evidence, might have had some practical justification in the context of battling the Raj to establish an independent India, but with the change of challenges and priorities, the retention of the same emphasis and reading today would be hard to justify.

The interpretation of India's past cannot but be sensitive to the concerns of today. Our identities cannot be defined independently of our traditions and past, but this does not indicate a linear sequence whereby we interpret our past first, and then arrive at our identity, equipped to face contemporary issues. On the contrary, our reading of the past and understanding of the present are interdependent, and the selectional criteria that are central to interpreting the past have to take note of the relevance of the different concerns in the contemporary world. While we cannot live *without* our past, we need not live *within* it either.

3

The Rhetoric of Democracy and Development in Late Colonial India

David Washbrook

political development

At first sight, the reasons for discussing democracy and development in the context of the late colonial Indian state may seem very curious. Not only did the latter do very little to advance the causes of either, but, being a 'British' colonial state, it held only the most limited understanding of them. The concepts of democracy and development are not the first to come to mind when considering the history of even the domestic British state during this, the inter-war, period.

Yet, from another angle, India's experiences in this era of democracy and development, and of the relationship between them, may have been extremely important in setting the agendas of the future. For, try as it might, the British colonial state could not shut out the insistent demands on its policies and practices made in the name of these core values of the twentieth century. A rising nationalist movement at home and deepening struggles with Fascism and Bolshevism abroad forced it to revive Britain's formal credentials as a liberal power; while depression, war and a rapidly changing structure of the international economy wrecked the old colonial system and obliged consideration of how India might be 'developed' within the framework of a new one. The epoch witnessed a broadening of 'representative', if not particularly democratic, forms of government in the economy.

If, however, the colonial state had to accommodate these pressures from the beginning of the twentieth century on and could not, as it undoubtedly would have liked, preserve indefinitely that combination of bureaucratic despotism and free market economics that had characterized the nineteenth, it was not without means of containing them. Institutionally, it retained a firm grip over the apparatuses of governance and, ideologically, it possessed far more experience than any of its opponents, at least inside India, at redefining the terms 'democracy' and 'development', those most flexible of concepts, to make them compatible with continuing authoritarian rule and the privileging of narrow vested interests. It conceived a series of strategies, symbolized perhaps by the amazing 1935 *Government of India Act*, designed to extend representation and promote economic growth without, apparently, changing any of the basic relations of power and wealth constructed under its long period of rule. Democracy and development here were meant to be imprisoned within the structures of the colonial past.

At one level, at least, the strategies plainly failed: in 1947 India acquired freedom with a commitment to universal democracy and to planned national development, which went far beyond anything evolved under the late colonial state and, indeed, represented policies deliberately conceived in opposition to its highly constraining influences. In many ways, the stroke of midnight on 15 August 1947 shattered the links between the colonial past and the national future. But at other levels these conservative strategies were extremely successful and may be seen to have come down to independent India, patterning some of her own responses to the problems of later years. The success derived from the extent to which the strategies became embedded in institutional practices and professional ideologies taken over wholesale by the newly independent state and exercising subtle, often unseen, restraints on the imagined freedoms which India's politicians thought they had won.

There is perhaps no clearer indicator of this subtle post-colonial influence than the ultimate fate of the 1935 *Government of India Act*, originally designed to undermine the national integrating functions of the Congress, to submerge the voices of *demos* beneath those of executive authority and aristocratic privilege and to keep India tied to the apron-strings of Westminster. The Act did not entirely die with the rule of the King-Emperor: when India wrote 'her own' constitution in 1950, she took more than 250 of its clauses straight out of the relevant Parliamentary publication. Included among those clauses were the ones which Mrs Gandhi later would use 'constitutionally' to suspend the constitution and to revive a form of President/Viceroy's rule first seen in 1939.

THE RHETORIC OF DEMOCRACY

Extensive though the contributions of British scholars to political theory may be, they have rarely offered much elucidation of the concept of 'democracy'. Even the most celebrated essay on the subject in the English language preferred the title 'On Representative Government' and, though regarded as radical in its mid-Victorian day, can scarcely escape the charge of elitism brought against it latterly by Maurice Cowling, among many others.[1] Over the course of the nineteenth century, the dominant British liberal tradition succeeded in appropriating the term 'democracy' from eighteenth-century popular radicalism and giving it a quite different set of meanings. 'Democratization' now came to refer to that slow process whereby ruling elites co-opted into the functioning of the state successive layers of 'sub-elites' who were to prove their 'responsibility' by providing consensual support for the judgements of their masters. And a very slow process it was too: Britain, 'the mother of liberty', achieved full adult suffrage only in 1928, scarcely a generation before India and many generations after the majority of societies in Western Europe and North America. Moreover, what relationship this suffrage has to organization and exercise of state power, and whether it is meaningful to conceive of the existence of democratic 'rights', as opposed to 'concessionary privileges', remain open questions. Britain possesses no written constitution and, in the light of several legal judgements of recent years, it is arguable whether 'subjects' possess any rights at all, even of interrogation, against the executive authority of the state.

Conceptually, the dominant British political tradition has always been inclined to conceive of the state as prior to the interest of any of its constituent members. As a result, arguments about the virtues and vices of democracy (even, for that matter, Mill's) have tended to be couched in terms, not of inalienable human rights, but of what would better facilitate the functioning of the state and the maintenance of social order. This has had several serious consequences for the nature of British political structure.

First, it has meant that the symbolic and the executive elements in the state have taken precedence over the representational and the legislative. The former (the monarchy, bureaucracy, law and armed forces) stand for continuity, order and guardianship over 'the whole of society'. The latter are merely transient and particularistic which, if not watched carefully, will bring about disruption (i.e. change) and chaos (i.e. a re-alignment of the social order). This position has two corollaries: first, of course, it imputes a demeaned function to 'politics', including democratic/representational politics. These last are held to reflect only sectional, if not individual, sets of interests, to be potentially corrupt and to threaten the workings of 'good' government. In the British state

---

[1] See Maurice Cowling, *Mill and Liberalism* (Cambridge: Cambridge University Press, 1963).

tradition, being 'above politics' (as the monarchy, the civil service, etc.) represents a higher, more legitimate, condition than being 'in' them; and the final accolade sought by every major politician is to be regarded as 'a statesman' who has risen out of the day-to-day, hurly-burly of the political process to join the other metaphysical beings protecting the continuity of 'the state'. The second corollary is that, in the British tradition, representational/democratic politics take place inside a highly conservative institutional and ideological straitjacket designed to constrain most of their urgings. The tightness and strength of the straitjacket may be judged from the extent to which it has enabled an extremely narrow 'gentry' stratum of society to repel, or accommodate, the challenges of industrialization, urbanization and 'mass' society until very recently, without losing its cultural hegemony.

A further consequence for British political culture has been the tendency to conceive of democracy instrumentally, in terms of the ends which it will achieve rather than the rights which it reflects. And, most usually, those ends have been concerned with deepening state power and control over areas of society inaccessible to it before. The co-option of sub-elites and their incorporation into state processes as 'representatives' for wider constituencies has been particularly efficacious in this regard. While, at one level, modern British history may be a history of progressive democratization, at another it is also a history of expanding state authority and coercion. In a large number of cases, ranging from local government to school boards to police committees, the two have been but opposite sides of the same coin.

These rather lengthy remarks about the meanings of democracy in British ruling culture may seem out of place in a paper supposedly dealing with India. But they gain their relevance from the extent to which the pressures and strains pushing late colonial India towards democratization were mediated by a state apparatus heavily influenced by this culture. In India, no less than (indeed somewhat more than) in Britain, the executive elites sought to deflect demands for democracy into recipes for representation and to preserve the supposed autonomy and integrity of 'the state' from the insistent importunings of mass politics. As in Britain too, one part of the tragedy of modernity may be the remarkable extent to which they succeeded.

Institutionally, India's pathway to democracy could hardly have been less promising. The first representative institutions were introduced to strengthen the colonial state after the shocks caused by the Mutiny. Most famously, they consisted of Governors' Councils where prominent notables were invited to offer advice to the ICS so that the latter could keep in touch with 'native opinion'. The notion that the real function of representation was advisory, while 'policy' was made by the bureaucracy, remained basic to British schemes of democratization right up to the Montagu–Chelmsford reforms of 1919, if not indeed the *Government of India Act* of 1935. It was, of course, later challenged and in large part overturned by the very different conception of representative democracy held by the national movement. However, at least two legacies of this initial ideology of representation were bequeathed to India even beyond 1947.

It was over the question of who had the right to represent whom that the issue of 'communalism' first entered the structure of the state. Familiarly, the introduction of principles of separate representation for 'Hindus', 'Muslims', landholders, etc., has been seen as a peculiarly colonial device constructed by the British for the purposes of 'divide-and-rule'. From a broader angle, however, it may be seen, more simply, to reflect British ruling elite ideas about the nature of representation itself. By definition, members of civil society could only represent specific and sectional interests since it was axiomatic that societal integration took place only through the state and thus the state executive alone could represent the 'whole' society. To conceive of the possibility that any member of civil society, 'Indian' or other, could represent his 'whole' society would have been to undermine the functions and legitimacy of the entire British ruling tradition. It was, and remains, a crucial strategy of this kind of state, to preserve its authority, that civil society be seen as 'naturally' divided. When independent India inherited a large part of the ideology and apparatus of the late colonial state, it also inherited this necessary strategy. In seeking to understand the post-colonial intensification of 'communal' strife, it may be important to consider not only developments in civil society but also the sources wherein the post-colonial state tries to ground its legitimacy.

The second and related legacy was the inflated role accorded to itself by the bureaucracy (and judiciary) as the proper makers of policy and the guardians of society. Although, from the time of Cornwallis, bureaucrats and judges had tried to give themselves this status, their success had been limited by the fact that they were, technically, the employees of a joint stock Company whose primary function was to make money. This situation changed with the abolition of the Company and with the introduction of representative institutions against whose implications the bureaucracy now had to define its own place. (It also changed, it might be added, at this time with the rise to power over Oxford schools of Jowett and the beginnings of a 'service' ideology for the British civil 'service' itself.) The later Victorian ICS, as the whole of the British 'establishment', developed a high-flown rhetoric of impartiality and guardianship, which served to protect its moral authority, and quasi-hereditary elite status, from the challenges of rising democracy. To a degree, that rhetoric, and the ideology behind it, continued into the post-colonial era where it was used to delegitimate programs of radical change in everything from the law to the linguistic bases of the state. Indeed, once the Indian National Congress became the state, the pretence of being 'above politics' plainly passed into its own ideology of leadership.

Yet perhaps the most significant paths towards Indian democracy (as opposed to democracy in India) were laid by post-Mutiny developments in much humbler areas. The Mutiny created not only a moral and political crisis in the colonial state but also a financial and economic crisis. The new Crown state was saddled with burgeoning debts but had to be cautious in increasing taxation lest it foment further revolt. It also had to abandon the highly extractive fiscal policies of the Company era, which had brought several parts of the Indian economy to ruin, and to find ways of reviving and stimulating an economic growth without which India would have been a very poor imperial asset. To help it out of these problems, the colonial state turned to 'democracy', or rather to representation, at the local level—thereby initiating a series of strategies which continue to affect the Indian polity.

The task here was to extend and off-load many of the petty functions—for roads, sanitation, primary schools—onto locally elected and co-opted 'native' boards and municipalities. Once these were in place, taxation could be increased by means which made it appear that Indian society was taxing itself; and much time-consuming local administration could be passed to unpaid 'politicians'. That the extension of these responsibilities should not involve any meaningful shift in power, however, was guaranteed by a complex system of controls, which kept budgets and administration under central surveillance and dependent upon handouts of official patronage; and by a construction of local political structures, which kept them parochial, divided and distant from the real centres of power.

As early as the 1860s, the British began to discover forms of representative government, which were largely compatible with their continuing overrule and which, over the next several generations, they steadily expanded, in part to meet cheaply the many new tasks being

Structural summary of Dev

asked of government but also in part as a response to oppositional demands for the widening of democracy. The hope was that India's democratic urges could be contained and ensnared in these institutions, which serviced the colonial state's needs; that they were incapable (except in a few cases, such as Calcutta[2]) of providing launching pads for a broader oppositional politics and were controllable through networks of resource distribution. In the later colonial period, whenever the national movement asked for 'democracy', the British replied by offering 'devolution' and their model, conceived after World War One, for their progressive 'withdrawal' from India was based upon steadily expanding the principles of so-called local self-government from the bottom of the Indian political pyramid upwards.

As a strategy for preserving British authority to the last possible minute, for undermining the functioning of any meaningful 'national' politics and for creating a context of relations in which the jibes of bureaucrats at the corruption and particularism of politicians became almost self-fulfilling prophecies, it needs to be said that these ploys were only too successful. In 1937, the Indian National Congress, albeit against the advice of its 'high command', voted to buy the British conception of democracy as devolution and 'entered' the institutions of 'representative' local and provincial self-government. The result was a very sorry period in the history of the national movement. Concern to offer consistent and united opposition to the British disappeared amidst unseemly scrambles for patronage, bitter factional feuds over the status and fruits of office and sharpening communal antagonisms. Gandhi's call in 1939 for 'the resignation of the Ministries' came not a moment too soon to rescue the Congress from itself and to restore the ideals of the freedom struggle. However, the political model had been established and, after 1947, it was clearly used by the new Congress state to develop 'the machine' system of politics, based upon patronage links between central and local government, which sustained its power until the 1960s.

A further corollary to these politics was the elaboration of a highly problematic system of pseudo-federalism. Faced with the uncomfortable prospect, after World War One, of having to concede broader rights of representation, the colonial state developed a strategy of 'retreating to the centre'. It seemed to concede the principles of democratic right by establishing franchises, legislatures and ministries in the various provinces

---

[2] C.R. Das and his followers were successful to an extent in the 1920s in subverting the institutions of local and municipal governments to achieve their own nationalist ends.

and, after 1937, even handing over powers of what it called 'self-government' to them. This gave the emergent Indian constitution the appearance of a kind of federalism. But it was a very peculiar kind for, of course, all the most important powers of government (fiscal, military, foreign policy, etc.) were held 'reserved' at a centre which, itself, was virtually outside any democratic control. The system was actually more dualistic than federal; it passed administrative responsibility, and little else, to democracy in the provinces, while keeping real power firmly in the hands of the bureaucracy (and, it was hoped, aristocracy) at the centre.

The implications of 1937 for the development of an Indian politics were very serious. Democratic aspirations were fanned in provincial legislatures with promises of meaningful self-government. Yet the provincial legislatures, which were designed to divert attention away from the centre more than anything else, had not the means of meeting these aspirations. They were also designed to offset demands for a national polity by promoting divisive regionalist sentiments. What the would-be 1935 constitution offered was a recipe for expanding internal political conflict, between centre and provinces over their respective roles, between executives and legislatures over their respective powers, between democracy and oligarchy over their respective principles. It represented the last-ditch stand of a waning colonial state trying, against reason and history, to define some continuing place for itself.

last gasps of Empire?

The events of 1947 finally aborted the 1935 proposals but, problematically, those of 1950 brought more than a fair share of them back again. As noted before, the authors of the Indian Constitution put an extraordinary degree of faith in the political wisdom of the British and drew heavily on the 1935 Act. By so doing, they thus drew quintessentially 'colonial' forms of political relationship into the core of their emergent national democratic state. That issues concerning the design of provincial states and their relationship to the centre, concerning the uneasy relations between executive and legislature and concerning the provenance of democratic authority should subsequently have bedevilled the history of the Indian nation cannot be regarded as wholly surprising. They came as part of a colonial inheritance which was all too readily accepted.

THE RHETORIC OF DEVELOPMENT

In many ways, several of India's major problems of development also can be seen to derive from a failure to question seriously enough the colonial inheritance. Although inclined to pose as a *laissez-faire* state for much of the later nineteenth century, and to allow Britain's industrial monopoly to bring its own rewards through the market-place, the British Raj also possessed a strongly interventionist side. The eagerness of the Company to lay claim to all possible sources of land revenue meant that, from an early date, its government found itself simultaneously charged with responsibility for providing irrigation and various support services to agriculture. The needs of the military and of emergent plantation economies required large-scale involvement in a variety of labour and factor markets. India's massive railway building programme was also closely directed by the state. It is arguable, however, whether the nineteenth-century colonial state thought of any of these activities immediately in terms of their implications for socio-economic 'development': they were conducted, and costed, much more for reasons of 'state' profit and power. Indeed, even the elaboration of the famine code was promoted as much by concern for the losses of revenue, which famine brought, as for the loss of life.

The First World War dramatically changed both the political context within which issues of economic growth and social welfare were considered and the economic context within which they had to be resolved. On the one hand, a nascent domestic public opinion and a rising national movement demanded greater accountability and policies geared more obviously to India's, rather than Britain's, interests. On the other, the decline of the colonial staples and a shift in India's relations with the rest of the world economy necessitated a radical restructuring of her systems of production and trade. At one level, the colonial state responded to these changes purposefully. It progressively abandoned its (albeit selective) stance on non-interference in markets; it instituted wide-ranging inquiries into areas of the economy about which it had previously been in blissful ignorance; it drew up plans and recruited experts and technicians; most noticeably, it even found itself defining and defending a notionally 'Indian' national economy, replete with its own tariff barriers, Reserve Bank and industrialization strategies. Many of the instruments and controls with which independent India was to try to 'manage' her own economy were forged in the last years of the British Raj, particularly in the 1930s and 1940s under the successive strains of depression and war.

At the same time, however and perhaps obviously, these instruments and controls were never designed simply to promote India's economic welfare and the development of her 'national' economy. They also served a variety of other purposes: in part, to keep going for as long as possible the residual benefits of the colonial system and to slough off the additional costs which it now was incurring; in part, to safeguard the authority of the bureaucracy itself; in part, to secure the social bases of privilege on which the Raj was founded. Although the cause of Indian development was enthusiastically embraced by the late colonial state, amidst a paper shower of committees and reports, plans and promises, the rhetoric was often meant to mislead, or to disguise the extent to which the embrace encircled India's throat. What was achieved was less the provision for India of a new economic dawn than the prolongation of a long post- or neo-colonial night.

In the first place, the inter-war era of emergent planned development was marked by a spectacular decline in levels of state, and state supported, investment in the economy. Major programmes of railway building came to an end; changing military priorities reduced the need for investment in support structures for the army; perhaps most significantly of all, with the completion of the major riverine irrigation projects, capital investment in agriculture dried up. By the early 1930s, Sir George Schuster could proudly proclaim the state's capital expenditure commitments cut to a mere Rs 6 crores from an average of Rs 24 crores in the 1920s and, in real terms, many times more than that in the later nineteenth century. This was to be an era of planned development without money.

Given both the unstable international financial climate and the prospect of foreseeable British 'withdrawal', the reasons for the colonial state's parsimony in capital investment seem clear enough. More interesting, perhaps, is how, in the context of nationalist opinion, the state was able to get away with it. In part, this seems to have been due to conceptual illusions created by the invention of new categories: with planning and development spawning their own rhetoric, departments and bureaucracies, sight seems to have been lost of the many implications for development of other forms of government activity. 'Specialization' here produced tunnel vision. In part, however, the colonial state was able to 'get away with it' because of severe limitations in the conceptual apparatus of its principal political opponent, the Indian National Congress. Congress's economic thinking remained locked into the nineteenth century, viewing India's problems primarily in terms of distributional relations with Britain and within Indian society itself. Its own programme centred on forcing industrialization behind protection and on promoting land reform. It failed to see that the economic cheese of capital investment, particularly in agriculture, was being stolen from under its nose. This blindness continued into the 1950s, creating a situation in which an agriculture, starved of capital investment for, by then, a generation, threatened to creak to a halt.

With the thorny issue of agricultural productivity, in an epoch of declining prices and dwindling markets, removed, apparently by mutual agreement, from the agenda of development, the colonial state could look much more happily on the problems of planning. Its concession of the case for selective tariff reform (by then, hardly the issue in British politics which once it had been, save in the Labour Party which had been taken over by J. Hobson's anachronistic free trade ideals) opened opportunities for protecting colonial markets, for promoting new styles of imperialism and for forging new relations of mutual support with India's rising industrial capitalists. The tariff policies which emerged in the 1920s and 1930s were aimed primarily at keeping the Japanese, and other 'foreign' competitors, out of Indian markets while judiciously dividing the remaining cake between British and indigenous interests. The resulting tariff barriers provided as much cosy protection for British, as for Indian, industrial capital to find safe profits for itself. Indeed, so safe that, as A. K. Bagchi has seen, many new Indian industries rapidly reached positions of overcapitalization as resources flooded in to take advantage of the artificial security.[3]

This situation was no doubt ironic for a capital-short economy like India's but it was one whose lesson was only partially learned after 1947 by a post-colonial state which continued to confuse state-sponsored industrialization with state-protected profitability. The results were to provide very expensive and very lopsided trajectories of development for India and ones whose political implications went a long way towards altering the social complexion of the state. The conduct of the economy during World War Two made plain how close the relationship had become between the interests of private industrial capital and the public policies of the late colonial state. After independence, this relationship carried on and, indeed, was greatly strengthened. It was no accident that the very first bill introduced into independent India's new legislature should have been one to emasculate free trades unionism nor that the 'socialist' industrialization policies of the early five-year plans should have

[3] A. K.Bagchi, *Private Investment in India 1900–39* (Cambridge: Cambridge University Press, 1973).

spawned some of the largest privately owned industrial conglomerates in the non-Western world.

At least, however, the development strategies of the late colonial state produced some industrial benefits, if at considerable political price. Why this is remarkable is that, for the most part, these strategies were aimed at not producing, or changing, anything at all. The greater part of the state's interventions in the market place had as their objective the keeping of things going, which otherwise would have fallen down. The successive shocks of depression and war destabilized a wide variety of commodity, credit and food markets, threatening to wreak havoc not only with the economic relations which they expressed, but also with the social relations. The inter-war years saw deepening tensions, marked by conflict and riot, between groups at every level of the social system. To preserve order, as much to prevent breakdowns in the economy, the bureaucracy found itself having to intervene and coming, whether it liked it or not, to take over the regulation of large areas of India's complex and multiple systems of exchange.

Arguably, the underlying causes of these breakdowns went deeper than the international events which were often the occasions of them and reflected changes in structural conditions. On the land, population growth in the context of technological stagnation was altering the balance between capital and labour, pressing down the latter's share of the social product. In commodity markets, new monopsonistic conditions of demand, both at home and overseas, were eating into producers' returns. If these problems were satisfactorily to be resolved, at least to the point at which the market could be 'restored' and buyers and sellers command sufficient returns to reproduce both themselves and their material production, a radical social re-structuring of the distribution of resources and labour power was necessary.

Such a radical re-structuring, however, was practically impossible for the late colonial state, whose bases of social power lay with groups privileged by the present distribution, even to consider. Three corollaries flowed from this: first, having initially intervened in various markets as a short-term expedient, the state found it impossible ever to get out again. It was obliged to take an ever-widening responsibility for the regulation of exchange, spawning an ever more elaborate system of controls and licenses. Second, to explain its activities, it began to generate an anti-market ideology which put the blame for its predicament on the greed of, particularly, petty merchants rather than the structural conditions under which they had to work. In a curious elision of apparently opposite philosophies, for example, the highly conservative late colonial state of the 1930s began to propagate Fabian socialist ideas about the irrationalities of the market-place and the evils of 'the middle-man'.

And third, it hid its essentially political purposes behind a rhetoric of development aimed at helping the already-privileged groups, whose support it courted, rather than those most desperately in need. These last consisted principally of what it called 'the peasantry' and which, by European social reference, were supposed to represent the bottom of the social heap. But, of course, by Indian reference, landholding 'peasants' were the elite groups of village society with whom the colonial state, abandoning its erstwhile affection for rentier landlords, had been seeking a closer alliance since the later nineteenth century. Policies of aid, subvention and development aimed at 'the peasantry' helped further to support those groups who had done best out of the colonial economy but ignored the landless masses beneath, whose plight progressively worsened.

Once more these 'interventionist' instruments and ideologies, originally designed to serve the specific needs of the colonial state and to arrest decay in the socio-economic structures on which it was founded, seem to have had a long after-life beyond 1947. Of course, the post-colonial state came into existence with a mandate to effect a far more radical re-distribution of social resources than its predecessor had dared consider. But the terms of the mandate were at least confused by the degree to which the nation's new leaders subscribed to the colonial myth that rural India was at base a 'peasant' society. Extra resources (taken principally from a landlord class whose significance had long dwindled) were thus given to those groups in rural society who, arguably, needed them least and the structural problems, which had necessitated state intervention in the first place, went unresolved. In these circumstances, the new state no more than the old could withdraw from the market place and it found itself having to take yet greater responsibility for holding the exchange system together as imbalances in the relative market positions of different economic groups deteriorated further. Moreover, it also adopted that curious ideological mixture of Fabianism and conservatism to legitimise its actions and, for a long time, set out to hunt down the middle-man and the entrepreneur as the principal enemy of 'the people'. The new state, like the old, devoted a disproportionate share of its 'developmental' energies to keeping things going and ameliorating the consequences of change rather than leading it in more novel and constructive directions.

CONCLUSION

Democracy and development, which ought to be mutually supportive, stand today in sharp and antagonistic juxtaposition. Given their respective histories, of interpretation and institutionalization, in the late colonial state, this situation can hardly be deemed surprising. Democracy was 'conceded' in ways meant to separate power from responsibility, to diffuse opposition and to protect elite authority. Development was a synonym for conservation, for interposing state power to protect privileges and relations of erstwhile dominance, which changing conditions in the market-place were undermining. A starting point for a re-definition of these concepts would be to emancipate them from the historical legacies of the late colonial era.

4

Nation as Mother: Representations and Contestations of 'India' in Bengali Literature and Culture[1]

Sugata Bose

'Our history,' wrote the Swadeshi leader Bipin Chandra Pal, 'is the sacred biography of the Mother. Our philosophies are the revelations of the Mother's mind. Our arts—our poetry and our painting, our music and our drama, our architecture and our sculpture, all these are the outflow of the Mother's diverse emotional moods and experiences. Our religion is the organized expression of the soul of the Mother. The outsider knows her as India. . . . It is, I know, exceedingly difficult, if it be not absolutely impossible, for the European or American to clearly understand or fully appreciate this strange idealization of our land, which has given birth to this cult of the Mother among us.'[2] A cornerstone of what Pal described as his 'constructive study of Indian thought and ideals', this narration of the nation as mother was the literary and cultural patent of the Bengali political generation of 1905 as they strenuously sought to 'unsettle' the 'settled fact' of Curzon's partition of Bengal.[3]

[1] Earlier versions of this essay were presented at the seminar on 'Languages, Literatures and Societies in South Asia' at the University of Pennsylvania and at St. Antony's College, University of Oxford. I am grateful for comments by Ranajit Guha, David Ludden, Ayesha Jalal, Sumathi Ramaswamy, Gayatri Chakravorty Spivak and David Washbrook. I have benefited from the important theoretical and historical work on nationalism by Partha Chatterjee even though my disagreements with certain, key aspects of his method and conclusions will be evident. Needless to say, I bear sole responsibility for any errors and for any contentious arguments and interpretations I have chosen to advance.

[2] Bipin Chandra Pal, *The Soul of India: A Constructive Study of Indian Thoughts and Ideals* (4th edn, Calcutta: Yugayatri Prakashak, 1958), p. 134.

[3] Surendranath Banerjee's challenge to Curzon's confident assertion about the done deal of partition was phrased in these terms.

By the time of Mountbatten's more far-reaching partition of India a generation later, many political attitudes had changed and many roles reversed. In the spring of 1947 the erstwhile votaries of Indian unity started demanding the partition of Bengal and Punjab. In an editorial entitled 'Banga-bhanga Andolan' ('The Agitation to Divide Bengal') on 11 April 1947 the newsmagazine *Millat* (*Nation*) accused the Congress and the Hindu Mahasabha of performing the role of Parashuram as they 'together raised a sharpened pickaxe to slice "Mother" into two'. The Hindu Mahasabha's matricidal tendencies were more readily explicable. They had, according to *Millat*, been 'born mad' ('janma-batul' was the Bengali word used) and had always wanted to 'drive the Muslims to the shores of the Arabian Sea'. 'But Congress!', exclaimed Millat,... 'For half a century they had talked big and had preached many high ideals.... What had happened to them so suddenly that having taken off their mask they were dancing on the same platform with the Hindu Mahasabha?'[4]

THE PARASHURAM MYTH

The allusion to Parashuram refers to Puranic Hindu mythology. According to the Puranas, the *rishi* Jamadagni ordered his five sons, one by one, to murder their mother Renuka. The four elder sons refused to commit such a heinous act. The fifth, Ram, was made of sterner stuff and obeyed without displaying any qualms. He lifted his *parashu* (or *kuthar*, axe, in simpler Bengali) and struck the fatal blow. Parashuram, as he came to be called, was widely recognized in the Puranas as the sixth *avatar* (incarnation) of Vishnu, the immediate predecessor of the more famous seventh *avatar*, Dasarath's son Ram, whose exploits were narrated in the epic *Ramayana*.[5] *wowza*

ENGENDERING THE NATION

In a macabre twist to the narrative of the Indian nation the apparently triumphal moment of independence coincided with a gory dismemberment, if not the death, of the Mother. This was particularly ironic since the awakening of a nation from slumber, if not its actual birth, was

[4] *Millat*, 28 Chaitra, 1353; 11 April, 1947, p. 2.
[5] Those who are not steeped in Puranic mythology may wish to refer to Sudhir Chandra Sarkar (ed.), *Pouranic Abhidhan* (A Dictionary of the Puranas, Calcutta: M.C. Sarkar and Sons, 1963), pp. 289–92.

believed to have occurred when its children were blessed with a
revelation—the magical vision of the Mother. As Aurobindo Ghosh
argued in 1907, it was only when 'the Mother had revealed herself' that
'the patriotism that work[ed] miracles and save[d] a doomed nation [wa]s
born'. He credited Bankim Chandra Chattopadhyay with having caught
the first modern glimpse of this grand spectacle: 'It was thirty-two years
ago that Bankim wrote his great song and few listened; but in a sudden
moment of awakening from long delusions the people of Bengal looked
round for the truth and in a fated moment somebody sang *Bande
Mataram*. The mantra had been given...'[6]

Bankim's hymn to the Mother, originally written and printed in 1875
as a filler for a blank page in his journal *Bangadarshan* (Vision/Philosophy
of Bengal), had a chequered and controversial career in the service of
the nationalist movement. It was inserted into Bankim's novel *Anandamath*
in 1882 and set to music and sung publicly for the first time by
Rabindranath Tagore at the Calcutta session of the Indian National
Congress in 1896. I quote the first verse of this remarkable song:

Bande Mataram

Bande mataram,
sujalaang suphalaang, malayaja sheetalang,
shasya shyamalaang mataram.
Shubra-jyotsna-pulakita-jamineeng,
phullakusimita-drumadala-shobineeng,
suhasineeng sumadhura bhashineeng
sukhadaang baradaang mataram.
saptakotikantha-kalakala-ninada-karale,
dwisaptakotibhujaidhritakharakarabale,
abala keno ma eto bale!
Bahubaladhaarineeng, namami taarineeng,
ripudalabaarineeng mataram.

---

[6] Aurobindo Ghosh, 'Rishi Bankim Chandra' in *Bande Mataram*, 16 April,
1907. Aurobindo overlooked the contributions of Bhudeb Mukhopadhyay who
preceded Bankim in crafting the image of the mother in nationalist fiction. Of
course, Bhudeb missed the 'fated moment' and did not have the same impact
on Bengali nationalist consciousness as 'Rishi Bankim' (the sage Bankim).

I bow to you, Mother,
well-watered, well-fruited,
breeze cool, crop green,
the Mother!
Nights quivering with white moonlight,
draped in lovely flowering trees,
sweet of smile, honeyed speech,
giver of bliss and boons, the Mother!
Seven crore voices in your clamorous chant,
twice seven crore hands holding aloft mighty scimitars,
Who says, Mother, you are weak?
Repository of many strengths,
scourge of the enemy's army, the Mother![7]

The magic number of seven crores refers, of course, to Bengalis and the
Mother whom Bankim had in mind in 1875, even though there is no
specific mention, is Bangamata or Mother Bengal. The name Bharatavarsha
for the subcontinent as a whole was commonly used in the political
discourse of Bengal, certainly since the Hindu Mela of 1867.[8] One of
the earliest literary evocations of the concept of Bharatmata was
Dwijendralal Roy's song:

Jedin sunil jaladhi hoite uthile janani Bharatavarsha,
Shedin bishwe she ki kalarab, she ki ma bhakti, she ki ma harsha.

The day you arose from the blue ocean, Mother Bharatvarsha,
The world erupted in such a joyful clamour, such devotion, mother,
and so much laughter.

An early visual evocation came in 1905 with Abanindranath Tagore's
painting 'Bharatmata'. Visualized as a serene, saffron-clad ascetic woman,
the Mother carried the boons of food, clothing, learning and spiritual
salvation in her four hands. A conscious creation of an 'artistic' icon of
the nation, Abanindranath tells us in a memoir that he had conceived
his image as Bangamata and later, almost as an act of generosity towards

[7] I have read Aurobindo's translations of this poem in verse and prose in
Karmayogin, 20 November, 1909 and have borrowed from him. But I have made
quite a few changes in an attempt to give a more accurate and simpler rendering
of the Bengali original.

[8] There is mention of this in Rabindranath Tagore, *Jibansmriti* in *Rabindra
Rachanabali*, Vol. 17, (Calcutta: Viswa-Bharati, 1965), pp. 348–53.

the larger cause of Indian nationalism, decided to title it 'Bharatmata'.[9]
I will directly address the contradictions between the linguistic region,
Bengal, and the overarching nation, India, later in the paper, but for the
moment it is necessary to probe a little further into the relationship
between nation and gender.

The figure of gender has been central to a large array of modern and
post-modern readings of the colonial encounter. Ashis Nandy, among
others, has underscored the theme of male anxiety and fantasy in the
projection of colonial knowledge and power and its attempted inversion,
if not subversion, in Gandhian resistance.[10] Thoroughly 'Westernized'
nationalists like Jawaharlal Nehru relied heavily on the metaphor of
sexual aggression and rape in their critiques of the violence perpetrated
by the colonial masters. Recently, Sara Suleri has objected that 'the
continued equation between a colonized landscape and the female body
represents an alteritist fallacy that causes considerable theoretical damage
to both contemporary feminist and post-colonial discourses'. She points
out that the 'colonial gaze' was not directed to 'the inscrutability of an
Eastern bride' but rather to 'the greater sexual ambivalence of the
effeminate groom'. '[N]o intelligent feminism,' she contends, 'should be
prepared to serve as the landscape upon which the intimacy of
homoerotic invitation and rejection can be enacted.'[11] Yet there was more
to the casting of the nation in the image of mother than is captured by
the metaphors of heterosexual aggression and resistance and homoerotic
invitation and rejection. The mother complex (I use the term 'complex'
simply to refer to an engaging social-psychological phenomenon and not
to mean any sort of disorder or neurosis) in Bengal and some other
linguistic regions in India had fairly deep psychological and cultural
roots.

It is tempting to interpret 'the concept of the Motherland—Deshmata',
as Tanika Sarkar has done, as a 'cultural artefact'.[12] But to nationalist
thinkers like Bipin Pal the Mother in what had come to be called
Motherland by modern Western-educated Indians was in origin 'not a

---

[9] Cf. Tapati Guha-Thakurta, *The Making of a New 'Indian' Art: Artists,
Aesthetics and Nationalism in Bengal, c. 1850–1920* (Cambridge: Cambridge
University Press, 1992), pp. 255, 258.

[10] See Ashis Nandy, *The Intimate Enemy: Loss and Recovery of Self under
Colonialism* (Delhi: Oxford University Press, 1983).

[11] Sara Suleri, *The Rhetoric of English India*, (Chicago, 1992), pp. 16–17.

[12] Tanika Sarkar, 'Nationalist Iconography: Image of Women in 19th Century
Bengali Literature' in *Economic and Political Weekly*, 21 November, 1987, p. 2011.

[handwritten: literal understanding of India as a mother]

mere idea or fancy, but a distinct personality. The woman who bore them and nursed them, and brought them up with her own life and substance was no more real a personality in their thought and idea than the land which bore and reared, and gave food and shelter to all their race.' While European expressions like fatherland were 'clearly metaphorical', the 'real concept Mother as applied to India' had 'no metaphor behind it'. The 'full truth and reality of this concept' could only be grasped, in Pal's view, 'in the light of the entire Nature Philosophy of the Hindus', especially the conception of the Earth as Prakriti.[13]

That the conception of the earth as mother was not peculiarly Indian is suggested by recent work on European environmental history which has posited a strong correlation between the earth and the nurturing mother before the historic rupture of the scientific revolution of the sixteenth and seventeenth centuries altered an organic view of the cosmos. Until that happened the onslaughts on nature were restrained by the culture of a nature-mother equation for, the Parushurams of the world excepted, men did 'not readily slay a mother, dig into her entrails for gold, or mutilate her body...'[14] A relatively undisturbed 'cosmic balance' was, however, not the only bridge between the love of mother and devotion to the motherland, but was importantly mediated by specific cultures and ideologies and articulated by the vernacular languages of nationalism.

Did the element of 'reality', stressed by Pal, in the 'imagination' of the nation as mother lend a special quality to the 'profoundly self-sacrificing love'[15] inspired by this particular devotional movement? I will turn later in this paper to young Bengali revolutionaries who sacrificed their lives in the cause of the mother-nation. But it would be a grave error to treat the narrative of the nation as mother related by men like Pal as constituted outside the domain of ideology. Pal was not above resorting to analytical sleights of hand to locate a Prakriti-Ma or Nature-Mother equation within his particular project of cultural nationalism.[16] The ideological construction of the nation as mother was vectored on

[13] Pal, *Soul of India*, pp. 102–5, 108–9.

[14] Carolyn Merchant, *The Death of Nature: Women, Ecology and the Scientific Revolution* (San Francisco: Harper and Row, 1980), pp. 2–3.

[15] See Benedict Anderson, *Imagined Communities: Reflections on the Origin and Spread of Nationalism* (London: Verso, 1991), p. 141.

[16] I am grateful to Ranajit Guha and Gayatri Chakravorty Spivak for encouraging me to take a sceptical view of Pal's ideological construction.

to a dynamic, discursive field previously unmarked by political values. The mobilizers and mobilized necessarily stood in different positions in relation to this construct.

In the cultural context of Bengal the nationalist cult of the Mother, not surprisingly, emphasized the female principle as Shakti or the source of strength. Consequently, a certain concordance came to be drawn between the Mother Goddess, whether in the form of Durga or Kali, and the mother country. Tanika Sarkar suggests that a contradictory image, that of the mother as an 'archetypical, hapless, female victim' was also present in the nationalist iconography. As an example she cites the 'Bharatmata' painted by Abanindranath—'pale, tearful, frail'.[17] This may not be a particularly good example. To me, at any rate, 'Bharatmata' looks fairly radiant, calm and reassuring. But 'srinkhalita Bharatmata', the Mother bound in chains, was a widely used emotive image in nationalist posters and the contrast between 'ma ki chhilen' (the way mother had been) and 'ma ki hoiachhen' (what mother has become or been reduced to) was quite enough to fire the nationalist ire. In addition to her glorious past and her sorry present, the utopia of 'ma ki hoiben' (what mother will be) constituted a powerful temporal sequence that boosted nationalist morale.

The concept of the nation as mother could not of itself even begin to address many problematic aspects of the relationship between nation and gender, not least the question of the social emancipation of women. Even though the most commonly used Bengali term for the mother's children—'santan'—was not gender-specific, early ideologues of national- ism implicitly, if not explicitly, portrayed a son-mother relationship. 'Matribhakti', devotion to the mother, was clearly not the monopoly of sons, but the psychological and cultural nuances and complexities of the daughter-mother relationship appears to be conspicuously sparse in early nationalist discourse. A few women like Sarala Devi and Kamini Roy, of course, composed panegyrics to the motherland; a few others performed Swadeshi service of various kinds for the Mother. The feminization (and peasantization) of the ideal type of the Mother's nationalist devotees, nevertheless, involved the imputation of certain values by men and elites to women (and peasants).

Even in the literature that glorified the nation as mother, the ideals of womanhood were mythical characters such as Sati, Savitri, Sita, Lilavati, Khana and Arundhati who were often distinguished by high

[17] Sarkar, 'Nationalist Iconography', p. 2012.

learning, wisdom or other accomplishments that was tempered by devotion to their husbands as well as a desire not to outshine them.[18] In one very famous Swadeshi song the wandering rural composer and singer Charankabi Mukundadas exhorts the women of Bengal to throw away their silk and glass bangles. He asks them not to be deceived by the false glitter of imported goods and not to wear *kalanka* (shame) instead of *shankha* (the white *chank* bangle, symbol of chastity). That they don't have real gold bangles is hardly a cause for mourning, he tells them. The daughters of Bengal must see to it that the Mother's wealth is not drained away any further.

Another sort of problem could stem from the intolerable burden placed on women who were idealized as mothers. This point was made forcefully in Prabhat Mukhopadhyay's story and Satyajit Ray's film *Devi* in which the family patriarch persuaded himself that his daughter-in-law was an incarnation of the Mother Goddess.[19] The loss of value of woman as human being that this entailed was considerable. The tyranny of divinity could only be countered by an invocation to humanity. When Abanindranath painted 'Bharatmata', he had in mind his daughter's face. It was the coming together of human intimacy and divine inspiration that gave not just the picture but the idea of the nation as mother its overpowering appeal.[20]

NATIONALIST THOUGHT AND COLONIAL KNOWLEDGE

How far was the narrative of nation as mother trapped within the 'essentializing' project of colonial knowledge as power and reduced to the status of a 'derivative discourse'? Making a distinction between the 'problematic' and the 'thematic' of nationalist thought, its claims and its justificatory structures, Partha Chatterjee in his seminal book *Nationalist*

[18] Khana cut off her tongue rather than utter pearls of wisdom that cast her husband into the shade.

[19] Jung's observation that 'the consequence of increasing Matriolatry was the witch hunt' in the European Middle Ages was not wholly irrelevant to Bengal in terms of social consequence. But the psyche underlying the collective worship of the Virgin Mary was qualitatively different from the adoration of the Mother Goddess.

[20] Sister Nivedita, Swami Vivekananda's famous Irish disciple, stressed this point in 'The Function of Art in Shaping Nationality: "Notes" on "Bharatmata"' in *The Modern Review*, February 1907, cited in Guha-Thakurta, *The Making of a New 'Indian' Art*, p. 255.

Thought and the Colonial World has suggested that it constituted a 'different' but 'dominated' or derivative discourse.[21] In his equally important and learned book *The Nation and its Fragments* which 'carries forward an argument begun in' *Nationalist Thought* Chatterjee draws a sharp dichotomy between the inner, spiritual and outer, material domains. Arguing that anti-colonial nationalism 'creates its own domain of sovereignty' in the former, he asserts that the history of nationalism as a political movement by focusing on 'the material domain of the state' has 'no option but to choose its forms from the gallery of "models" offered by European and American nation-states: "difference" is not a viable criterion in the domain of the material'.[22]

Chatterjee also sets out in *Nationalist Thought* a 'theory of stages in the constitution of a nationalist discourse': the 'moment of departure' representing 'the encounter of a nationalist consciousness with the framework of knowledge created by post-Enlightenment rationalist thought'; the 'moment of manoeuvre' requiring the 'mobilization of the popular elements in the cause of an anti-colonial struggle' and 'distancing of those elements from the structure of the state'; and the 'moment of arrival' when nationalist thought becomes 'a discourse of order' and of 'the rational organization of power'.[23] Taking Bankim to be the exemplar of the 'moment of departure', Chatterjee asserts that he and, by implication, the moment, 'accepted entirely the fundamental methodological assumptions, the primary concepts and the general theoretical orientation of nineteenth century positivist sociology and utilitarian political economy'. So, in Bankim there was 'a reversal of the Orientalist problematic, but within the same general thematic'. 'Imprisoned within the rationalist framework of his theoretical discourse and powerless to reject its dominating implications', Bankim could merely 'dream' of 'a utopian political community in which the nation was the Mother, once resplendent in wealth and beauty, now in tatters. Relentlessly, she exhorts

---

[21] Partha Chatterjee, *Nationalist Thought and the Colonial World: A Derivative Discourse?* (London: Zed Press, 1986), p. 42.

[22] Partha Chatterjee, *The Nation and its Fragments* (Princeton and Delhi, 1994), pp. xi, 6, 9. Chatterjee is quite on target in underlining the attempt in nationalist discourse to separate the two domains. But he then makes a discursive shift to rather unquestioningly utilize this dichotomy in his own analysis. I discuss Chatterjee's assertion about the unviability of difference in the material domain of the state in the section entitled 'Nation and State' below.

[23] Chatterjee, *Nationalist Thought*, pp. 43, 50–1.

a small band of her sons, those of them who are brave and enlightened, to vanquish the enemy and win back her honour'.[24]

This sort of a formulation misses a nuance or two concerning the relationship between nationalist thought and colonial knowledge at the moment that the discourse of nation as mother was fashioned. First, the 'positivism' of nineteenth-century Europe which appealed to early Bengali nationalist thinkers was a more complex phenomenon than is acknowledged by Chatterjee. As Jasodhara Bagchi has shown, Comteist Positivism after 1848 showed a marked 'shift towards the Affective side (as contrasted with the Intellectual side) of human nature in his plan of social regeneration'. Women and the proletariat, the two 'underprivileged partners of the male patriciate' were accorded privileged positions 'in a harmonious scheme of social regeneration'. Such a scheme of 'order and progress' had its attractions for Bengal's nationalist patricians. The other 'specific feature about the Positivist programme, not adequately noticed so far, that recommended this model to the emerging Nationalist ethos' was 'its anti-imperialist stance', articulated by Comte's disciples like Richard Congreve.[25]

Second, the authors of the narrative of nation as mother attempted, not without some contortions, to draw as much (if not more) on rationalist traditions of pre-colonial India as on European post-Enlightenment reason. Bipin Chandra Pal, for instance, claimed as part of his ideological project to have taken the dialectic of *Purusha* and *Prakriti*, the principles of permanence and change, from the Sankhya system of philosophy. 'No rational interpretation of cosmic evolution is possible,' he wrote, 'except upon the hypothesis of these two fundamental principles... The conception of Mother associated with our geographical habitat is filiated to this old, old, universal Hindu conception of *Prakriti*; but of *Prakriti* conceived especially as Shakti.'[26]

[24] Ibid., pp. 61, 73, 79.

[25] Jasodhara Bagchi, 'Positivism and Nationalism: Womanhood and Crisis in Nationalist Fiction—Bankimchandra's *Anandamath*' in 'Review of Women Studies', *Economic and Political Weekly*, October 1985. What is not clear, however, in Bagchi's analysis is the extent to which Bankim may or may not have been conversant with the various shifts in Comtean thought.

[26] Pal, *Soul of India*, pp. 109–10. Pal was, of course, conversant with nineteenth-century European philosophy. While comparing Christian Trinity and Hindu Purusha-Prakriti, he wrote: 'To quote a well-known saying of one of your own European philosophers, in every act of knowledge or reason, "the self separates itself from itself to return to itself to be itself." And if this be the logic

In analysing nationalist thought it may be best to abandon any ahistorical quest for indigenous authenticity. Many current post-colonial readings of nationalist thought run the risk of being captivated within the stark binary dichotomies of colonial knowledge that they wish to critique.[27] The nineteenth-century colonial encounter was a messy, historical process, which inevitably imparted a measure of imbrication to the domains of nationalist thought and colonial knowledge whether in terms of their content or form. Only the most prosaic critic would listen to Swadeshi songs set to tunes influenced by European music and sung to the accompaniment of the organ and relegate them to the status of 'dominated discourse'. Dwijendralal Roy's highly popular 'Banga Amar, Janani Amar, Dhatri Amar, Amar Desh' (Bengal mine, Mother mine, My Protector, My Country) experimented with straight notes borrowed from European melodies and introduced the concept of the chorus lines hitherto unused in Indian music.[28] Atul Prasad Sen set his famous 'Utho go Bharatalakshmi' (Arise, Bharatalakshmi) to a tune he had heard on a gondola in Venice. Nationalist thought, even at the moment of departure, may well have found idioms of articulation that overlapped with European forms and yet at the same time opposed both the problematic and the thematic of colonial knowledge. An overemphasis on the nation and the novel has prevented the exploration of this

of rational life, and if the Ultimate Reality, by whatever name be called, whether God, or Allah, or Brahman, or Isvara, be intelligent and self-conscious, then you must posit in the very Being of that Reality an element of differentiation which, without cancelling the Divine Unity, supplies the object of Divine thought, through which the Divine realizes his own consciousness. The Ultimate Reality being infinite, the object through which that Reality can realize its infinite reason, must also be infinite. As it is true of the rational, so also is it true of the emotional and the volitional life. Love also demands with a view to realize itself an object not different from, yet not absolutely identified with, the lover.' Pal, p. 111.

[27] As Sara Suleri puts it, '...if colonial cultural studies is to avoid a binarism that could cause it to atrophy in its own apprehension of difference, it needs to locate an idiom for alterity that can circumnavigate the more monolithic interpretations of cultural empowerment that tend to dominate current discourse'. Suleri, *Rhetoric of English India*, p. 4. For a powerful, if occasionally strident, Marxist critique of the indigenist (among other) fallacies of 'colonial discourse theory', see Aijaz Ahmad, *In Theory: Classes, Nations, Literatures* (London: Verso, 1992).

[28] See Sarvani Datta, 'The Songs of Dwijendralal Roy: Its Sources and Lyrics', (M. Phil. dissertation, University of Calcutta, 1989).

possibility through the careful sifting of the poetry (and drama) of nationhood.[29]

NATION AND CLASS

The charge of elitism hurled at nationalist thought at the moment of departure has more force to it than the charge that it was completely subordinated to the colonial sociology of knowledge. Before the 'popular mobilization' resorted to at the moment of manoeuvre with its 'many contradictory possibilities', the nationalist ideal, Partha Chatterjee argues, implied an 'elitist programme'.[30] But, as Tanika Sarkar has noted, 'food and cloth, the two basic necessities, were the two strongest metaphors' of nationalism even in its early phase.[31] This provided a potential link between the elite and subaltern arenas of politics. To my mind, the materiality of nationalist ideology called as much for a 'declassing' of the privileged than a straightforward invitation to subordinated and marginalized groups to take equal part in nationalist rituals.

The evocation of nation as mother encompassed an inculcation of the ethic of *mota chal* and *mota kapar* (coarse, simple rice and thick, homely cloth). One of the best-known Swadeshi couplets by Rajanikanto Sen went:

> *Ma-er deya mota kapar, mathay tule ne re bhai,*
> *Ma je amar deen-daridra, er beshi aaj sadhya nai.*

> The Mother has given us this simple cloth, wear it with pride,
> She is poor and destitute today, and can afford no more.

The connection between a *mota khabo, mota porbo* (we will eat 'mota' and wear 'mota') attitude and devotion to the nation as mother was made

[29] Partha Chatterjee provides some insightful glimpses into the variations between the written and spoken word as well as the role of the theatre in middle-class nationalism in *The Nation and its Fragments*, pp. 7–8, 55–8. Poetry has not received the same attention as prose from students of nationalism. The novel was arguably *the* literary vehicle that transmitted the content and forms of 'Western' nationalism to colonial settings. Poems and songs, despite borrowings of Western forms, represented alternative modes of expression that might suggest a different accent on the question of derivation in particular and the languages of nationalism in general.

[30] Chatterjee, *Nationalist Thought*, p. 51. In *The Nation and its Fragments*, however, he advances an argument about the 'subalternity of an elite', referring to the Calcutta middle class, p. 37.

[31] Sarkar, 'Nationalist Iconography', p. 2012.

more explicit in another of his songs *'amra nehat gorib, amra nehat chhoto'* which may be roughly rendered in English as follows:

> We may be poor, we may be small,
> But we are a nation of seven crores; brothers, wake up.
> Defend your homes, protect your shops,
> Don't let the grain from our barns be looted abroad.
> We will eat our own coarse grain and wear the rough, home-spun cloth,
> What do we care for lavender and imported trinkets.
> Foreigners drain away our Mother's milk,
> Will we simply stand and watch?
> Don't lose this opportunity, brothers,
> Come and congregate at the feet of the Mother.
> Giving away from our own homes and begging from foreigners,
> We will not buy the fragile glass, it breaks so easily,
> We will rather be poor and live our simple lives,
> No one can then rob us of our self-respect.
> Don't lose this opportunity, brothers,
> Come and congregate at the feet of the Mother.

Hardly a bugle call for class-based politics, the narrative of nation as mother nevertheless left a small opening for the poor and obscure to enter the story and perhaps even alter its denouement.

NATION AND RELIGIOUS COMMUNITY

Much more problematic was the question whether the concept of nation as mother left any space whatsoever for the accommodation and expression of the religious diversity of the Bengali and Indian nations. Certainly on this issue the narrative started off on the wrong foot. The final verse of Bankim's song 'Bande Mataram' could not resist a conflation of the mother country with the Mother Goddess:

> *twang hi durga dashapraharana-dhaarinee,*
> *kamalaa kamala-dala-biharinee,*
> *banee bidyadayinee,*
> *namaami twaam.*

> You are Durga bearing ten weapons of war,
> Kamala at play in the lotuses,
> Goddess of Learning, giver of knowledge,
> I bow to you.

The equation of nation with goddess understandably left many Muslims cold. What compounded the problem further was the appearance of the song in Bankim's novel *Anandamath* that was dripping with anti-Muslim prejudice. A peculiar apologia that has been offered ever since suggesting that Bankim meant British when he said Muslim simply added insult to injury.

The narrative of the nation as mother that unfolded during the late nineteenth century and throughout the course of the twentieth century became much more complex and even flowed into divergent streams. Bengali Muslims were familiar with and understood the concept of the nation as mother even if they did not fully share the Bengali Hindus' mother complex. Perhaps the most powerful evocations of the nation as mother were made by the Bengali Muslim revolutionary poet Kazi Nazrul Islam. In one of his most popular nationalist songs he exhorts the leader imagined as the captain of a ship in peril to face up to the challenge of saving his nation or religious community and to say unambiguously that those who were drowning were all Mother's children.[32] Much later the Bengali Muslim nationalists who led the movement of independence for Bangladesh drew upon the entire corpus of early twentieth century nationalist literature, goddesses and all. In addition to Tagore's ode to Mother Bengal *'Amar sonar Bangla, ami tomay bhalobashi'* (My golden Bengal, I love you) which became the national anthem, another Tagore song very popular in 1971 explicitly drew the goddess imagery:

> *Bangladesher hridoy hote kakhan aponi,*
> *Tumi ki aparup rupe bahir hole janani.*
> *Dan hate tor kharga jwale, ban hat kare shankaharan*
> *Dui nayane sneher hashi, lalat netra agunbaran.*

> From the heart of Bangladesh spontaneously
> You have emerged with such breathtaking beauty, Mother.
> In your right hand flashes the scimitar, your left hand dispels fear
> Your two eyes radiate a loving smile, the third eye on your forehead is a fiery glow.

Quite apart from Bengali Muslim creative imagination contributing to the narrative of the nation as mother, many of the creative writers,

---

[32] The relevant lines from the song *'Durgama giri kantar maru'* are *'jatir athaba jater karibe tran, kandari balo dubichhe manush santan mor mar'*. Kazi Nazrul Islam, *Nazrul Rachanabali* (Bangla Academy, Dhaka, 1993), pp. 288–9.

nationalist ideologues and political revolutionaries of the early twentieth century did not agree with Bankim's attitude towards Muslims or his fictionalized version of the history of Muslim rule. Swami Vivekananda, who had a powerful influence on Bengali youth at the turn of the century, preached the equal truth of all religions, held on the whole a positive assessment of Islam and looked forward to a millenium when the Sudra and other downtrodden social groups would rise to power. The views of Aurobindo, who did more than anyone else to propagate the political cult of the mother-nation, are even more instructive. 'The vast mass of the Mussulmans in the country,' he wrote, 'were and are Indians by race, only a very small admixture of Pathan, Turkish and Mogul blood took place, and even the foreign kings and nobles became almost immediately wholly Indian in mind, life and interest.' As for the Mughal empire, it was, according to Aurobindo, 'a great and magnificent construction and an immense amount of political genius and talent was employed in its creation and maintenance. It was as splendid, powerful and beneficent and, it may be added, in spite of Aurangzeb's fanatical zeal, infinitely more liberal and tolerant in religion than any medieval or contemporary European kingdom or empire and India under its rule stood high in military and political strength, economic opulence and the brilliance of its art and culture.'[33]

A very motley crowd of nationalists holding a variety of attitudes to other religious communities went to prison and detention camps during the first half of the twentieth century. It is hard, if not impossible, to draw up a balance-sheet of bigotry and broad-mindedness. But among the revolutionaries who went to the gallows with 'Bande Mataram' on their lips there was clearly no need and no sense of another religious community as the 'other' to substantiate their own affective bond with the mother-nation. What evidence there is points to a substantial measure of generous eclecticism in the mental make-up of these revolutionaries. Dinesh Gupta, one of the three young men who stormed Writers' Building in Calcutta in December 1930, wrote to his sister-in-law days before he was hanged: 'If one believes in any of the world's religions, one has to believe in the indestructibility of the soul. That is, one has to accept that the body's death does not signify the end of everything.

[33] Sri Aurobindo, *The Spirit and Form of Indian Polity* (Calcutta: Arya Publishing House, 1947), pp. 86, 89. This volume consisted of chapters extracted from 'A Defence of Indian Culture', a series of essays written in response to William Archer's strictures upon Indian culture and civilization and published in the Arya in 1918–21.

We are Hindus, we know something of what the Hindu religion has to say about this. Islam also says when human beings die, 'khuda's fereshta', God's angel, comes for his/her 'rukbaz' and calling upon the soul of the human being says, 'Ay rub nikal is kalib se chal khudaka zannat me' —meaning leave this body to be with God. So it can be understood that everything does not end when human beings die, Islam has faith in this. Christianity says, 'Very quickly there will be an end of the here, consider what will become of the next world'.... If I have faith in any one of these three religions, I have to believe that I cannot die. I am immortal. No one has the power to kill me.' What follows in Dinesh's letter is a blistering attack on social ills and injustices perpetrated in the name of religion: 'In a country where a fifty-year old man can marry a ten-year old girl in the name of religion, where is religion in such a country. I would set fire to the face of religion in such a country. Where touching another human being is polluting, one should drown the religion of such a country in the Ganga and be done with it.... For a trivial cow or a bit of music played on drums we are murdering each other's brothers. For doing that will 'bhagaban' open the doors of 'baikuntha' for us, or will 'khuda' give us a place in 'behesht'.'[34] Having had his say on religion and having assured his mother that she was from now on the mother of all India, Dinesh Gupta calmly accepted 'the garland' of the hangman's noose.

By the time the 'bande mataram' controversy exploded with full force at the all-India political level in 1937, there were at least three contexts in which the matter had to be seen. The most immediate context was the element of triumphalism inherent in the singing of 'bande mataram' in the legislatures 'thereby demonstrating Congress victory'. Since the Gandhian Congress was infected with Hindu communalism at the regional level in many provinces, this was bound to outrage many Muslims. The original context, referred to by Jawaharlal Nehru, was provided by Bankim's unfortunate novel. Nehru took the trouble to procure an English translation of the book and did not need much time to figure out that the background was 'likely to irritate the Muslims'. Stretched out between the original and immediate contexts was the context of sanctification of a problematic cultural icon through sacrifice,

[34] Dinesh Gupta to his *boudi* (sister-in-law), 18 June, 1931; see also Dinesh Gupta to his mother, 17 June, 1931 and 30 June 1931. Originally published in *Benu*, a Bengali monthly literary magazine in 1931, these letters have been quoted in full in Sailesh De, *Benoy, Badal, Dinesh* (Calcutta: Biswas Publishers, 1970), pp. 154–6, 158.

in the case of the revolutionaries, supreme sacrifice. The question, therefore, was whether the song should be performed as a national anthem at Congress gatherings. At the suggestion of Subhas Chandra Bose it was decided to seek the advice of Rabindranath Tagore in an attempt to resolve this question at the meeting of the All India Congress Committee at Calcutta in October 1937.[35]

Rabindranath Tagore wrote privately to Subhas Chandra Bose that the song containing adoration of Durga was wholly inappropriate for a national organization that was the meeting place for different religious communities. He wrote, 'Bengali Hindus have become restless at this debate, but the matter is not confined to the Hindus. Where there are strong feelings on both sides, what is needed is impartial judgment. In our national quest we need peace, unity, good sense—we don't need endless rivalry because of one side's obstinate refusal to yield'. In a measured press statement the poet explained that he had found the feelings of devotion and tenderness as well as evocation of the beauty of Bharatmata in the first verse of the song appealing. But he had had no difficulty in detaching this verse from the whole song as well as the book in which it had appeared. He had never entertained any love for the whole song. Once 'bande mataram' was transformed into a national slogan many noble friends had made unforgettable and huge sacrifices for it. At the same time the song as a whole and the history associated with it hurt Muslim feelings. Tagore argued that the first part of the song stood on its own and had an inspirational quality which was not offensive to any religious community.[36] The Congress accepted Tagore's advice and resolved that henceforth only the first part of the song would be sung in national meetings. Bengal's two luminaries, Rabindranath Tagore and Subhas Chandra Bose, were showered with abuse by a sizeable section

[35] See Subhas Chandra Bose to Jawaharlal Nehru, 17 October 1937, in Sisir K. Bose and Sugata Bose (eds), Netaji Subhas Chandra Bose, *Collected Works Vol. 8 1933–7* (Netaji Research Bureau, Calcutta, and Oxford University Press, Delhi, 1994), pp. 226–7; and Jawaharlal Nehru to Subhas Chandra Bose, 20 October, 1937 (Nehru Memorial Museum and Library).

[36] Rabindranath Tagore to Subhas Chandra Bose, 19 October, 1937, and Tagore's press statement on 'Bande Mataram', 30 October, 1937, cited in Nepal Majumdar, *Rabindranath O Subhaschandra* (Calcutta: Saraswati Publishers, 1987), pp. 56–57, 59–60. Nearly three decades prior to this direct political intervention, Tagore had subtly subverted the blind adoration of the mother-nation on the part of Gora, the hero of the most 'nationalist' of his novels, through a revelation of his Irish parentage. See Rabindranath Tagore, *Gora* (English translation, Madras: Macmillan, 1924).

of Bengali Hindu literary and political circles. But in the year of his birth centenary, 1938, Bankim's equation of the mother-nation with Durga was banished from the platform of India's premier nationalist party. Subhas Chandra Bose did close his presidential speech with the slogan 'bande mataram', but he refused to entertain any controversy sought to be raised by some Hindu politicians over the decision to abridge the song.[37]

The problem posed by the narrative of nation as mother in its relationship to the history of relations between religious communities was that it was sought to be directed, if not hijacked, in different directions. It could be sanctified by those prepared to die in the cause of the mother-nation and defiled by those ready to kill in the name of religion. The trouble was that as the narrative reached its denouement it was the living rather than the dead who had any chance of capturing political power.

NATION AND LINGUISTIC REGION

In a dramatic overstatement of the case for nationalist thought being ensnared by the cunning of reason and positivist knowledge, Partha Chatterjee has written in *Nationalist Thought*: 'The 'subject' is a scientific consciousness, distanced from the 'object' which is the Indian, the Bengali, the Hindu (it does not matter which, because all of them are defined in terms of the contraposition between the Eastern and the Western).' On this view, nationalist thought, certainly at its moment of departure and to a lesser extent at the later stages too, makes 'no attempt' to 'define the boundaries of the Indian nation *from within*'.[38] In *The Nation and its Fragments* Chatterjee devotes a mere three pages to a strand in nationalist thought that 'raises doubts about the singularity of a history of India'. He accepts that '[t]here is a great disjuncture here between the history of India and the history of Bengal' and speculates that 'there were many such alternative histories for the different regions of India'. Yet in a startling intellectual abdication to the votaries of a singular nationalism who managed to capture state power Chatterjee pleads that 'we do not yet have the wherewithal to write these other [suppressed] histories'.[39]

Far from being completely tied up in knots by Orientalist discourse, nationalist thought retained a certain awareness of multiple social

[37] See Majumdar, pp. 60–6.

[38] Chatterjee, *Nationalist Thought*, pp. 58, 55.

[39] Chatterjee, *Nation and its Fragments*, pp. 113–5. One interesting dimension of these alternative regional histories of Bengal (written mostly by Hindus) is that they contain generally favourable assessments of the rule of independent Muslim sultans and nawabs of Bengal.

identities and the freedom of manoeuvre to stress one over another in
politics. Yet the language and idiom of nationalism operated in the late
nineteenth and early twentieth century with the greatest potency at the
level of the linguistic community and region. The predominant vision
of the mother-nation in this period was the image of Mother Bengal.
There could be gifts made to Mother India and a keen awareness of
the dangers for the nationalist cause of evoking a Hindu Mother. But
the conception of the mother-nation was in inspiration and exposition
that of Mother Bengal. The all-India nationalist movement sought to
harness the energy of this phenomenon by seeking to make measured
concessions to linguistically based provincial organizations in 1920 and
came to fear its strength in the course of efforts to enforce central
discipline on the way to grasping centralized state power. In the end,
the potential threat posed to central authority by linguistic nations played
a role in the Congress's compromise on partition along lines of ostensibly
religiously-based communalism.

We have seen how the mother in Bankim's 'bande mataram' and
Abanindranath's 'Bharatmata' were originally conceived as Mother
Bengal and then ungrudgingly offered in the service of a wider Indian
nation. Aurobindo in an essay entitled 'Desh o Jatiyata' (The Country and
Nationhood), written in 1920, candidly acknowledged that during the
heyday of the Swadeshi movement they had seen the vision of Bangamata.
Aurobindo believed that this was an undivided vision and over-optimis-
tically predicted that unity and progress of 'Bangadesh' were inevitable.
But, he wrote, 'Bharatmata's undivided image has not yet been
revealed... the Bharatmata that we ritually worshipped in the Congress
was artificially constructed ('kalpita' was the Bengali word used), she was
the companion and favourite mistress of the British, not our mother... The
day we have that undivided vision of the image of the mother... the
independence, unity and progress of India will be facilitated'. But he kept
warning that the vision had to be one that was not divided by religion. He
concluded, '... if we hope to have a vision of the mother by invoking the
Hindus' mother or establishing Hindu nationalism, having made a cardinal error we would be deprived of the full expression of our nationhood.'[40]

The interchangeable use of Mother Bengal and Mother India in poetic
imagination makes it difficult to clinch the argument about the relative
strength of the idea of the mother-nation at the level of the linguistic

[40] Sri Aurobindo, 'Desh o Jatiyata' in *Dharma o Jatiyata* (Sri Aurobindo
Ashram, Pondicherry, 1957, originally written in 1920), pp. 80–3.

region. But the emotive appeal of the linguistically defined mother-nation
is compelling. Consider a letter written by Pradyot Bhattacharya, a young
man who had assassinated one of Midnapur's British district magistrates
in 1932. A day before he was hanged he wrote: 'Mother, you cannot
ask me for any justification for what I have done. Perhaps you do not
know that you have created us for your own purpose. But I am letting
you know that for thousands of years we were being quietly created in
your minds, the minds of Bengal's mothers. Today we are slowly
revealing ourselves. And I have always known that I am Bengali and
you are Bengal, the same element, could never think of us separately....
Through the ages you have endured insult, humiliation and
oppression... the undercurrent of revolt against these that was flowing
deep within you, I am that accumulated revolt.... If that revolution
achieves self-expression today why should you shed tears.... Mother,
can your Pradyot ever die? Look around today, lakhs and lakhs of
Pradyots are smiling at you. I'll continue to live, Mother, imperishable,
immortal. Bande Mataram.'[41] It is hard not to be persuaded that this
young life was being sacrificed at the altar of Mother Bengal.

A few years later in 1939 Rabindranath Tagore and Subhas Chandra
Bose came together for the foundation-laying ceremony of a house to
be called 'Mahajati Sadan' which they hoped would be home to an
enlightened and dignified idea of a 'great nation'. As part of his speech
on the occasion, Tagore recited a prayer he had composed in the
Swadeshi era:

> The Bengalis' faith, the Bengalis' hope,
> The Bengalis' work, the Bengalis' language,
> Bless them with truth, O Lord.
> The Bengalis' heart, the Bengalis' mind,
> All the brothers and sisters in Bengali homes,
> May they be one, O Lord.

After a short pause he said: 'And let this word be added: may Bengal's
arm lend strength to India's arm, may Bengal's message make India's
message come true.'[42]

---

[41] The complete Bengali original of this letter from Pradyot Bhattacharya to
his mother is reproduced in Sailesh De, *Ami Subhas Balchhi*, Vol. 1 (Rabindra
Library, Calcutta, 1970), pp. 316–19.

[42] *Ananda Bazaar Patrika*, 20 August, 1939.

NATION AND STATE

Literary and cultural representations of the nation are often disfigured
by hard historical and political realities. In 1947 the leadership of the
Indian National Congress accepted the transfer of power from British
hands at the apex of a unitary and centralized structure of the Indian
state. Bengal paid a hefty price to enable the Congress to inherit the
strong centre of the British Raj. The official ideology of the Indian state
came to rest on a monolithic concept of sovereignty borrowed from
modern Europe and denying the multiple identities and several-layered
sovereignties that had been its complex legacy from its pre-colonial past.[43]

Partha Chatterjee has provided an insightful analysis of nationalist
thought at what he has called its 'moment of arrival' when its discourse
is conducted not only in 'a single, consistent, unambiguous voice' but also
'succeeds in glossing over all earlier contradictions, divergences and
differences'. Yet a flaw creeps into his method in seeking to 'give to
nationalist thought its ideological unity by relating it to a form of the post-
colonial state'.[44] This sort of reasoning backwards denudes nationalist
thought of 'all earlier contradictions, divergences and differences' and can
have the unintended effect of playing into the hands of the post-colonial
state's ideological project which it promises to question and critique. A
post-colonial state, unitary in form, could only accommodate the one
strand of singular nationalism. Although Chatterjee is not unaware of its
dangers, he still resorts to a kind of teleology that leaves not enough
theoretical space for the recovery of contested visions of nationhood and
alternative ideological frameworks for the post-colonial state. It assumes
and asserts a conflation of nation and state where it can be argued that
none existed, at least not until very late in the colonial era.

Here it is relevant to absorb the nuances of Edward Said's thesis that
'*at its best*, nationalist resistance to imperialism was always critical of itself'.
While recognizing the insights provided by Chatterjee's critique of
nationalism, Said points out he 'does not emphasize enough ... that the
culture's contribution to statism is often the result of *a* separatist, even
chauvinist and authoritarian conception of nationalism. *There is also*,
however, a consistent intellectual trend within the nationalist consensus
that is vitally critical, that refuses the short-term blandishments of

---

[43] See Ayesha Jalal, *Democracy and Authoritarianism in South Asia: A Comparative and Historical Perspective* (Cambridge: Cambridge University Press, 1995).

[44] Chatterjee, *Nationalist Thought*, pp. 49, 51.

separatist and triumphalist slogans in favor of the larger, more generous human realities of community...' So 'we must also focus on the intellectual and cultural argument within the nationalist resistance that once independence was gained new and imaginative reconceptions of society and culture were required in order to avoid the old orthodoxies and injustices.'[45]

If not all nationalist thinkers were having megalomaniacal dreams of the bourgeois acquisition of power in a centralized nation-state, how did they view the relationship between nation and state? While the affective bond of Bengali nationalists at the 'moment of departure' was stronger with the nation conceived as Mother Bengal, they did ponder and think about political arrangements covering all India. But the kind of Indian unity they aspired for and the type of state structure and ideology they believed to be appropriate on a subcontinental scale may have been in many instances quite different from the centralized monolith that was declared to be sacrosanct in 1947. The structural and ideological underpinnings of 'India, that is Bharat' of the Indian constitution of 1950 were a far cry from theories of the state articulated by generations of nationalist thinkers. A multiplicity of visions of Indian unity and the nature of the state lent nationalist thought an important dimension of ideological disunity and discontinuity.

Most nationalists since the late nineteenth century claimed, of course, that an at least inchoate sense of Indian nationhood and Indian states wielding authority on a subcontinental scale had existed prior to the imposition of British rule and administrative unification. India or Bharat, they asserted, signified much more than geographic location. Bipin Pal wrote, '...while the stranger called her India, or the Land of the Indus, thereby emphasizing only her strange physical features, her own children, from of old, have known and loved her by another name.... That name is Bharatavarsha. To clearly understand and grasp the nature and reality of the fundamental unity in which all our divergent and even apparently conflicting usages and customs, cults and cultures, our racialities and provincialities, have almost from the very beginning of our history been rationally reconciled, you must try to realize the deep significance of this old and native name of the land which the foreigner has so long called and known as India.' Even though Pal left many points of ambiguity, he did not proceed to make an argument about Hindu religious or Aryan

---

[45] Edward W. Said, *Culture and Imperialism* (New York: Alfred A. Knopf, 1993), pp. 217–19.

racial unity. In fact, he argued strongly against political and administrative centralization. What he did do was to read cultural meaning and a 'federal' idea into Bharatvarsha which was 'not a physical name like India or the Transvaal, nor even a tribal and ethnic name like England or Aryavarta, but a distinct and unmistakable historic name like Rome'. Pal recognized that Bharata (a Vedic personage) and Romulus were, 'strictly speaking', 'more legendary than perhaps historical' but felt that 'the profound significance of the name which they gave to these two great countries of the ancient world' was 'by no means affected by their legendary or even mythical character'. Bharata had been described in ancient texts as *rajchakravarti*. Pal took some pains to explain that the 'literal meaning of the term is not emperor, but only a king "established at the centre of a circle of kings." King Bharata was a great prince of this order.' His position was 'not that of the administrative head of any large and centralised government, but only that of the recognized and respected centre' which was the 'general character' of all great princes in ancient times. Under Muslim rule, according to Pal, Indian unity, 'always more or less of a federal type', became 'still more pronouncedly so'.[46]

Aurobindo's analysis of the ideal type of the Dharmarajya described in the epics suggested that it was 'not an autocratic despotism but a universal monarchy supported by a free assembly of the city and provinces and of all the classes'. The ancient ideal recognized that 'unification ... ought not to be secured at the expense of the free life of the regional peoples or of the communal liberties and not therefore by a centralised monarchy or a rigidly unitarian imperial State'. Aurobindo suggested that 'a new life' that 'seemed about to rise in the regional peoples' in the eighteenth century was 'cut short by the intrusion of the European nations'. The 'lifeless attempt' to 'reproduce with a servile fidelity the ideals and forms of the West' was 'no true indication of the political mind and genius of the Indian people'.[47] Whatever else Bipin Pal and Aurobindo Ghosh may have been doing, they were not borrowing wholesale, as Chatterjee asserts they must have been condemned to doing, from modular forms offered by European and American nation-states.[48] If there was a measure of such borrowing in nationalist thought at the 'moment of departure' in the material domain

[46] Pal, *Soul of India*, pp. 62–3, 65, 68, 92.

[47] Aurobindo, *Spirit and Form of Indian Polity*, pp. 77–8, 91.

[48] See Chatterjee, *Nation and its Fragments*, pp. 6–9.

of the state, there seems to have been a powerful critique as well of
Western ideals and forms. Tagore's writings on nationalism and modernity disdainfully rejected European forms of the nation-state while
accepting universalist ideals of humanism. Steering a creative path
between an unthinking eulogy of European 'enlightenment' and an
undiscriminating assault on the 'modern', the more imaginative strands
of anti-colonial thought fashioned a cultural and political space where
there was no necessary contradiction between nationality and human
community. Chatterjee's analytical binarism sharply separating the inner,
spiritual from the outer, material domain leads to an ahistorical
exaggeration of the 'sovereignty' of anti-colonial nationalism in the former
and its deterministic subservience in the latter.

A thoroughgoing nationalist critique of the entire Western concept of
civil society was, of course, available in Gandhian thought at the so-called
'moment of manoeuvre'.[49] The problem with Gandhi was that he did
not offer any theory of the state. His was a relentless nihilism, a
celebration of extreme anarchy and the pursuit of decentralization to the
point of atomization. In 1908 Gandhi had written in *Hind Swaraj*: 'India's
salvation consists in unlearning what she has learnt during the past fifty
years or so. The railways, telegraphs, hospitals, lawyers, doctors and such
like have all to go, and the so-called upper class have to learn to live
consciously and religiously and deliberately the simple life of a peasant.'[50]
By 1945 Gandhi had made many political compromises with the
'modernists' but only slightly modified his ideological stance: '...I still
stand by the system of Government envisaged in Hind Swaraj ... I am
convinced that if India is to attain true freedom and through India the
world also, then sooner or later the fact must be recognized that people
have to live in villages, not in towns, in huts, not in palaces ... I do not
want to draw a large scale picture in detail. It is possible to envisage
railways, post and telegraph offices etc. For me it is material to obtain
the real article and the rest will fit into the picture afterwards.'[51] There
is much that is valuable in the critique of modernity in the anti-modern

[49] See Partha Chatterjee's brilliant analysis in *Nationalist Thought*, Ch. 4. It
could be argued, however, that Gandhian thought was 'derivative' of certain
nineteenth-century misperceptions of India's ancient 'village communities'.

[50] See M.K. Gandhi, *Hind Swaraj* in *The Collected Works of Mahatma Gandhi*
Vol. 10 (Publications Division, New Delhi, 1958).

[51] Mahatma Gandhi to Jawaharlal Nehru, 5 October, 1945, in Jawaharlal
Nehru, *A Bunch of Old Letters* (Delhi: Oxford University Press, Centenary
Edition, 1989), pp. 505–6.

Gandhi which post-modern cultural critics can and have drawn on. Yet Gandhi's unwillingness 'to draw a large-scale picture in detail' has made him especially appealing to a particular brand of post-modernism which uncritically exults over the fragment. There were other nationalist models of the state, such as C.R. Das' draft Swarajist constitution, which offered, by contrast, something of a blueprint of a decentred democracy where there was room for a dialectic between fission and fusion, centrifugal and centripetal tendencies.[52]

The conception of a state of union reflecting and presiding over the balance and harmony of free regional peoples and religious communities was a major theme running through Bengali nationalist thought. As Rabindranath Tagore put it, 'Where there is genuine difference, it is only by expressing and restraining that difference in its proper place that it is possible to fashion unity. Unity cannot be achieved by issuing legal fiats that everybody is one.'[53] When Rabindranath and Subhas Chandra came together in 1939 to give expression to their idea of a 'mahajati' (great nation), the poet said: 'The shakti (strength) of the Bengali nation that we have resolved to establish today is not that rashtrashakti (state power) which instils fear and doubt in friends and foes alike.'[54] While Subhas' belief in Samyavada (socialism) occasionally led him to praise the virtues of a strong state in implementing a radical social and economic programme, he seemed more willing than Nehru to build that state on the foundations of regional autonomy and an equitable sharing of power among religious communities. The irony of the twentieth-century intellectual and political history of Bengal is that the powerful strand in nationalist thought that had stressed a federal unity and cross-communal understanding was defeated at the critical moment of the post-colonial transition. The insistence of a large section of paranoid and pulverized Bengali Hindu educated classes on the partition of Bengal facilitated the Congress High Command's acquisition of centralized state power. Those who stood for unity of Bengal till the very end could only lament the denial of an opportunity 'to work from the bottom and bring into being

[52] Chittaranjan Das, 'Swaraj Scheme, January 1923' in *The Oracle*, IV, 1 (Jan 1982), pp. 63–80. This remarkable 'constitution' held that the 'ordinary work' of a 'Central Government should be mainly advisory'. It called for 'a maximum of local autonomy, carried on mainly with advice and coordination from, and only a minimum of control by, higher centres...'

[53] Rabindranath Tagore, 'Bharatbarsher Itihas', *Bharatbarsha* in *Rabindra Rachanabali*, vol. 4 (Viswa-Bharati, Shantiniketan, 1965), p. 382.

[54] *Ananda Bazaar Patrika*, 20 August, 1939.

an Indian Union of our free choice' once the British attempt 'to impose an Indian Union from the top had failed'.[55]

Most of the 'brave and enlightened sons' must have died, literally and metaphorically, in the service of the Mother. This had left the field wide open for the Congressmen and Mahasabhaites with their matricidal tendencies. At the end of the day the partitioner's axe had been wielded by the mother's own sons.

RAM, PARASHURAM AND MOTHER INDIA

Although Jamadagni's son Ram and Dasarath's son Ram were the sixth and seventh avatars of Vishnu respectively, they had overlapped for a while in cosmic time. Parashuram had been banished eventually after several murderous sprees for the ultimately unpardonable crime of murdering his mother. But, according to the Ramayana, he found his way back and confronted Ram as he returned to Ayodhya after marrying Sita. Ram had just won Sita in a contest by performing a marvellous feat with the Haradhanu, Shiva's bow. Putting forward another formidable bow, the Vaishnavdhanu, Parashuram challenged Ram to break it or use it if he could. Ram did so with ease, upon which powerless, impotent and inert, Parashuram retired to Mahendraparbat, the Himalayas, and Ram for the moment enjoyed his patrimony. Not an unfair outcome (only to be expected of good story-teller like Valmiki), since Parashuram was guilty of matricide and Ram could not as yet be accused of misogyny. Much later in the story—on their return to Ayodhya from their lengthy forest exile—Sita, who had already walked through fire unscathed once, was asked by her noble husband to go through the test a second time to satisfy the inhabitants of the kingdom of Ayodhya. Having had enough, Sita asked Mother Earth to save her from the humiliation. Mother Earth opened up and took Sita back into her womb. As the Parashurams of the 1990s hurled their pickaxes in Ayodhya and the votaries of Ramrajya and Shiva's soldiers demanded shuddhi or extermination, one could not but muse over *Millat*'s 1947 warning that the Congress and the Hindu Mahasabha, beset by Curzon's ghost, had raised a sharpened parashu to 'slice "Mother" into two'.

interesting

[55] Sarat Chandra Bose, *I Warned My Countrymen* (Netaji Research Bureau, Calcutta, 1968), p. 196.

5

Exploding Communalism: The Politics of Muslim Identity in South Asia

Ayesha Jalal

Farewell O Hindustan, O autumnless garden
We your homeless guests have stayed too long

Laden though we are today with complaints
The marks of your past favors are upon us still

You treated strangers like relations
We were guests but you made us the hosts
....

You gave us wealth, government and dominion
For which of your many kindnesses should we express gratitude

But such hospitality is ultimately unsustainable
All that you gave you kept in the end

Well, one has a right to one's own property
Take it from whoever you want, give it to whoever you will

Pull out our tongues the very instant
They forgetfully utter a word of complaint about this

But the complaint is that what we brought with us
That too you took away and turned us into beggars
....

You've turned lions into lowly beings, O Hind
Those who were Afghan hunters came here to become the hunted ones

We had foreseen all these misfortunes
When we came here leaving our country and friends

We were convinced that adversity would befall us in time
And we O Hind would be devoured by you

. . . .

So long as O Hindustan we were not called Hindi
We had some graces which were not found in others

. . . .

You've made our condition frightening
We were fire O Hind, you've turned us into ash.[1]

Altaf Husain Hali (1837–1914) in his inimitable way captures the
dilemma of Muslim identity as perceived by segments of the *ashraf*
classes in nineteenth century northern India. Steeped in nostalgia for
Islam's past glories and a wry sense of the Muslim predicament, Hali's
Shikwa-e-Hind, or complaint to India, cannot be dismissed as simply the
bigoted laments of a man who has accepted social closure on grounds
of religious difference and antipathy towards non-Muslims. To challenge
Hali's questionable reading of the history of Islam in the subcontinent
or his spurious representations of Indian Muslims in undifferentiated
terms as descendants of foreign immigrants is to concentrate on the
obvious and miss out the richness of the poetic nuances. What is
instructive about the poem is how a committed Muslim with more than
a surfeit of airs was hard pressed to deny the decisive and irreversible
impact of India on his co-religionists. As the metaphor of fire to ashes
makes clear, this is an assertion of a cultural identity, once distinctive
but now all too faded. Hali's grievance is precisely the loss of
distinctiveness which he believes had given Muslims a measure of dignity
and humanity. Bereft of any qualities of friendship or fellowship, Muslims
had become selfish, inward looking, indolent and illiterate. None of this
is the fault of India. Hali instead blames *qismat* which brought Islam to
the subcontinent and made certain that, unlike the Greeks, the Muslims
did not turn away from its frontiers in failure.

India without Islam is an ingenious idea. It would certainly have
obviated the need for endless scholarly outpouring on communalism. But
however much Muslims may take Hali's lead in blaming *qismat*, Islam
in India, united or divided, is a fact of history and an intrinsic feature

[1] Altaf Husain Hali, 'Shikwa-e-Hind', (1888) in *Jawhar-e-Hali*, compiled by
Iftikhar Ahmed Siddiqui (Lahore: Kereven-e-adab, 1989), pp. 314–30.

of the subcontinent's future. What is less clear is whether communalism should continue to serve as a descriptive or analytical clincher in representations of the Muslim past, present and future in the South Asian subcontinent. In the 1990s it has once again taken centrestage in academic and political debates, a consequence of the resort to what has been called Hindu majoritarian communalism seeking to preserve or capture centralized state power. Successive Congress regimes in the 1980s surreptitiously invoked a nebulous form of Hindu majoritarianism which has been crafted into a more potent political ideology by the forces of Hindutva. Neither the Congress nor the RSS, BJP and VHP combination would plead guilty to the charge of communalism. Not only the self-professedly secular Indian state and the Congress regimes at its helm, but also their challengers claim the appellation of nationalist. The original sin of being communalist for the most part has been reserved for the subcontinent's Muslims. Notwithstanding the compromises of secular nationalism with Hindu communalism, the burden of this negative term in the history of late colonial India has fallen on the Muslim minority. The establishment of a Muslim state at the moment of the British withdrawal added immeasurably to the weight of the burden. In the post-colonial scenario in general, and the conjuncture created by the Ayodhya controversy in particular, the Indian secularist response has been to tar both Hindu majoritarianism and Muslim minoritarianism with the brush of communalism. This asymmetry has expressed itself not only in state policy but also in secular academic discourse. Muslim minority 'communalism' has occupied a critical location in academic texts organized around the binary opposition between secular nationalism and religious communalism. If this neat but misleading dichotomy is to be dismantled, the entire notion of a Muslim minority 'communalism' at the subcontinental level needs to be subjected to a probing analysis.

This task has become especially urgent since such an overarching and loaded term as communalism ends up essentializing the very religiously informed identities, politics and conflicts it purportedly aims at explaining and combating. It is not as if this danger has escaped the attention of scholars engaged, as many of them have been, in disturbing and decentering notions of monolithic religious communities and singular identities.[2] What is remarkable, however, is the continued usage of a

---

[2] For instance Romila Thapar, 'Imagined Religious Communities? Ancient History and the Modern Search for a Hindu Identity', *Modern Asian Studies*, 1989, 23, 2, pp. 209–31.

term in a debate which widely acknowledges communalism as at best the pejorative 'other' of nationalism and at worst a borrowing from the colonialist project of essentializing Indian society and history.[3] Even those who deploy it as a matter of convention, while inveighing against its analytical utility, have to concede that as the accepted designation for religiously based cultural identities, politics, ideology or conflict, communalism lays emphasis on the peculiarly Indian aspects of what is a global problem of negotiating and accommodating social differences. Whether this compartmentalization of one of the subcontinent's most gnawing and lingering problems–the shifting politics of religiously informed identities–is not an unwitting form of academic communalism remains an open question.

This paper is an attempt to spot the blots in the historiographical discourse on Muslim communalism. While exploring the nexus of culture and political power the argument avoids presuppositions which erroneously link a religiously informed cultural identity with the politics of cultural nationalism. By contrasting the 'inevitability' of a Muslim identity, variously defined, with the 'impossibility' of a supra-regional and specifically Muslim politics in the subcontinental context, the paper aims at demonstrating the largely arbitrary, derogatory and exclusionary nature of the term 'communal' as it has been applied to individuals and political groupings claiming to represent the interests of Indian Muslims.

Such an argument requires a new typology of Muslim political thought, one that goes beyond the facile and rigid distinctions between 'liberals' or 'traditionalists', 'modernists' or 'anti-modernists', 'communalists' or 'secular nationalists'. The chronological starting point of the argument is the late nineteenth century when many of the salient features of a Muslim political discourse began to be worked out by members of the north Indian *ashraf* classes smarting under the loss of sovereignty on the one hand, and the onset of Western colonialism and 'modernity' on the other. Written in an accessible 'new' Urdu, the dissemination of the discourse was facilitated by a rapidly expanding print media. Popular among Muslim middle and upper classes in Muslim-majority provinces like the Punjab and, to a lesser degree, Bengal, the prose and poetry of this era bears the marks of the regional and class identity of its Muslim-minority province exponents. A historical investigation of Muslim identity and politics in the majority and minority provinces of colonial

---

[3] See Gyanendra Pandey, *The Construction of Communalism in Colonial North India*, Delhi: Oxford University Press, 1990.

India will be followed by an analysis of the implications of the post-colonial transition for Muslims scattered across separate sovereign states. By both historicizing and conceptualizing the twin issues of Muslim cultural difference and a Muslim politics, the purpose is to show why exploding communalism may not be a wit too late and is perhaps the only hope of genuinely rethinking and renegotiating the perennial problem of difference and identity in South Asia as a whole.

DIFFERENCE, EXCLUSIVISM OR COMMUNALISM: THE LATE 19TH AND EARLY 20TH CENTURIES

A more than common preoccupation with their distinctive religious identity has been a feature shared by upper and middle class Muslims in the subcontinent, irrespective of their 'liberal', 'modernist', 'conservative' or 'anti-modernist' leanings. This sense of distinction from non-Muslims has led to the suggestion that 'communal consciousness' is an intrinsic, indeed a normative, part of the Muslim socio-religious and political world view. The elision of religious difference with an essentialized Indian Muslim community is explained in terms of the legitimizing ideals of Islamic solidarity and the necessary subordination of the individual will to the *ijma* or consensus of the community.[4] It is extraordinary, but also revealing, that a decidedly elitist discourse should be seen as not only reflective of Indian Muslims but also their 'communal consciousness'. The politics of Muslim identity in the subcontinent cannot be reduced to a mere rationalization of normative Islamic discourse. There is much variation even within this elite discourse, not all of which focused on the knotty issue of electoral representation, and still greater evidence of Muslim willingness to differ from rather than defer to the consensus of the community, however construed, in the rough and tumble of practical politics.

Before the 1920s when Congress' inclusionary secular nationalist paradigm gained wider currency, the assertion of difference even when bordering on cultural exclusivism did not automatically translate into Muslim 'separatism' or minority 'communalism'. Remarkable as it may seem from the vantage point of today, Hali's *Shikwa-e-Hind* did not stir a public controversy over his, or for that matter his community's, putative lack of allegiance to India. This raises the cardinal question: were

[4] Farzana Shaikh, *Community and Consensus in Islam: Muslim Representation in Colonial India, 1860–1947* (Cambridge: Cambridge University Press, 1989).

concerns about the Muslim community as a distinctive religious entity
destined to keep the adherents of this perception on a separate, if parallel,
track with those engaged in the project of invoking an inclusionary idea
of a single Indian nation? Apparently not if one considers that in 1874
Hali himself had written feelingly in his poem *Hubb-i-Watan* or love of
the motherland that a patriotism which went no further than mere
attachment to the community was nothing short of selfishness. A true
patriot was one who regarded all the inhabitants of India, whether
Muslim, Hindu, Buddhist or Brahmosamaj as one:[5]

> If you want your country's well being
> Don't look upon any compatriot as a stranger[6]

Granted the range of moods that are the wont of a poet, there is no
evident tension or contradiction in Hali's mind between an affinity to
the people of India and pride in a selectively imagined and recreated
Islamic past. Less inclined to glorify Islamic history but equally conscious
of his Muslimness was Hali's mentor, Sayyid Ahmed Khan. Not a
religious scholar by training, his rational approach to Islamic theology
and law earned him the lacerating abuse of orthodox Muslim *ulema*
bunched in the theological seminaries at Deoband and, less vociferously,
Farangi Mahal in Lucknow.

The *ulema* were not alone in opposing Sayyid Ahmed's new-fangled
views. His ardent promotion of Western knowledge and culture as well
as loyalty to the Raj drew acerbic comments from Muslims attached to
their societal moors and the ideal of a universal Muslim *ummah*. Among
Sayyid Ahmed's fiercest critics was the Persian Islamic scholar Jamaluddin
al-Afghani who lived in India between 1879 and 1882 and called for
Hindu-Muslim unity as the first step to dislodging British colonialism. The
contest between Muslims moved by Islamic universalism and those for
whom the immediacy of the colonial context constituted the overwhelming reality was to be played out on the political stage during the first
few decades of the twentieth century.

For now it was Sayyid Ahmed's policy which held sway. The Aligarh
movement which he fathered became the source of modernist and
rational thinking among the Muslim elite and, ironically enough, also

[5] Cited in Mushir U. Haq, *Muslim Politics in Modern India, 1857–1947*
(Lahore: Book Traders, n.d.), p. 35.

[6] *Jawhar-e-Hali*, pp. 200–9.

provided the catalyst for latter day Muslim political 'separatism' and 'communalism'. By contrast, his more culturally exclusive Muslim opponents, harbouring anti-colonial and Islamic universalist sentiments, immersed themselves in religious strictures at traditional educational institutions like *madrassahs* and *maktabs* only to end up squarely on the side of an inclusionary and 'secular' Indian nationalism. Identifying the twisted knots in these two contending and overlapping strands in Muslim thinking highlights the curiosity that passes for minority 'communalism' in subcontinental history.

Unabashedly elitist in his thinking, Sayyid Ahmed has been hailed as the author of the notorious 'two nation' theory by the officially subsidized historians of Pakistan and condemned for being the evil genius who helped carve out a separate niche for India's Muslims within the sphere of colonial policy and political discourse. Yet despite his resolute stance against the Indian National Congress, Sayyid Ahmed was more concerned with dissuading his fellow Muslims from the plague of religious bigotry. Like Hali's, Sayyid Ahmed's Muslimness was rarely at odds with his Indianness. Quite as much as the Hindus, Muslims too 'consider[ed] India as their homeland'. Presaging Hali's *Shikwa-e-Hind* five years earlier without the romanticism or the complaint, he confessed that by living together in India 'the blood of both have changed, the colour of both have become similar, the faces of both, having changed, have become similar.... We mixed with each other so much that we produced a new language—Urdu, which was neither our language nor theirs'.[7] The essence of Sayyid Ahmed's message to his co-religionists was to keep religion and politics on separate tracks. It was *mazhabi tahsab* or religious bigotry which was preventing Muslims from partaking of the new education.[8]

This was Sayyid Ahmed's strategy for the uplift of a demoralized, disparate and disunited 'Muslim community' which his aristocratic imaginings in combination with colonial census enumeration were in the process of giving more supra-local substance than warranted by the empirical reality. Yet Sayyid Ahmed with his arrogant belief in the superiority of *ashraf* culture was palpably uninterested in mobilizing the

[7] Speech at Patna on 27 January, 1883, in Shan Mohammad (ed.), *Writings and Speeches of Sir Syed Ahmad Khan* (Bombay: Nachiketa, 1972), pp. 159–60.

[8] Sayyid Ahmed Khan, 'Tahsab', in *Mazameen-e-Sir Sayeed: Muntakhab Tehzib-ul-Akhlaq*, compiled by Dr Ghulam Hussain Zulfikar (Lahore: Sange-e-Meel, 1993), pp. 44–9.

Muslim *ajlaf* classes. To confuse his ideas on electoral representation with Muslim politics in an era which required at least a partial mobilization of the subordinate social classes is unacceptable teleology. Sayyid Ahmed's understanding of the position of Muslims in the colonial context was more relevant than the normative aspects of Islamic political theory. Since the British saw the Indian Muslim community as unified, if not united, by the common bond of religion, Sayyid Ahmed couched his appeal accordingly.

His rejection of the Congress, which he regarded as a creation of the more advanced Bengali 'nation' and not of Hindus as such, stemmed in large part from the uneven impact of colonial economic and educational policies in the different regions of India.[9] Just a year before the formation of the Congress, Sayyid Ahmed Khan had asserted unequivocally that 'Hindu and Mussalmans are words of religious significance, otherwise Hindus, Mussalmans and Christians who live in this country constitute one nation'. In his 'opinion all men are one'; he did 'not like religion, community or group to be identified with a nation'.[10] That a call for Muslim non-participation in the early Congress should have qualified Sayyid Ahmed for the role of a 'separatist' and anti-nationalist underscores the political nature of the distinction between a 'communalist' and 'non-communalist' posture in retrospectively constructed nationalist pasts.

Sayyid Ahmed may have been the most prominent spokesman of a north Indian regionally based Muslim elite. Yet his sharpest critics were also Muslim. His emphasis on *ijtihad* or independent reasoning and disapproval of *taqlid* or adherence to the four authoritative schools of Islamic jurisprudence set him apart from the *ulema* who saw in his modernist intellectual stance a barely disguised attack on their pre-eminent status in Muslim society. While sharing an *ashraf* culture, an affinity for Urdu and a core of Islamic beliefs with Sayyid Ahmed's modernist associates at Aligarh, the guardians of the faith kept these *la-dini* or irreligious Muslims at an arms' length.

If issues of religious interpretation divided Muslim from Muslim, Sayyid Ahmed's policy of subservience to the British Raj and reception of Western modernity and culture elicited contempt from a section of

[9] See his speeches at Lucknow, 28 December, 1887 and Meerut, 16 March, 1888 in Mohammed (ed.), *Writings and Speeches of Sir Syed Ahmed Khan*, pp. 180–94 and pp. 204–20.

[10] Ibid., pp. 266–7.

his co-religionists. Sayyid Akbar Husayn (1846–1921), better known as
Akbar Allahabadi, in his bitingly humorous and brilliant satirical verses
developed a powerful critique of modernity, mercilessly ridiculing Sayyid
Ahmad Khan and his associates for their shallow imitation of Western
culture:

> The venerable leaders of the nation had determined
> Not to keep scholars and worshippers at a disadvantage
> Religion will progress day by day
> Aligarh College is London's mosque[11]

Scathing and relentless in his criticism of a modernity wanting in
spirituality, Akbar Allahabadi neither fits the bill of a diehard anti-
modernist enamoured of obscurantist *maulvis* nor of a religious bigot.
He recalled that as a child, a *maulvi* tried teaching him knowledge and
he in turn tried teaching the *maulvi* reason; the enterprise ended in tears,
neither the *maulvi* learned reason, nor Akbar knowledge. It was the
degenerate state of the community rather than threats to its existence
which agitated him. He could declare with equanimity that India was
neither an Islamic country nor of Lakshman and Ram. Every Indian was
the pliant well-wisher of the English and Hind simply the warehouse of
Europe.[12] It is a measure of Allahabadi's distinctiveness as a poet that,
while enormously popular in Urdu literary circles on both sides of the
1947 divide, he forms no part of either the Indian or the Pakistani
nationalist pantheon.

Maulana Shibli Numani (1857–1914) also defies categorization as a
'liberal modernist' or 'anti-modern conservative' and appropriation into
mainstream Indian and Pakistani nationalist narratives. An associate of
Sayyid Ahmed Khan, Shibli adopted the idioms of modernity without
disavowing the basic grammar of Islamic learning. His thematics spawn
a rich and varied corpus of writings on Islamic history, theology, law as
well as literary criticism and poetry. Not an Islamic universalist, Shibli
endorsed Sayyid Ahmed's line that Indian Muslims were British subjects
and not bound by religion or Islamic history to submit to the dictates
of the Ottoman Caliphate. Yet on matters closer to home, Shibli's Islamic
sentiments led him to take political paths different from those charted

---

[11] *Kulliyat-e-Akbar Allahabadi*, Vol. 1 (Delhi, n. d.), p. 95.

[12] See *Intikhab-e-Kalam-e-Akbar*, compiled by Dr Ghulam Hussain Zulfikar
(Lahore, 1966), pp. 110, 112.

by Sayyid Ahmed Khan. By 1895 he was publicly opposing Sayyid Ahmed Khan's policy of Muslim non-participation in the Congress.[13] Shibli's perspectives reflect the new and competing trends in Muslim discourse at a time when Sayyid Ahmed Khan's intellectual influence, if not his legacy, had been overshadowed by events.

By the late 1880s British imperial policies in India and the Islamic world were leading more and more Muslims to eschew Sayyid Ahmed Khan's policy of non-participation in the Congress and loyalty to the Raj. Yet during the closing decades of the nineteenth century Hindu revivalist activities, especially in northern India centring on the issue of Urdu versus Hindi in the Devanagri script and cow slaughter, seemed to lend substance to colonial and *ashraf* notions of an Indian Muslim 'interest' that needed articulation and representation. But while the interests of the 'majority' religious community could be subsumed under the umbrella of the emerging Indian 'nation', those of the largest religious 'minority' remained marooned in the idea of the 'community'.

Instead of stopping to challenge the formulations of majoritarianism and minoritarianism in the evolving discourse of Indian nationalism, scholars seem to have been more fascinated by the 'separatist' and 'communal' claims of a privileged and pretentious segment of the Muslim community. It would not be too far-fetched to suggest that communalism in the subcontinent has been more a function of interpretation than of the actual phenomenon in its manifold dimensions. A shared core of Islamic ideals had never prevented Muslims from taking oppositional positions in relation to one another even at the level of elite discourse. This can be made light of if one regards the strategic essentializing of religious community as more important than its utility as a point of reference for the assertion of cultural difference. To wholly concentrate on the Islamic dimensions of the discourse, as if these are unproblematically singular in meaning, is to ignore key aspects of historical change and the new contradictions and contestations within the Indian 'Muslim community'.

The partition of Bengal in 1905 may have provided the main impetus for the orchestration of the Muslim claim to separate political representation and the establishment of the self-professedly 'communal' All-India Muslim League in December 1906. But it was the Morley-Minto reforms of 1909 which institutionalized what until then had been a dominant

[13] Mehr Afroz Murad, *Intellectual Modernism of Shibli Nu'mani: an Exposition of his Religious and Political Ideas* (Lahore: Institute of Islamic Culture, 1976), p. 100.

colonial perception of the importance of religious divisions in Indian
society by granting Muslims separate electorates in representative bodies
at all levels of the electoral system. A momentous step, it gave Muslims
the status of an all-India political category but one effectively consigned
to being a perpetual minority in any scheme of constitutional reforms.
The structural contradiction between communally compartmentalized
electorates and the localization and provincialization of political horizons
was to have large consequences for India's regionally differentiated,
economically disparate and ideologically divided Muslims and, by
extension, for Congress' agendas of an inclusionary and secular nationalism. If the shared idioms of an otherwise varied discourse appear to
substantiate the colonial construction of Muslims as a separate and
identifiable 'communal' category, the actual politics of Muslims in the
different local and regional settings uncovers how common ideas led to
uncommon deeds.

After 1911, the annulment of the partition of Bengal, the crisis in the
Balkans and the Kanpur mosque incident of 1913 created the conditions
for major reformulations of the discourse and politics of upper and
middle class Muslims. Voicing the mood in certain Muslim elite quarters,
Shibli wrote a series of polemical poems against the All-India Muslim
League, rejecting the very notion of a separatist and loyalist politics, and
endorsing the establishment of a joint Hindu-Muslim front. Well versed
in the normative aspects of Islam, Shibli refused to treat religion as a
code for Muslim participation in politics.

This was a stretch removed from the stance being advocated at the
time by Abul Kalam Azad through his organ *Al-Hilal*. By far the most
important Muslim 'traditionalist', Azad's somersaults on religion and
politics convey the paradoxes of 'communalism' in the subcontinental
context. Azad is celebrated in the tomes of Indian nationalist historiography for his steadfast opposition in the forties to the Muslim League's
inexorable drift towards 'separatism' and 'communalism'. This is why
his early writings on religion and politics make for fascinating reading.
Islam was not only the vital component in Azad's identity but also the
main source of his intellectual and political orientation. In 1904 he
described the Congress as a Hindu body. 'There will be nothing left with
us', he wrote, 'if we separate politics from religion'.[14] Azad was crestfallen
to see that his co-religionists were 'not united and organised as a
community'; they had 'no *quaid* (leader)', a mere 'rabble scattered among
the population of India' they were living an 'un-Islamic and irreligious

---

[14] Cited in Haq, *Muslim Politics in Modern India*, p. 72.

life'.[15] The more than explicit exclusivism and separatism, to say nothing of the implicit sense of superiority, was tempered only by Azad's consistent anti-British posture and support for the Congress.

Azad's Islamism led him to even greater excesses in the name of religion. In 1920 at the height of the Khilafat agitation Azad, backed by the newly founded Jamiat-ul-Ulema-i-Hind, issued a *fatwa* declaring that under the Shariah it was an 'Islamic obligation' for Muslims to 'quit India'.[16] According to the most prominent Muslim spokesman of Congress' secular nationalism and notion of composite culture, given the choice between country and faith, Indian Muslims could only opt for the latter. These utterances for the most part have been swept under the carpet. Politically 'correct' alignments, not the integrity or substantive content of the thinking, have been the more important factors determining the allotment of titles 'nationalist' or 'communalist' to would-be spokesmen of India's Muslims.

An assessment of the political positions of that other champion of Islamic universalism and the Khilafat, Maulana Mohamed Ali, will suffice to make the point. In 1912 he castigated Congress 'nationalists' for refusing to accept that the educated Hindu 'communal patriot' had turned Hinduism into an effective symbol for political mobilization and Indian 'nationality'. The Hindu 'communal patriot' simply 'refuse[d] to give quarter to the Muslims unless the latter quietly shuffles off his individuality and becomes completely Hinduised'.[17] This was a powerful indictment of Indian 'nationalism' from a man who during the non-cooperation and Khilafat agitation of the early 1920s was closely allied with Gandhi. Nothing dissuaded Mohamed Ali from speaking freely and fearlessly as a Muslim 'communal patriot'. Not even the honour of delivering the presidential address at the Congress session in December 1923. Mohamed Ali ascribed his belated entry into the Congress in 1919 to the 'political history of the community' to which he belonged. Making political capital out of Congress's acceptance of separate electorates for Muslims in its Lucknow pact of 1916 with the Muslim League, Mohamed Ali called the Simla deputation a 'command performance'. Separate electorates were 'the consequence, and *not* the cause of the separation between Muslims and their more numerous Hindu brethren'. India's

[15] Ibid., p. 108.

[16] Ibid., p. 124.

[17] Mohamed Ali, 'The Communal Patriot', February 1912, in Afzal Iqbal (ed.), *Writings and Speeches of Maulana Mohamed Ali*, first edition 1944, revised edition, (Lahore, 1987), pp. 75–7.

most hopeful future lay in becoming a 'federation of faiths', not in a 'misleading unity of opposition'.[18] Stated uncategorically from the Congress pedestal, this was a command performance indeed!

Yet few historians of Indian nationalism trace Mohamed Ali's 'communal' lineage to this period. It was only after his falling out with the Congress on the issue of the Nehru report in 1928 that his communal colours begin to be spotted. So even the statements of a self-styled 'communal patriot' enunciated from within the Congress are 'nationalist'; outside its ambit they acquire the ignominious status of 'communal reaction'. For those who participated in the Khilafat agitation, the collapse of the movement amidst heightened social conflict along communitarian lines became a litmus test for their allegiance to Indian nationalism. Azad, whose political speeches during the campaign had been peppered with verses from the Quran, 'kept himself aloof from the murky communal politics of the twenties'.[19] By contrast, Mohamed Ali became a rabid 'communalist'. The assertion that he belonged to 'two circles of equal size ... which are not concentric—one is Indian and the other is the Muslim world' is seen as the 'tragedy' of Mohamed Ali's life.[20] Not particularly convincing as a tragic figure, in November 1930 he made an impassioned plea for Indian freedom while strongly advocating the 'Muslim case' for separate electorates, safeguards and majority provinces:

> I have a culture, a polity, an outlook on life
> —a complete synthesis which is Islam. Where God
> commands I am a Muslim first, a Muslim second, and
> a Muslim last, and nothing but a Muslim.... But where
> India is concerned, where India's freedom is concerned,
> where the welfare of India is concerned, I am an Indian
> first, an Indian second, an Indian last, and nothing but
> an Indian.[21]

A respectable 'nationalist' position in an earlier period, by the 1930s such an expression of the multiple identities of India's Muslims from outside the Congress fold entailed being called a 'communalist'.

---

[18] Mohamed Ali's presidential address to the Indian National Congress at Cocanada, 26 December, 1923, in Ibid., pp. 111–8.

[19] Nanda, *Gandhi-Pan-Islamism, Imperialism and Nationalism* (Bombay: Oxford University Press, 1989), pp. 391–2.

[20] Ibid., p. 390.

[21] Mohamed Ali's speech at the fourth plenary session of the Round Table Conference in London on 19 November, 1930, in Iqbal (ed.), *Select Writings and Speeches of Mohamed Ali*, p. 356.

The arbitrariness of sifting 'nationalists' from 'communalists' becomes a trifle more glaring once the spotlight is shifted away from the level of discourse onto the formal political arenas. Anyone not belonging to the Congress and articulating a politics of 'Muslim interests' is a communalist, not a nationalist. So while the unity of religion and politics at the level of discourse and pro-Congress 'nationalist' activity does not make for a communal position—for instance during the Khilafat movement—the most explicitly non-religious manoeuvrings and machinations in the name of a 'community' are sufficient for a reputation as a communal politician. Bickering over the loaves and fishes of office in local and provincial councils, hardly proof of religious concerns, throws up a colourful medley of Muslim political sinners, one more 'communal' than the other. The main qualification for 'communalism' appears to be the pursuit of power politics, least engaged with specifically religious issues.

Different historians have examined the growth of 'communalism' in the provinces under the Montford reforms, correctly attributing it to the structural imperatives of the representative institutions created by the colonial state. Yet without a consideration of the politics of Muslims qua Muslims, these interpretations run the risk of becoming tautological. Under separate electorates Muslims voted for Muslims; the elected representatives worked in the interest of their constituents with the result that the politics of Muslims were thoroughly 'communalized'. It might be more even handed to condemn all politics within the inadequate representative institutions of the colonial state as reflecting the religious divide. But that would mean abandoning the binary opposition between secular nationalism and religious communalism. So the slanted logic ends up insinuating that an elected Muslim had to make a real hash of representative office to escape being a 'communalist'. No such difficulties pin down 'nationalists' drawn from the majority community if elected on the Swarajist or the Congress ticket.

Underplayed in analyses of the Montford reforms is the extent to which the provincial dynamic in electoral and representative activities countered the process of 'communalizing' Muslim politics at the all-India level. The essentialization of religious difference implicit in 'communalism' has clouded any sense of maintaining an analytical distinction between levels of politics. Identifying the well-springs of 'communalism' in distinct locales and provinces does not add up to an undifferentiated political dynamic of all-India proportions. The convergence of Muslim and Punjabi or Muslim and Bengali did not mean exchanging provincial interest for a common religious identity. With their identities bounded

by region and informed by religion, the interests of Indian Muslims did
not pour neatly into all-India 'communal' moulds. This is brought out
in stark form by the conflict of interests between Muslims in the majority
and the minority provinces. Supra-communal alliances were forged not
only in the U. P. where Muslims were in a minority but also in the Punjab
and Bengal where they had bare majorities.

In the Punjab the Unionist leaders Fazl-i-Husain and Sikander Hayat
Khan, and in Bengal the Krishak Praja leader Fazlul Haq, had made
sure that by 1937 the provincial imperative had prevailed over a
specifically Muslim communal line within the domain of representative
Muslim politics. The pursuit of power, not the preservation of religious
distinctiveness, tended to empty an elite political discourse of its
normative and substantive content, leaving the Indian Muslim category
as an unlikely vehicle for cultural nationalism. The All-India Muslim
League's dismal performance in the 1937 elections reveals the complete
bankruptcy of any notion of an all-India Muslim 'communalism'. It was
the perceived threat from the singular and uncompromising 'nationalism'
of the Congress to provincial autonomy and class interests which gave
the discourse and politics of the Indian Muslims as a subcontinental
category a fresh lease of life.

FROM COMMUNITY TO NATIONHOOD: SEPARATISM
OR EXCLUSION?

A teleological view of history would interpret the transformation of the
discourse and politics of a minority religious community into a demand
for nationhood as the logical culmination of the 'communal' tendencies
among Indian Muslims. Those who subscribe to the 'two nation' theory
are among the more notorious practitioners of this approach. But their
sharpest opponents have been no less culpable. Reading 'composite
culture' for 'nation', assimilation for distinctiveness, does not banish the
telos of partition for those wedded to the convention of perceiving
historical trends in the binary mode of secular nationalism and religious
communalism. The subaltern thunder in South Asian historiography has
certainly struck fear in the minds of historians beyond the pale of this
select circle. But it has not shed much useful light on how to link
'communal consciousness' and periodic outbursts of inter-communal
violence among marginal social groups in the public arenas of localities
with the partition of India along ostensibly religious lines. Subaltern
consciousness is shaped by too many contending identities to allow for
an unquestioning privileging of the 'communal' element within it.

'Communal consciousness' itself has been subject to far greater recent and dramatic historical change than is acknowledged by these historians. Asserting the autonomy of the subaltern subject from elite manipulations in the making of history can be a meaningful proposition only if based on an assessment of the inter-connections between different levels of politics. Short of holding subaltern consciousness and violence responsible for the partition of India, and that is surely not the intention, there can be no adequate explanation of the post-colonial transition which does not address the calculations and miscalculations of those located at the highest level of politics.

What such an explanation cannot afford, however, is the historiographical error of treating the end result of the 1947 partition as the ultimate goal of Muslim politics and also of broader historical trends subsumed under the theme of 'communalism'. If discrepancies based on class, regional and ideological differences permeated the discourse and politics of Muslim identity in the late nineteenth and early twentieth century, the metamorphosis of a minority community into a 'nation' was designed more as a powerful rhetorical device than an accurate statement of the reality.

The idea of a Muslim state, albeit within India and restricted to the north-western Muslim-majority provinces, had been voiced in December 1930 by Mohammad Iqbal at the All-India Muslim League's annual session. A critic of Western nationalism, Iqbal did not declare Indian Muslims a 'nation' when he initially called for a state based on the territorial amalgamation of the Punjab, the North-West Frontier Province, Sind and Baluchistan. This was a proposition that, for a change, bore the marks of Punjabi Muslim rather than Muslim minority province interests. Islam as a living cultural force in India demanded its 'centralization in a specified territory' and was the only sure 'basis of a permanent communal settlement'. None of this was actuated by 'narrow communalism' or 'any feeling of ill-will towards other communities'. There were 'communalisms and communalisms' and it was not the 'low and ignoble' communalism based on antipathy towards other communities but the 'higher aspect of communalism' as culture, which even the Nehru report had endorsed, that Iqbal had in mind.[22] Yet the demand for a state within India where only a fraction of Muslims could live according to their

---

[22] Mohammad Iqbal's presidential address to the All-India Muslim League at Allahabad, December 1930 in Syed Sharifuddin Pirzada (ed.), *Foundations of Pakistan, All-India Muslim League Documents: 1906–1947* (Karachi: National Publishing House, 1970), Vol. 11, pp. 158–61, 166.

culture and religious traditions was too obviously in the interests of the majority provinces, particularly the Punjab, to excite an All-India Muslim League council dominated by Muslims from the minority provinces. So Iqbal's ideas were dismissed as mere poetics in established Muslim political circles.

The famous resolution passed at the Muslim League's Lahore session marked the transition of the Indian Muslims from a minority to a 'nation'. One point of view which needs putting to rest is that in declaring the Indian Muslims a 'nation', the League was inspired by a normative ideal in Muslim consciousness, namely that the preservation of the religious identity of the community demanded the exercise of political power by representatives of the Faithful.[23] Given the varied uses Muslim thinkers make of the normative ideals of Islam, arguments focusing on discourse do not offer satisfactory explanations of changing historical dynamics. The statement of Muslim 'nationhood' which emanated from Lahore in March 1940 was, to quote one critic, 'an extreme step for solving communal problems'.[24] An explicit revolt against minoritarianism, it was also an implicit *coup* against the dominant binary mode which extolled Congress' 'secular nationalism' as legitimate and denigrated Muslim difference as illegitimate 'religious communalism'. Declaring the Indian Muslims a 'nation', Jinnah confessed that the idea of being a minority had been around for so long that 'we have got used to it ... these settled notions sometimes are very difficult to remove'. But the time had come to unsettle the notion since 'the word "Nationalist" has now become the play of conjurers in politics'.[25]

No amateur conjurer himself, Jinnah came away from the League's session with a mixed bag of tricks. The weightiest was the demand that all future constitutional arrangements be reconsidered 'de novo' since Indian Muslims were a 'nation' entitled to equal treatment with the Hindu 'nation'. But in attempting to give territorial expression to the Muslim claim to nationhood, Jinnah and a mainly minority province based All-India Muslim League had to make large concessions to the autonomy and sovereignty of the majority provinces, not a very tidy beginning to

[23] Shaikh, *Community and Consensus in Islam*, Ch. 6.

[24] Dr Radha Kumad Mookerji, *A New Approach to the Communal Problem* (Bombay: Padma Publications, 1943), p. 59.

[25] Jinnah's presidential address to the All-India Muslim League, Lahore, March 1940 in Pirzada (ed.), *Foundations of Pakistan, All-India Muslim League Documents: 1906–47*, Vol. 11, p. 335.

the search for statehood. If reconciling the contradictory interests of Muslims in majority and minority provinces had thwarted the All-India Muslim League's representative pretensions in the past, the sheer impracticability of squaring the claim of nationhood with the promise of statehood required something more than an artful conjuring trick.

The historiographical debate has deliberated on the issue of Muslim 'nationhood' rather more than on the ambiguities surrounding the demand for Muslim 'statehood'. This has to do with that other *telos* which presumes the orchestration of separate nationhood as an inevitable overture to exclusive statehood. Recent revisionist historiography on partition, including my own,[26] has noted the uneasy fit between an assertion of Muslim 'nationhood' and the uncertainties and indeterminacies of politics in the late colonial era that led to the attainment of sovereign 'statehood'. While the insistence on national status for Indian Muslims became a non-negotiable issue after 1940, the demand for a wholly separate and sovereign state of 'Pakistan' remained open to negotiation as late as the summer of 1946. The scholarly blindness to this is a product of the double mental barrier, both against maintaining an analytical distinction between 'nation' and 'state' and expunging the *telos* of partition from interpretations of the historical evolution of the demand for a 'Pakistan'.

The claim that Muslims constituted a 'nation' was perfectly compatible with a federal or confederal state structure covering the whole of India. With 'nations' straddling states, the boundaries between states had to be permeable and flexible. This is why Jinnah and the League remained implacably opposed to the division of the Punjab and Bengal along religious lines. It was the veritable absence of an all-India Muslim 'communalism' which had given rise to the claim for Muslim 'nationhood'. This did not translate into a secessionist demand for a Muslim nation-state, but was intended as the building block for a confederal arrangement with the Hindu-majority provinces, or Hindustan, at the subcontinental level.

In the event the strategy went awry, resulting in the exclusion from India of the leader and the party which had staked a claim on behalf of all Indian Muslims. Communally compartmentalized electorates had helped transform the case of Muslim distinctiveness into an assertion of 'nationhood' at the level of all-India political discourse. But the emphasis

---

[26] See Ayesha Jalal, *The Sole Spokesman: Jinnah, the Muslim League and the Demand for Pakistan* (Cambridge: Cambridge University Press, 1985).

on provincial and local arenas of politics pitted Muslim regional interest
against those raised on behalf of a subcontinental 'community' or 'nation'.
The resort to Islam was a mobilizational technique to generate momentum for a political movement seeking a substantial share of power for
Muslims in an independent India. If the League's politics lent a
'communal' colouring to the demand for a 'Pakistan' at the social base,
there were Muslim groups opposed to its strategy who made an ever
greater play of Islam as a religious ideology.

After 1940, the Muslim League did a better job manipulating the
discourse than in rivetting control over the politics of Muslims in the
majority provinces. Yet even at the level of the discourse, the League
was not the most convincing pretender in the race for the Islamic trophy.
As late as the final decade of the British Raj in India, prominent Muslim
thinkers, including 'Nationalist Muslims' like Maulana Azad and Maulana
Husain Ahmad Madani of the Jamiat-ul-Ulema-i-Hind, promoted
muttahiddah qawmiyyat or composite nationalism with the same passion
as their belief in religious and cultural differences between Muslims and
non-Muslims. With the exception of Azad, the most ardent believers in
the *ummah vahidah* or one nation theory patented by the Congress were
ulema who could not imagine an independent India without *shariah* rule.
The irony of this non-secular vision co-existing harmoniously with the
Congress' secular programme underscores the political motivations
behind the binary opposition between secular nationalism and religious
communalism. More ironic still was the enthusiastic support for the
Pakistan demand by Muslim communists and socialists, especially those
associated with the Progressive Writers movement.[27] The participation
of ungodly socialists in the Pakistan movement fuelled charges by Islamic
ideologues that the demand for 'Pakistan' was no more than a 'secular
charade. Yet having fiercely opposed Jinnah and the Muslim League,
a good number of these religious ideologues and organizations adopted
Pakistan as the terrain to launch their crusade for *shariah* rule. The
rabidly religious Jamat-i-Islami, the bigoted Majlis-e-Ahrar and the
idiosyncratic Khaksars are all examples of this legion.

Unable to resolve the contradictions among Muslims at the level of
discourse, the League did even more miserably in the realm of actual
politics. At the end of the day the singular nationalism of the Indian

---

[27] See Khizar Humayun Ansari, *The Emergence of Socialist Thought Among
North-Indian Muslims (1917–47)* (Lahore: Book Traders, 1990), Ch. 6.

National Congress got the better of both the Muslim claim to 'nation-hood' and the majoritarian provincialism of Muslims in the north-western and eastern extremities of the subcontinent. The Congress leadership, keen on grasping the centralized apparatus of the colonial state, was prepared neither to share power with the Muslim League at the all-India level nor accommodate Muslim majoritarian provincialism within a loose federal or confederal structure. It was ready instead to wield the partitioner's axe—in concert one might add with the Hindu Mahasabha—to exclude both the League and the Muslim-majority areas from the horizons of the secular Indian nation-state. Cast against its will into the role of a seceding state, Pakistan was left to begin its independent career with an ideology of Muslim 'nationhood' which could not plausibly be squared with the mutilated and moth-eaten territorial contours of its truncated statehood.

DIVIDED NATION, RIVAL STATES AND THE MUSLIM QUANDARY

The anguish of partition for the subcontinent's Muslims has been captured by poets and writers on both sides of the 1947 divide. Despair at the masterly deception that had turned the dream of independence into one of brutal separation pervades the literature written in the very Urdu language which many extremist Hindus hold responsible for stoking the fires of Muslim 'communalism' since the late nineteenth century. In his *Khoon ki Lakeer* or 'The line of blood', Sardar Jaffari, one of India's leading leftist poets, rejected the newly demarcated boundary as an imperialist artefact:

Who is this cruel person who has with his burning pen
Cut a deep line of innocent blood across the motherland's breast
What happened? Suddenly all the instruments have changed
    their tune at this gathering.[28]

Across the border in Muslim Pakistan, Ahmad Riaz boldly repudiated the religious loyalty which had brought about the tragedy to reassure his friends in India:

[28] My adaptation of Sardar Jaffari cited in M.Yusuf Abbasi, *Pakistani Culture: A Profile* (Islamabad: National Institute of Historical and Cultural Research, 1992), p. 76.

The dawn of independence has come,
but still the paths of past and present are in darkness.
We are neither infidels nor Muslims.
Crushed by famine and hunger, we are the rejected ones.
Comrades, hold out your hands, even today we are together.
Who could ever divide the estate of literature?
Cities can be divided, the streets closed
but who can imprison intensity of feeling.[29]

Such warmth of feeling was to become rare as Muslims in India and Pakistan set about renegotiating their identity according to the dominant idioms of the two nation-states. With the Indian and the Pakistani states turning the binary opposites of secular nationalism and religious communalism into ideologies of legitimacy, the dilemma of a subcontinental Muslim identity was to become irresolvable. The imperatives of citizenship in mutually hostile nation-states meant that Muslims were no longer simply a divided community but declared enemies of co-religionists beyond the nearest international check point. Under such inauspicious circumstances even a Hali might have settled for the ashes than the politically injudicious task of breathing fire into the partitioned hearts and minds of Muslims with a rousing *Shikwa-e-Azadi*.

Far from being an indivisible property and a symbol of Muslim cultural identity, the Urdu language became an early and unrelieved victim of attack by the Hindu Mahasabha, the Jan Sangh and the RSS. They demanded a Hindi-only policy in the very region which had nurtured Urdu as its lingua franca. The willingness of the U. P. Congress to go along with these Hindu nationalist organizations dealt a grievous blow to the cultural pretensions of India's Urdu-speaking Muslim elite. The cruelest cut was the charge that by insisting on Urdu as their cultural heritage, now that the majority community had made the sacrifice of partition to settle the problem of difference once and for all, Muslims were furnishing evidence of their inveterate disloyalty to the Indian nation-state. Being born and raised in India, the Muslims learnt to their horror, was no longer sufficient evidence of their Indianness. Those whose faith in the secularism encoded in the Indian constitution made this a questionable proposition had only to be reminded of Sardar Vallabhbhai Patel's chilling exhortation to Muslims: 'I want to tell them frankly that mere declaration of loyalty to [the] Indian Union will not help them at this critical juncture. They must give proof of their declaration'.[30]

[29] Ibid., pp. 77–8.
[30] Cited in Moin Shakir, *Politics of Muslim Minorities* (Delhi, 1980), p. 137.

The taunt of disloyalty came from unexpected quarters. Abul Kalam Azad, the Muslim paragon of secular nationalism, reprimanded his co-religionists for vesting their trust in an undeserving leadership and party which had now tossed them to the winds. Nothing less than a complete change of heart was required to win the certificate of loyalty. But with Pakistan as a permanent albatross signifying their negative identity, switching the Turkish fez for the khadi cap and innumerable other such gestures to India's composite culture and secular nationalism—for instance reluctantly giving up separate electorates and sullenly agreeing to let their children learn Hindi instead of Urdu—could not confirm the Muslim minority's positive affiliation to the nation-state. Even if segments of the elite saw political advantages in distancing themselves from the more controversial symbols of their religiously informed cultural identity, there were few such incentives for the mass of poor and illiterate Muslims. Confounding the dilemma of Muslim identity were the religious and political aspirations of that motley collection of *ulema* who, because they had chosen the Congress instead of the Muslim League, had somehow to be accommodated within the framework of a secular and democratic India. Having purchased tickets for the train purportedly taking India's Muslims to a secular nationalist destination, the *ulema's* ideological world view could obstruct coherent communication between passengers in the first and third class compartments. Irritations with the never-ending journey of India's Muslims led to the menacing suggestion that the train would be better off on tracks leading straight across the sealed border.

Hali's *Shikwa-e-Hind* had come to haunt the Indian Muslims with a vengeance. Under suspicion in India and unwelcome in Pakistan, their predicament has been an unenviable one. The distortions of the historical evidence in both states have inculcated among the educated few a congenital animosity towards the country for whose creation they are held responsible. That there has been so little love lost between upper and middle class Indian and Pakistani Muslims is hardly cause for surprise.

The decision to make Urdu the state language of Pakistan harkened back to an overarching conception of Muslim identity which found few echoes in the regionally based cultural identities of its people. Reduced to being a subaltern language in its own regional setting, Urdu came to be regarded as an instrument of neo-imperialist domination. Bengalis in the eastern wing put up stout resistance against encroachments on their cultural autonomy. On 21 February, 1952 students protesting the language policy were gunned down by the police. A common religious identity had never meant the denial of a separate cultural tradition. Proud of belonging to the same literary heritage as Rabindranath Tagore and

Kazi Nazrul Islam, Bengali intellectuals deplored the official policy of deprecating their Islamic beliefs. There was 'no inherent contradiction in being a Bengali, a Muslim and a Pakistani—all at the same time'.[31] Bengalis were not alone in bearing the brunt of linguistic and cultural denial. In the Punjab, supposedly the political nerve-centre of Pakistani imperialism, intellectuals working to promote their regional language and culture were declared 'anti-state'. After the military coup of 1958, the state clamped down further on regional literary associations. Bengali resentments found their fullest expression in the establishment of an independent state of Bangladesh. Shamsur Rahman conveyed the long-standing cultural alienation of Muslim Bengal in a poem written during the liberation struggle:

> Freedom:
> you are Tagore's ageless poetry,
> his immortal songs.
> Freedom:
> you are Kazi Nazrul, wild-haired sage
> trembling with the thrill of creation.
> Freedom:
> you are that meeting at the martyr's monument
> on the eternal twenty-first of February.[32]

The brief populist interlude in what remained of Pakistan came as something of a boon for regional language movements. Resistance themes in regional folklore were among the symbols of protest against the military regime of General Zia-ul-Haq. One Punjabi poet conveyed the growing disdain for the state's attempts to forge a singular national identity on the basis of an alien culture and language:

> In vain you are looking for your identity in the imperial courts of Delhi?
> Why do you ask deserts to provide you the shadows of pipal?
> You cannot find your own perfumes in other's gardens.[33]

If the Pakistani state's language policy generated more resentment than enthusiasm for Urdu as one of the dominant idioms of national identity, the response of a predominantly Muslim but regionally differentiated population to its ambiguous recourse to Islam proved utterly divisive.

[31] Cited in Anisuzzaman, *Creativity, Reality and Identity* (Dhaka: International Centre for Bengal Studies, 1993), p. 104.

[32] Ibid, p. 115.

[33] Nirvan Noori cited in Shafqat Tanveer Mirza, *Resistance Themes in Punjabi Literature* (Lahore: Sange-e-Meel, 1991), p. 201.

The emphasis on religion by its early managers was never intended as a commitment to the establishment of an Islamic state. At the helm of state power, the erstwhile Muslim 'communalists' were not about to pass the mantle of Pakistani 'nationalism' to the religious guardians. In fact the term 'communalism' disappeared from the discourse as 'nationalists' of all hues and colours jockeyed for political ascendancy.

The embattled politics of Pakistan's Islamic ideology scuttled any sort of consensus on national identity. Even as a military-bureaucratic state strained its nerves to keep the Islamicists as bay, it saw attractions in plumping for policies privileging the common religious bond of an otherwise culturally distinctive and economically disparate people. More successful in deluding itself than large segments of a society comfortably positioned to simultaneously live out multiple layers of identity, the inefficacy of the Pakistani state's Islamic card is a powerful indictment of the argument that the religious factor in 'Muslim consciousness' outweighs all other considerations. As electoral results consistently showed up the weak appeal of an exclusively Islamic ideology in politics, it was left to the military-bureaucratic state to embark on policies of Islamization in its search for legitimacy. Yet the most paradoxical legacy of Zia-ul-Haq, the self-proclaimed soldier of Islam, was the intensification of regional, linguistic and sectarian tensions. Whatever the preferred discourse, the politics of identity in Muslim Pakistan have been structured around decidedly non-religious and non-communal considerations.

If a state-supported Islam has been unable to lend any sense of commonality to the politics of identity in a predominantly Muslim country, its political utility for secular India's besieged Muslim minority appears even more uncertain. Apart from declaring the political uses of religion illegal, the Indian constitution by scrapping separate electorates removed the principal institutional barrier to the articulation of Muslim politics in other than 'communal' terms. Although there is scant evidence of Indian Muslims voting on the basis of religious considerations, the notion of minority 'communalism' remains enmeshed in Indian political discourse. This has given pro-Hindu as well as ostensibly secular parties the moral pretext to issue periodic condemnations of the narrow mindedness of Muslims on the question of personal law and other matters to do with their religiously informed cultural identity. The tolerant secularist and the bigoted Hindu are really after the same pound of flesh—Muslims have to stop drawing upon the religious and cultural strands of their identity if they want complete integration in the secular and democratic framework of the Indian nation-state.

Discomfort with difference is a function of the inclusionary nationalism and, its concomitant, equal citizenship which are among the defining features of modern nation-states. But despite ample evidence on the ground, the paradox of inclusionary nationalism ending up as a narrative construction of an exclusionary majoritarian identity has rarely commanded attention from the votaries of the nation-state. In India matters are further complicated by the fact that the inclusionary idiom is expressed in an artificial binary opposition between secular nationalism and religious communalism. To be secular and nationalist for a Muslim entails publicly disclaiming too close an association with the specific traits of the minority community, religious and cultural. Otherwise there is no escaping the pejorative label of 'communalism'. But the protagonists of Hindutva can get away critiquing the state's pseudo-secularism while pitching their bid for the nationalist mantle.

Finding ways to accommodate a distinctive Muslim identity without launching a frontal assault on the contradictory official idioms of the Indian state can result in perilous logic. The inclusionary idiom flows from a singular conception of Indian nationalism whose ideological basis is a secularism with religion left out. Yet there is also the accompanying conception of a composite nationalism deriving its justification from India's pluralist religio-cultural tradition. The idea of a composite nationalism was in some ways an advance on the notion of India as a 'federation of faiths'. It entertains the possibility of the co-existence of religious communities without adequately addressing the problem of difference among them. Secular nationalism, on the other hand, avoids through erasure the problem of difference by projecting a singular narrative construction of Indian identity. Collapsing the pluralism implied in the 'composite' of nationalism with a 'secularism' devoid of religion leads to serious confusion of conceptual categories. This confusion which is expressed in varied ways in academic and political debates flows largely from an inability to retain an analytical distinction between Muslim identity and a Muslim communal politics. A Muslim identity, however one might choose to package it, makes a claim on difference denied by the singular secular nationalist ideal. But in the absence of any neat equation between a Muslim identity and a Muslim 'communal' politics, beyond a handful of electoral constituencies where voting patterns might occasionally reveal such an overlap, there is no reason for a secular nationalist discourse to acknowledge, far less accommodate, difference.

So it is one thing to applaud the declining influence of religious obscurantism on the politics of the Muslim masses and quite another to see this as a triumph of the secular-modernist initiative recently launched by a voluble and variegated segment of the Indian Muslim elite. A socially and economically underprivileged and politically divided minority which is the target of bigotry and organized violence from a determined section of the majority community could do with some measure of electoral solidarity to force the agendas of the state. Dismissing this as 'communalism' of the sort which brought about the partition of the country, the new generation of the Indian Muslim elite in a leap of faith from an all too awkward reality firmly believes in the secular and democratic ideals of their state and polity. Yet forging a secular modernist Indian Muslim identity without dabbling in power politics may require more reason than faith. It is somewhat difficult to imagine how a Muslim elite which has maintained a studied aloofness from their regionally fragmented underprivileged co-religionists are going to mobilize support for a secular conception of identity 'outside the communitarian framework'. Blazing Azad's old trail 'to posit composite nationalism' against 'appeals based on religious solidarity' is a noble secular hope.[34] But it runs counter to the singular secular nationalist idiom insofar as it admits a problem of Muslim identity.

The Muslim quandary in post-independence India is an especially acute one. Needing the very political solidarity which the secular nationalist idiom damns as 'communalism' and the electoral scene in any case renders impossible, the secular modernists can at best try and influence Muslim elite discourse. But as in the past that discourse has never been of a singular or homogeneous cast. Reforming Muslim personal law to fit a secular modernist ideal, hung and drawn by tensions in the composite and secular conceptions of Indian nationalism, without being quartered by the inescapable intervention of the religious guardians is a daunting task. The tragedy of the new breed of Muslim secular modernists in India quite as much as in Pakistan is their lack of facility in Islamic learning. Better trained in Marxist and Weberian paradigms than in the Quran, theirs are not necessarily pens more powerful than the sword. With no Sayyid Ahmed Khan, Syed Ameer Ali, Shibli or Azad waiting in the wings, the words of the insular and bigoted *fatwah*—giving bearded men will ricochet on any debate surrounding Muslim personal law. Indian Muslims with their multiple voices and splintered politics will undoubtedly continue to resist threats to their religiously

---

[34] Mushirul Hasan, 'Minority Identity and its Discontents: Response and Representation', *Economic and Political Weekly*, 19 February, 1994, pp. 441–51.

informed cultural identity. Taking on a variety of forms, it will be a
resistance so multifarious as to justify exploding 'communalism' and
rescuing the problem of difference from essentialization as well as
extinction.

CONCLUSION

An exploration of the discourse and politics of Muslim identity over a
period stretching more than a century reveals the grave flaws in
categorizing the multiple articulation of difference as 'religious communalism' or cultural nationalism. Muslim identity as difference has been
riven with too many internal contradictions to be capped by an all
encompassing 'communalism'. Historicizing and conceptualizing the
related issues of Muslim difference and Muslim politics has suggested
the inevitability of the one and the impossibility of the other. A common
source of reference in the normative ideals of Islam does not warrant
the essentialization of Muslimness implied by 'communalism'. But by the
same token, ideological and political disagreements among Muslims do
not nullify the case for difference. What it indicates is that the problem
of Muslim difference and identity in South Asia has been more complex
and nuanced than permitted by the protagonists of the 'two nation' theory
or the practitioners of a historiography based on a binary opposition
between secular nationalism and religious communalism.

The problem of difference in South Asia as a whole and of Muslim
identity in particular cannot begin to be addressed without forsaking the
dichotomies between 'secular' and 'religious' as well as 'nationalism' and
'communalism'. Just as the first set of opposites can be found blending
into the thought of a single individual, the second binary pair shares a
common conception of majoritarianism and minoritarianism in the
privileging of religious distinction. The majoritarian premises of Indian
and Pakistani 'nationalism' derive equally from the colonial project of
religious enumeration. While Indian nationalism asserts its inclusionary
idioms in the secular garb and Pakistani nationalism in an inclusionary
religious mode, neither avoids the pernicious process of exclusion
resulting from the implicit denial of difference. It is the singular and
homogenizing agendas of both nation-states which have wittingly or
unwittingly created the space for religious bigots seeking political power
to target vulnerable minorities. To call bigotry 'communalism' is to
implicate in the actions of the few the inactivity of the many. So while
there can be no denying the rampant bigotry of so-called Hindu

majoritarian 'communalism' in India and religious 'fundamentalism' in Pakistan, their politics of oppositional identity construction need to be exposed to the full glare of analytical scrutiny. The self-defence of baited minorities produces its own venomous narratives and versions of bigotry. But dubbing the outrage of the Indian Muslim minority to the actions of the Hindutva brigades 'communalism' is to deny legitimacy to any strategy aimed at protecting or accommodating the problem of difference and identity. In much the same way, the regional counter-narratives of difference in Pakistan have to be seen as strategies of resistance seeking release from the fetters of an uncompromising discourse of Islamic identity rather than as a denial of Muslimness.

That the dominant idioms of states, and the ways in which these are reflected in elite discourse, so often fly in the face of the shifting structural contours of politics at the base is reason enough for abandoning some of their more questionable premises. Exploding 'communalism' to uncover the manifold and contradictory interests driving the politics of Muslim identity in South Asia might enable a better appreciation of difference as a lived cultural experience, one that is forever changing in response to broader historical dynamics, rather than an abstract, sterile and essentialized category awaiting a fresh round of scholarly bandaging.

6

'Hindu Nationalism' and the Crisis of the Indian State: A Theoretical Perspective[1]

Sumantra Bose

Sixth December 1992 was a significant conjunctural moment in independent India's history. The demolition of the Babri Mosque, razed that day in Ayodhya by 'Hindu nationalist' militants, dramatically highlighted a grave crisis confronting contemporary India. However, there has been relatively little systematic effort to develop broader, theoretically-informed explanations of this crisis, and to situate the rise of the Hindutva (political Hinduism) movement within an overall contextual framework. After all, the Rashtriya Swayamsevak Sangh (RSS),[2] the ideological and organizational core of this movement, has been active since 1925, and its political affiliate, the Bharatiya Janata Party (BJP) has been in existence since 1951.[3] Till recently, however, the 'Hindu nation' on which the *sangh-parivar* ('family of organizations') headed by RSS premised its politics appeared to exist 'to a large extent within the party's imagination'.[4] What then might explain the considerably expanded popular appeal of a long marginal cause? What is the nature of India's 'crisis',

[1] I am grateful to Professor Lisa Anderson, Columbia University, and Professor Amrita Basu, Amherst College, for constructive criticism and warm encouragement.

[2] On the RSS and its central position within the Hindutva movement, see Walter Andersen and Shridhar Damle, *The Brotherhood in Saffron: The Rashtriya Swayamsevak Sangh and Hindu Revivalism* (Delhi: Vistaar Publications, 1987), and Tapan Basu et al., *Khaki Shorts and Saffron Flags: A Critique of the Hindu Right* (Delhi: Orient Longman, 1993).

[3] Between 1951 and 1980, the BJP was known as Bharatiya Jan Sangh (BJS).

[4] Bruce Graham, *Hindu Nationalism and Indian Politics: The Origins and Development of the Bharatiya Jan Sangh* (New York: Cambridge University Press, 1990), p. 255.

and why has that crisis become salient in the 1990s? And what is distinctive about the Hindutva movement that enables its proponents to 'sell' it (and with considerable success, especially in northern and western India) as the sole, definitive resolution to all of India's problems?

This article seeks to understand India's Hindutva upsurge within a broader frame of conceptualization and reference. This frame relates the expanded potential of Hindutva as *the* basis for collective Indian identity to what I call the 'organic crisis' of the post-colonial Indian state. This crisis has, I argue, been in the making for several decades, and inevitably has massive reverberations throughout civil society as well. My approach is therefore historically grounded, and my emphasis is on the *totality* of the Indian political and socioeconomic context, *within* (and *only* within) which it is possible to locate and discern the meaning and significance of the project of 'Hindu nationalism'. As Neeladri Bhattacharya puts it, 'the battle for Ramjanambhoomi is part of a wider *political* struggle for a constitution of 'Hindu' consciousness and identity...and for the assertion of 'Hindu' power over all other communities in India.'[5] This is quite correct, but the struggle to build a collective 'Hindu' consciousness itself acquires significance only when seen as the strategic pivot of a determined campaign to capture central state power in India. I argue that to comprehend why this campaign has acquired potency over the past several years, one must consider the organic crisis of the Indian state as a central explanatory factor. Thus, I will not only sketch the basic contours of this crisis, but also trace its genesis and evolution through an analysis of some of the most important and relevant long-term trends and developments in Indian politics.

My perspective further assumes that to explain the rise of Hindutva, we must critically dissect and challenge widely unquestioned dichotomies: such as the presumed antinomy, whether in theory or practice, between categories such as 'secularism'[6] and 'communalism'.[7] Indeed, as I will show, the relationship between secularism and communalism

---

[5] Neeladri Bhattacharya, 'Myth, History and the Politics of Ramjanambhoomi', in S. Gopal (ed.), *Anatomy of a Confrontation: The Ramjanambhoomi-Babri Masjid Dispute* (Delhi: Penguin India, 1991), p. 125. Emphasis added.

[6] The concept of 'secularism' can be understood in at least two ways—as state *neutrality* towards all matters religious (i.e. an *areligious* state), or as *equal respect* by the state towards all religions. In independent India, the latter interpretation (*sarva-dharma-sambhava*) has usually prevailed.

[7] The term 'communalism' was coined by the British in the mid-nineteenth century to describe highly plural, multi-religious societies such as those of the

in post-colonial India has been more complex, and *dialectical* rather than simply *adversarial*. A tendency to view 'communalism' as the binary opposite of Indian 'nationalism' (and that too from a nationalist/secularist ideological stance), as well as to study the communal phenomenon in abstraction from its historical and contemporary context, has marred the work of a number of authors on this subject.[8] Treating 'communalism' thus, as the antithesis of Indian 'nationalism', frequently results in the post-colonial 'secular' state (and the freedom movement before it) being absolved of most if not all culpability in the rise of 'communalism', and specifically of Hindutva. This lack of concern for structure and context, and the tendency to regard 'communalism' as *merely* a pernicious 'ideology' distilled by manipulative elites and swallowed by the ignorant masses, detracts from our understanding of the phenomenon in another crucial way. The 'privileging of communalism', and of 'the contradictions communalism *immediately represents*', has served to 'obscure and conceal [other] basic structural contradictions of Indian society'.[9] These contradictions, and their increasing salience over the past decade or two, are, I will argue, of central explanatory value in accounting for the Hindutva upsurge. The all too frequent overemphasis on Hindu-Muslim conflict, more a *manifestation* of India's crisis than a causal factor, tends to largely obscure the critical role played by growing caste, class, linguistic, regional and ethnic cleavages in the rise of 'Hindu nationalism'.

In constructing my theoretical framework, I have adapted and applied some of the concepts and analytical tools developed in the political writings of Antonio Gramsci,[10] and in the work of the political scientist

---

subcontinent and Malaya. In the post-colonial Indian context, the term denotes prejudice and hostility towards other religions, and 'communal politics' typically means mobilization which stokes and exploits such antipathy. In the post-1947 'secular' state, the term also came to bear strong pejorative connotations. Thus, even the BJP denies being a 'communal' party: it asserts that it is 'nationalist' ('nationalism', by contrast, still carries many positive connotations, partly because of the association of 'nationalism' with the anti-colonial struggle).

[8] For example, Bipan Chandra, *Communalism in Modern India* (Delhi: Vikas, 1979).

[9] Randhir Singh, 'Communalism and the Struggle Against Communalism: A Marxist View', in K.N. Panikkar (ed.), *Communalism in India: History, Politics and Culture* (Delhi: Manohar Books, 1991), p. 114. Emphasis added.

[10] As culled from David Forgacs (ed.), *An Antonio Gramsci Reader* (New York: Schocken Books, 1988).

Juan Linz on elements and processes of crisis and breakdown of democratic regimes.[11] My argument emphasizes the crucial role of the Indian state, and of Congress regimes, in facilitating the seemingly meteoric rise of 'Hindu nationalism'. As Linz puts it, 'the independent contributions made [to regime crises] by political incumbents' is 'an aspect all too often overlooked' because of a one-sided focus on the characteristics and activities of apparently radical opposition movements (such as the *Sangh Parivar*).[12] This is certainly true of India, where even some 'Marxist' writers have tended to be disturbingly ambivalent in assessing the implications of the culpability of the 'secular' state and democratic regime in creating the conditions and climate for, as well as actively encouraging, the politics of 'communalism'.[13] But as Gramsci wrote in his discussion of the rise of Italian fascism to power, it is the 'crisis... of the [Italian] unitary state... [that has] encouraged the rebirth of a confusedly patriotic ideology', not the other way around.[14]

Yet there has been widespread reluctance among scholars of contemporary India, and of the growing problem of communalism, to situate the rise of Hindutva within a broader, substantive critique of the modern Indian state. Even such otherwise unsparing critics as the 'anti-secularist' intellectual Ashis Nandy have tended to limit their critique to the hypocritical and self-serving 'secularism' of post-colonial regimes, and have consequently exaggerated the importance of the religious/communal dimension of the present crisis.[15] I believe, however, that the contemporary Indian crisis is a multidimensional one, of which communal conflict is but *one aspect*. Hence, a critique of the Indian state, if it is to explain the rise and appeal of 'Hindu nationalism', cannot restrict itself to this one aspect alone. It must extend its ruthlessness to encompass the totality of the Indian political universe.

[11] Linz, *The Breakdown of Democratic Regimes: Crisis, Breakdown and Re-equilibration* (Baltimore and London: Johns Hopkins University Press, 1978).

[12] Ibid., p. xi.

[13] See for instance Achin Vanaik, *The Painful Transition: Bourgeois Democracy in India* (London: Verso, 1990); and 'Reflections on Communalism and Nationalism in India', *New Left Review*, p. 196 (1992).

[14] Forgacs (ed.), *An Antonio Gramsci Reader*, p. 138.

[15] See Nandy's 'The Politics of Secularism and the Recovery of Religious Tolerance', in Veena Das (ed.), *Mirrors of Violence: Communities, Riots and Survivors in South Asia* (Delhi: Oxford University Press, 1990); and 'An Anti-Secularist Manifesto', in *Seminar*, 314, pp. 14–24.

That is precisely the purpose of this article. The following section
summarizes the main argument, and introduces and elucidates certain
central concepts and theoretical issues. The subsequent section, which
forms the bulk as well as the empirical heart of this essay, analyses the
emergence of 'Hindu nationalism' within an explanatory framework
which focuses on the crisis of India's democratic and 'secular' regime,
while relating this state-oriented approach to critically relevant long-term
changes in India's social structure and political economy. In the final
section, I briefly elaborate on what makes the Hindutva *ideological*
challenge particularly salient at this historical conjuncture, and enquire
into the nature of the 'alternative' offered to India by the 'Hindu
nationalist' movement.

THE ORGANIC CRISIS OF THE INDIAN STATE

The Analytic Framework: An Outline

This article seeks to understand the rise of Hindutva in the context of what,
following Gramsci,[16] I call the 'organic crisis' of the Indian state. This
overarching crisis, I argue, has two major dimensions: at the level of the
democratic regime, and in the sphere of the (multi)party system. At the
level of the regime, we have a situation that I, following Linz,[17] characterize

[16] By adapting and using Gramscian concepts and analytical techniques (or
gleaning insights into contemporary India from his historicist analysis of the post-
World War I crisis of the Italian state and the rise of Fascism), I am not endorsing
his privileging of the economic sphere, and of class forces and struggles. Instead,
I stress the primacy of the *political*, and see class as but one component (albeit
certainly not an unimportant one) of the highly complex and differentiated social
reality of modern India.

[17] A couple of caveats. Linz excludes a number of 'post-colonial democracies'
(though not specifically India) from the purview of his analysis, citing their lack
of 'institutionalization'. However, I believe that Linz's framework is clearly
applicable to contemporary India, which is a highly institutionalized democracy,
and substantially meets Linz's criteria for a 'democratic regime'. These are:
freedom to create political parties, freedom of speech and association, (reasonably) free elections at regular intervals, on the basis of 'at least universal male
suffrage,' and inclusion of effective political offices in the electoral process. Linz,
The Breakdown of Democratic Regimes, pp. 5–7.

Secondly, my use of Linz's work on regime breakdown does not mean that
I foresee an imminent demise of India's parliamentary democracy, which has
shown resilience over several decades. As Sri Lanka for example shows, even
extremely disruptive and chauvinistic forms of majoritarian mobilization are not

as a crisis of 'legitimacy'. This crisis, in turn, has two dimensions, which concern a severely impaired and deficient regime, 'efficacy' and regime 'effectiveness'. In the sphere of competitive party-politics, there is a 'crisis of hegemony' for the Congress Party, the pivot and principal beneficiary of post-independence India's one-party-dominant system. This in turn has generated a situation of unprecedented instability, unpredictability and flux in the multi-party system. It is this overall crisis, I contend, that has provided the context and opportunity for the Hindutva movement, through its political affiliate, the BJP, to mount a serious bid to capture state power.

In particular, the crisis has made salient old and new conflicts, contradictions and cleavages in India's vast and increasingly differentiated social structure, and has fostered profound dissatisfaction, disillusionment and anxiety among sections of the population. This, as I will show, is *especially* pronounced among certain relatively privileged, dominant and status-quo oriented social groups, who have begun to seriously doubt the capacity of Congress to hold the country together, and more important, ensure the survival and advancement of their own interests In this scenario, the majoritarian myth of Hindutva has, with its millenarian vision of an India which has resolved all its problems, political conflicts and social contradictions through an affirmation of the organic unity of a common 'Hindu' identity, acquired a new potency. In the present situation, the Hindutva movement is playing the role of (in Linz's terminology) a 'semi-loyal opposition' to the regime (as distinguished from a 'disloyal opposition'), and is waging its campaign through a strategy which is a combination of what Gramsci would call a 'war of position' and a 'war of movement', with the goal of staging, again in Gramscian terms, a 'passive revolution' in crisis-ridden India.

An organic crisis is *systemic* and *relatively permanent*. It has deep structural roots, and cannot be resolved, say, through mere changes in

---

incompatible with a continuation of electoral politics. This has, moreover, already been demonstrated in India's electoral arena over the past decade and more. Indeed, the competitive electoral system has been the pivot around which this mobilization has been undertaken, and the sphere where it has found articulated expression. What *cannot* be precluded is that at some point, the reduction of competitive democracy (especially in a highly diverse society) into a forum and vehicle for majoritarian-nationalist assertion will begin to seriously affect the autonomy and integrity of democratic institutions (also very noticeable in the Indian case).

the personnel of government. Organic crises tend to generate chronic social and political instability, and occasionally, major political realignments: in post-World War I Italy, for instance, it led to a fascist takeover. The crisis of regime legitimacy is defined by failures in the interrelated categories of efficacy and effectiveness. Efficacy 'refers to the capacity of a regime to find solutions to the basic problems facing [the] political system, and those that become salient in any historical moment.' Effectiveness is 'the capacity to actually implement the policies formulated, with the desired results.'[18] Further, legitimacy crises (and resulting 'extremist politics', as Linz calls it) have two salient aspects. First, they are not unfortunate accidents or aberrations but 'the result of structural strains'. Second, regime breakdowns, if and when they occur, are 'only the culmination of a long and complex process'.[19] A crisis of hegemony occurs when a force that has formerly exerted political, economic and ideological leadership over society is challenged from below and is no longer able to sustain a cohesive bloc of social alliances, i.e. when its claim to universal interest and value representation is no longer accepted by the previously 'hegemonized' groups.[20]

Disloyal oppositions are 'parties, movements and organizations [which] explicitly reject political systems based on... the authority of the state or [a] central authority with coercive powers', examples being 'anarcho-syndicalists' and 'secessionist and irredentist nationalist movements'.[21] The BJP is clearly *not* a disloyal opposition in this sense. It is, to the contrary, an *extremely* system-oriented party which exalts the centralization and the coercive role of the state. Good examples of Linzian disloyal oppositions in the Indian context are Kashmiri 'secessionists' and 'irredentists', or Sikh 'secessionists', who reject the present Indian state as a legitimate institutional framework. However, BJP *does* meet Linz's definitive criterion for 'semiloyalty,' which is

a willingness to encourage, tolerate, cover up, treat leniently, excuse or justify the actions of other participants that go beyond the limits of peaceful, legitimate patterns of politics in a democracy. Parties become suspect when, on the basis of ideological affinity, agreement on some ultimate goals [say, 'Hindu Rashtra'],

[18] Linz, *The Breakdown of Democratic Regimes*, pp. 20–2.
[19] Ibid., pp. 12, 80.
[20] Gramsci meant by 'hegemony' a dynamic process which presupposed active involvement by hegemonized groups, *not* static, totalizing and passive subordination. Thus, the parliamentary regime, a typical form of 'bourgeois hegemony', is to him based on a dialectic of coercion and consent, not simply coercion.
[21] Linz, *The Breakdown of Democratic Regimes*, p. 28.

or particular policies, they make a distinction between means and ends. They reject the means as undignified and extreme, but excuse them and do not denounce them publicly because of agreement with the goals so pursued... a frequent pattern is the radicalization of youth and student organizations of parties that the mature party leadership cannot disown without losing some of its most... enthusiastic supporters... ultimately, semiloyalty can be identified by a... system-oriented party's greater affinity for extremists on its side of the political spectrum than for system parties closer to the opposite side.[22]

This is precisely the relationship of the BJP to its allies such as the Vishwa Hindu Parishad (VHP) and Bajrang Dal, the groups more directly responsible for the mosque demolition.

Gramsci defined 'war of movement' as a series of frontal assaults on the ruling authority, and 'war of position' as a protracted organizational and mobilizational effort in civil society, whose objective is the formation of a collective will among the people, a prerequisite for the taking of state power. Civil society is thus crucial, since it is both the terrain in which the ruling authority organizes its hegemony, *and* the terrain in which opposition movements agitate and mobilize. The current 'Hindu nationalist' campaign is, in the main, a war of position, with sporadic elements of a war of movement. Finally, 'passive revolution', which Gramsci also calls 'revolution-without-a-revolution' and 'revolution-restoration', is a historical situation in which a new political formation comes to power without fundamentally reordering social relations, but rather by adapting to and gradually modifying the status quo. Gramsci regarded the *Risorgimento* as the archetypical nineteenth-century passive revolution, and fascism as its twentieth-century counterpart. Fascism took over when the parliamentary Italian regime proved incapable of reconciling and controlling, in the disturbed aftermath of World War I, the manifold contradictions, cleavages and conflicts of Italian society.

The Organic Crisis of the Indian State: Structural Roots and Basic Contours

The state-building and regime-consolidation enterprise of the political elite that took over following the 'transfer of power' (passive revolution?)[23] in 1947 had four primary goals. These were: (a) 'national integration' of a diverse mosaic of groups, communities and societies; (b) 'economic development' of a country decimated by 200 years of colonialism; (c) social equality in a land dominated by myriad forms of entrenched

---

[22] Ibid., pp. 32–3.
[23] On this issue, see Partha Chatterjee, *Nationalist Thought and the Colonial World: A Derivative Discourse?* (London: Zed Books, 1986).

inequality; and (d) consolidation of multi-party political democracy.

The balance-sheet of achievements and disappointments five decades later seems marked by serious systemic failure to resolve severe structural problems and dilemmas, some inherited from the Raj, but primarily others which have arisen and taken shape in course of post-colonial state-building. The parliamentary framework has endured, though of course it *is* rather unusual for a democracy to have been governed by three generations of the same family for 38 of its first 42 years. But on the other three counts, it is obvious that 'something has gone seriously wrong... even from the... perspective of parliamentary democracy, trickle-down philosophy of development and 'secularism' for dealing with diverse sectional groupings'.[24] The net consequence of such failure has been fairly unambiguous: heightened socio-political tensions, conflicts and cleavages, a climate of political violence, much of it state-sponsored, and widespread disgust with the ideological bankruptcy and endemic corruption of public life. In short, the ineptitude and degeneration of the state has been matched by growing dislocation and anomie in civil society.

While a sense of 'Indianness' is by no means absent among the citizenry, the project of integrating the 'nation' seems to have been a very partial success. This is manifested most graphically in the growth of powerful and popular secessionist insurgencies during the eighties and nineties in Kashmir, Assam, Punjab and elsewhere. But the tragedies of these 'disturbed areas' are but symptoms of a deeper structural malaise. As Paul Brass comments, the 'Punjab crisis reflect(ed)... a major structural problem in the Indian system that requires a broader political solution. That... problem arises from... the centralizing drives of the Indian state in a society where... the predominant long-term... tendencies are towards pluralism, regionalism and decentralization.'[25] And the seriousness of the 'communal question', undeniably much exacerbated by the recent depredations of 'Hindu nationalists', nevertheless predates the rise of Hindutva. The number of administrative districts affected by Hindu-Muslim violence rose from 61 in 1960 to 250 in 1986–87 (out of 425).[26]

---

[24] Rajni Kothari, *State Against Democracy: In Search of Humane Governance* (Delhi: Ajanta Books, 1988), p. 178.

[25] 'The Punjab Crisis and the Unity of India', in Brass, *Ethnicity and Nationalism: Theory and Comparison* (New Delhi: Sage Publications, 1991), p. 212.

[26] Cited in Zoya Hasan, 'Changing Orientation of the State and the Emergence of Majoritarianism in the 1980s', in Panikkar (ed.), *Communalism in India*, p. 143.

As for 'economic development', the dominant trend that has emerged seems to reflect a curiously skewed and uneven development. A substantial urban middle-class, estimated by some at 150 to 200 million, has emerged in the big cities and medium-sized towns. This group has expanded considerably, especially in the last decade or so, to the extent that it is now possible to speak of a reasonably cohesive 'urban middle class' with broadly shared values and aspirations. On the other hand, mass poverty and illiteracy have remained permanent features of much of the landscape of rural India. A growing urban underclass, especially susceptible to communal incitement, has also appeared in countless slums and shantytowns. This pattern of uneven development, which processes of 'economic liberalization' threaten to exacerbate, has been described as a 'phenomenon of two Indias', one 'on the path of "progress", having access to resources, information and technologies... the other very much left behind.'[27]

Uneven development is closely related to persistent, indeed deepening forms of social inequalities and attendant conflicts. Caste, far from being eradicated by the modernization impulse, has become an entrenched reality of social and political life, most glaringly among Hindi-speaking Hindus in northern India. Indeed, caste has become firmly established as *the* organizing principle of contemporary Indian politics, and this fact, as will become clear later, has much to do with the present appeal of Hindutva ideology to certain caste-based social groups.[28] Many of the poorest (though increasingly politically conscious) Indians are also the oppressed marginals of the caste-hierarchy, i.e. the *Harijans* ('untouchables') and tribal peoples. On the other hand, the elite career services, the Indian Administrative Service (IAS), Indian Police Service (IPS) and Indian Foreign Service (IFS) are quite disproportionately

---

[27] Kothari, *State Against Democracy*, p. 220.

[28] For a brief but useful discussion of the historical complexity and fragmentation of the Indian caste-system, and its reconfiguration and consolidation during the nineteenth and twentieth centuries in response to social modernization and the new centralized political power wielded by the colonial and post-colonial state-apparatuses, see Richard Fox, *Gandhian Utopia: Experiments with Culture* (Boston: Beacon Press, 1989), pp. 249–52. As Fox notes, 'independence accelerated the formation of this new caste-system, whose reality has to do with national and regional politics, vote banks and competition for government benefits.' There are, broadly-speaking, three such politically constructed caste-blocs: the 'scheduled castes' (ex-untouchables), the 'forward castes' (Brahmins, Rajputs, Kayasthas, Khatris etc.) and the vast and diffuse intermediate layer of 'backward castes' or 'other backward classes' (OBCs).

dominated even today by upper-caste Hindus, especially Brahmins.

These structural underpinnings, combined with various conjunctural developments, had resulted in an organic crisis of state power by the late 1980s. However, in order to show *how* this crisis unfolded, and *why* it fostered an atmosphere especially conducive to 'Hindu nationalist' mobilization, it is necessary to delve deeper and retrace the major trends in India's institutional politics and political economy since 1947.

INDIAN POLITICS SINCE 1947: THE DEMOCRATIC REGIME AND THE RISE OF MAJORITARIAN NATIONALISM[29]

The relative stability of the Nehru years (1947–64) has often been contrasted with the personalized and plebiscitary politics associated with Indira Gandhi. But there are problems with this dichotomy, especially given the limited and fragile structural basis of the 'Nehruvian consensus'. As Lloyd and Susanne Rudolph write:

The Nehru settlement [was] based on a coalition of urban and rural interests united behind an... urban-oriented industrial strategy. Its senior partners were India's... small but politically powerful administrative, managerial and professional urban middle classes and private-sector industrialists... the junior partners... were rural notables, mostly large landowners who survived intermediary abolition and blocked the... implementation of land-ceilings legislation.[30]

The rhetoric of modernization ('dams are the temples of modern India' etc) obscured that beneath the exterior, Nehru's regime was reproducing

[29] For the purposes of this paper, 'majoritarian nationalism' is defined as a political philosophy and programme of action that posits, and seeks to build electoral success on the basis of, a solidary 'majority' community defined and delimited by *ascriptive* (or near-ascriptive) factors such as race, language or religion. Majoritarian nationalism is, thus, qualitatively different from efforts to construct electoral majorities or pluralities by appealing, in a positive fashion, to a variety of social groups, ethnic, religious and racial communities and special interests, which are generally regarded as quite bonafide activity in parliamentary democracies. Perhaps the outstanding feature of majoritarian nationalisms is that their ideology and concrete strategy and agenda are *always* defined in negative terms, in opposition to an (usually hated, vilified) 'Other' (which frequently turns out to be a minority group within the boundaries of the state in question). In the contemporary South Asian context, two examples of majoritarian nationalism readily come to mind: 'Hindu nationalism' in India, and Sinhala-Buddhist nationalism in Sri Lanka.

[30] Lloyd and Susanne Rudolph, *In Pursuit of Lakshmi: The Political Economy of the Indian State* (Chicago: University of Chicago Press, 1987), p. 50.

traditional patterns of domination, and creating new ones. Substantive social change, as well as critical public debate on such unresolved issues as the gap between rich and poor, the relationship of the Union to its component ethnic and linguistic communities, *and* the 'communal question', were sought to be substituted, to borrow from Lahouari Addi's work on the decline of Algeria's once-popular National Liberation Front (FLN) regime, by 'slogans ["secularism", "Nehruvian socialism"] whose generality [apparently] bothered no one.'[31] And it was during Nehru's reign that the Congress organization in the countryside congealed into a preserve of the rural rich: ex-*zamindars* and wealthy farmers, who tended to be upper-castes. An elaborate system of patron-client networks developed, whereby agrarian dominants 'delivered' the votes of the 'subaltern' classes (as well as their own) to Congress during the elections of the fifties and sixties in return for guaranteed if implicit official sanction of their own hegemony at the local level (to a lesser extent, this endured into the seventies and eighties). Coupled with this came a rapid degeneration of the Congress party as a coherent ideological and organizational force. Indeed, by 'the 1960s... the dominant element in the party's outlook and practice' were those 'for whom politics was more... a way to make a living and get ahead in the world than a cause worthy of sacrifice.'[32] Gramsci would likely have characterized Nehru's Congress as 'revolutionaries of yesterday—today become reactionaries'.[33]

Little wonder, then, that fundamental and long-term failure in both efficacy and effectiveness fostered a crisis of regime legitimacy, as well as serious questions about the viability of Congress hegemony in competitive party-politics. This was reflected first in a dramatic decline in support at all-India, regional and provincial levels for Congress at the first general election (in 1967) after Nehru's death,[34] and in severe discord

[31] Lahouari Addi, 'Algeria's Democracy Between the Islamists and the Elite', *Middle East Report*, March-April 1992, p. 36.

[32] Rudolph and Rudolph, *In Pursuit of Lakshmi*, pp. 132–3.

[33] Forgacs, *An Antonio Gramsci Reader*, p. 255.

[34] The all-India Congress vote declined from 45 per cent in 1962 to 41 per cent in 1967; its parliamentary seats fell from 361 (of 488) to 283 (of 516). Congress was ousted from power in four provincial legislatures—Tamil Nadu, Kerala, Orissa and Delhi. In five others—Uttar Pradesh, Bihar, Rajasthan, West Bengal and Punjab, Congress, for the first time, failed to win outright majorities. Anti-Congress coalitions subsequently formed governments in Uttar Pradesh, West Bengal and Punjab. See David Butler, Prannoy Roy and Ashok Lahiri, *India Decides: Elections 1952–91* (Delhi: Living Media India Ltd., 1991).

within Congress, culminating in the famous split of 1969 into 'old guard' and populist-progressive Indira Gandhi factions. But 'it was the decline of the old Congress that explained the rise of Mrs Gandhi and not... the other way around.'[35]

The problem of recouping lost support was, for the post-Nehru Congress, a serious and complex one. The erosion in support covered the entire expanse of India, and the beneficiaries of this erosion were (for Congress) an infuriatingly disparate variety of anti-Congress groups. These included, in rural northern India, emerging political formations of rich peasants, who had begun to desert Congress for their own reasons.[36] In urbanized northern India, meanwhile, there occurred a consolidation of the petty-bourgeois *bania* (merchant/trader/shopkeeper/petty bureaucrat/low-level professional) vote behind the 'Hindu nationalist' Jan Sangh, forerunner of the BJP. In Tamil Nadu, the electorate gave a resounding mandate to the Tamil-nationalist Dravida Munnetra Kazhagam (DMK), whose social base consisted primarily of intermediate-caste small landholders, marginal farmers and rural artisans, as well as some urbanized petty-bourgeois of the same broad caste-category. In Kerala and West Bengal, left-wing coalitions led by communists, who had mobilized vast numbers of marginal peasants and the landless poor, wrested power. At one level, this factionalization of the opposition was a blessing for Congress, for it precluded any *immediate* threat to its power in New Delhi. But the short-term blessing was also a long-term problem. Unless Congress could recover its eroded base in the provinces, it would be only a matter of time before its hegemony at the centre would be effectively challenged.[37] It was here, in devising a coherent *all-India* strategy for recovery, that the diverse nature of the anti-Congress spectrum became, for the Congress leadership, a worrisome dilemma. A strategy that merely addressed voter alienation in, say, northern India, was unlikely to work in the south or east, and vice versa. Clearly, a programme and slogan was needed that would command resonance throughout India, and appeal to the broadest possible cross-section of the population.

Indira Gandhi showed considerable ingenuity in devising such a winning formula. She was consequently able to arrest Congress' decline as India's hegemonic party, and temporarily contain the regime's crisis of

[35] Vanaik, *The Painful Transition*, p. 85.

[36] For an explanation why, see Ibid., pp. 82–3.

[37] Of course, Congress is confronted with a magnified version of the same crisis in the 1990s.

legitimacy. She appealed to the vast masses of India's rural poor, who had 'demonstrated a new political consciousness and...participation in the 1967 elections',[38] and whose condition a quarter-century of 'independence' and 'socialism' had failed to alleviate. The new Congress strategy, breath-taking in its simplicity, was encapsulated in the slogan 'Garibi Hatao!' (Abolish Poverty!), and entailed cultivation of especially deprived and degraded social groups such as Harijans and tribals. On the whole, the rural 'masses' (as well as 'progressive' sections of the urban middle-class, especially youth) responded with much enthusiasm throughout India to the charismatic new leader and her promise of justice and an egalitarian society.[39] In the process, Mrs Gandhi established a style that 'prefigured the general political style of the seventies and eighties.'[40] This style, often termed 'populist', 'plebiscitary' etc., is, in my opinion, most accurately and evocatively characterized as one revolving around *majoritarian politics*: the 'majority', in this instance, being defined by a socio-economic criterion ('the poor', with Harijans, tribals and Muslims forming important subsets of this vast category). Ironically, however, it seems in retrospect that this new form of political mobilization, while successful in checking the regime's legitimacy crisis and reinstating Congress as the country's hegemonic party, eventually ended up sowing a considerable portion of the seeds of the even more serious institutional and ideological crises that gripped state authority in the eighties and nineties.

[38] Richard Fox, 'Hindu Nationalism in the Making, or the Rise of the Hindian', in Fox (ed.), *Nationalist Ideologies and the Production of National Cultures* (American Ethnological Society Monograph Series, No. 32), p. 76.

[39] The Congress recovery under Mrs. Gandhi was remarkable. The effective-ness of 'Garibi Hatao' as a slogan was enhanced by the inability of fractious anti-Congress coalitions to provide stable government in most of the provinces they had won in 1967. Throughout India, Congress polled 44 per cent in 1971, as opposed to 41 per cent in 1967, but the recovery in provinces where Congress had suffered heavy losses in 1967 was much more dramatic. In Uttar Pradesh, for example, Congress won 49 per cent of the vote (up from 33 per cent in 1967); in Bihar, 40 per cent (35 per cent); in Rajasthan, 50 per cent (40 per cent); in Orissa, 39 per cent (33 per cent); Delhi 64 per cent (39 per cent); Madhya Pradesh 46 per cent (41 per cent); Punjab 46 per cent (37 per cent). In the process, Congress retook almost all of the provinces 'lost' in 1967—Tamil Nadu excepted (by 1972, Congress had also regained power in West Bengal). In other provinces, too, the Congress vote climbed swiftly. For detailed statistics, see Butler, Roy and Lahiri, *India Decides*.

[40] Vanaik, *The Painful Transition*, p. 96.

A brief digression is in order here to note the main features of the considerably improved Jan Sangh performance in 1967, the electoral high-point for 'Hindu nationalists' till 1989. The BJS won 9.5 per cent of the vote countrywide, up from 7.5 per cent in 1962. But what is acutely significant (the precise nature of this significance and its relevance to contemporary politics will soon become clear) is the regional and social composition of the Hindutva support-base. 80 per cent of the 'Hindu nationalist' vote came from the Hindi-speaking Hindu belt of northern India, and 33 of the 35 parliamentary seats won by BJS were from this region. Of the 268 seats won by the party in various provincial assemblies, as many as 236 were from this region. The other interesting feature was the *urban bias* in the Jan Sangh voting base. Indeed, Jan Sangh candidates outpolled Congress in cities and towns of Uttar and Madhya Pradesh, and in the urban constituencies of Delhi, the party won a most impressive 47 per cent of the vote (from 33 per cent in 1962).[41] From these patterns, it seems clear that a movement that defined its politics in the idiom of pan-Hindu resurgence was confined in its appeal primarily to urban areas of Hindi-speaking north India. And who were these predominantly urban voters? They were 'small industrialists and businessmen, traders and employees in the lower ranks of the professions and civil service',[42] i.e. the petty-bourgeoisie. Indeed, this social base is an exact replication of that of BJP's parent-organization, RSS, which 'since its formation...has attracted support almost exclusively in urban areas [of north India], and largely from the salaried lower middle-class and small-scale shopkeepers.'[43] This social group, I believe, *continues* to form the critical core of the expanded Hindutva base of the 1990s. In an *all-India* context, then, 'Hindu nationalism' has historically been (and to a somewhat lesser degree, continues to be) very much the movement of a relatively small, socially and territorially circumscribed minority speaking the political language of integral majoritarianism.

For the time being, however, the *sangh-parivar*'s brand of majoritarian politics was stymied by Congress. In the 1971 elections, Jan Sangh, like most other non-Congress parties, lost ground. Interestingly, Jan Sangh fitfully attempted, after this setback, to compete with Congress' electoral strategy, formally adopting a populist, 'mass-oriented' socio-economic programme between 1972 and 1974. This prefigured a very similar but

---

[41] See Craig Baxter, *The Jana Sangh: A Biography of an Indian Political Party* (Philadelphia: University of Pennsylvania Press, 1969), pp. 270–89.

[42] Graham, *Hindu Nationalism and Indian Politics*, p. 254.

[43] Andersen and Damle, *The Brotherhood in Saffron*, p. 248.

far more successful copycat mobilizational effort in the late 1980s. However, given their ideology and social and organizational base, 'Hindu nationalists' were hardly the ideal candidates to compete with the regime at the game of *competitive populism*. They were to find far greater success in the late-1980s, though, in the deadly contest of *competitive chauvinism*.

In 1980, Indira Gandhi stormed back to office, riding a massive electoral rejection of the dysfunctional Janata coalition that had governed (or rather, failed to govern) the country between 1977 and 1980. However, given the continuing absence of regime efficacy and effectiveness, her mandate (43 per cent of the vote, 353 of 492 parliamentary seats) did not mean renewed stability. As her term progressed, the search for an alternative, abiding formula for popular mobilization behind Congress and its absolute leader became ever more urgent. 'Garibi Hatao' was hardly likely to work again on an India-wide scale; as Linz notes, 'the people can be fooled some of the time but not all of the time.'[44] But the massive backlash against Mrs Gandhi's Emergency regime (1975–77) clearly demonstrated that recourse to explicitly authoritarian measures to muzzle social discontent and political opposition was ultimately unsustainable and self-destructive in an institutionalized democratic polity.

This dilemma assumed serious proportions in 1983. In January, Congress lost heavily in provincial elections in two southern Indian provinces, Andhra Pradesh and Karnataka, party bastions that had stood solidly behind Mrs Gandhi even in 1977, when the north had defected *en masse*, and during the Janata tenure that followed.[45] Congress, despite

[44] Linz, *The Breakdown of Democratic Regimes*, p. 19.
[45] Especially in Andhra Pradesh, Mrs Gandhi's Congress had successfully constructed a formidable electoral coalition of intermediate castes (OBCs) and scheduled castes between 1971 and 1977 by instituting anti-poverty and social welfare programmes (as opposed to structural changes such as land reform) aimed at marginal farmers and landless labourers, who tended to belong to these caste-categories. However, this winning coalition had come unstuck by 1983. Congress was routed that year by *Telugu Desam* ('Telugu Nation'), a new party formed by a former film star named N.T. Rama Rao in Andhra, and by a resuscitated regional version of the disintegrated Janata Party in Karnataka. The defeats resulted directly from Mrs Gandhi's style of politics. Not only had the Congress governments in these provinces become notoriously inefficient and corrupt, but they were also subjected to constant manipulation by Mrs Gandhi, who appointed and dismissed Chief Ministers virtually at will. Telugu Desam, in particular, won the election on a plank of reasserting 'Telugu pride' against Mrs Gandhi's manipulative tendencies, and the total neglect of responsible government by her minions.

appearances, had only partially and temporarily recovered its position in the north in 1980.[46] Later that year, meanwhile, the situation in the major north-eastern province of Assam went completely out of control because of the regime's mishandling of a student-led ethno-linguistic movement that demanded enhanced regional autonomy, as well as genuine development in an area which remained desperately poor despite rich endowments of natural resources. While this movement did have separatist and chauvinist overtones (it asserted the rights of 'indigenous' Assamese over 'foreigners', especially Bengali migrants), the regime's response, a combination of repression and manipulation, only led to the deterioration of a tense situation into massive violence.[47] Encouraged by these election results and the regime's disastrous policy in Assam, various opposition parties, decimated in 1980, began to regroup. Non-Congress chief ministers of Andhra, Karnataka, West Bengal and Jammu & Kashmir organized several 'conclaves' with the

[46] In north Indian provinces like Uttar Pradesh and Bihar, the Congress provincial leadership and organization had, unlike in southern and western India, remained almost totally under the control of upper-caste groups, especially Brahmins and Thakurs. In 1980, Congress still won these provinces by constructing an alliance between these groups and the scheduled-caste Harijans, thereby outmanoeuvering, for the moment, rising political formations of the intermediate castes. But the apparent re-establishment of Congress hegemony presented a rather misleading picture. As Francine Frankel writes, 'the early 1980s only appeared similar to ... the beginning of the seventies ... the upper castes clung precariously to [political] power [in U. P. and Bihar] through increasing use of corruption and coercion.' 'Middle Classes and Castes in Indian Politics: Prospects for Political Accommodation', in Kohli, ed., *India's Democracy: An Analysis of Changing State-Society Relations* (Delhi: Orient Longman, 2nd edition 1991), p. 258. Meanwhile, the voting patterns of supposedly 'pro-Congress' groups like Muslims had become much less predictable. In U. P. and Bihar, Charan Singh's OBC-based Lok Dal ('People's Party') did very well in constituencies with large Muslim populations in 1980. The north also continued to record strong support for Lok Dal and BJP in provincial elections. In West Bengal, meanwhile, the Communist Party of India-Marxist (CPI–M), capitalizing on a limited land reform programme, was firmly entrenched in power.

[47] In 1983, the regime tried to force through an assembly election in the troubled province. This farce, boycotted by practically all 'indigenous' Assamese, precipitated a polarization of Assam's divided people into antagonistic communities, and led directly to terrible massacres. Bengali Muslims were the worst sufferers in the violence.

explicit purpose of recreating a united anti-Congress front. Even more threatening for a leader who placed a premium on centralized power, the opposition began demanding fundamental changes in the constitution of the Indian state. A thorough renegotiation of centre-state relations and the vesting of greater powers in the provincial authorities topped their agenda. With parliamentary polls due by end-1984, the renewed opposition challenge simply could not be ignored.

The character of the Congress counter-offensive became clear by mid-1983. It was premised, once again, on majoritarian appeal—with the crucial difference that this time, the definition and content of the 'majority' was very different. In elections to the Jammu & Kashmir provincial assembly, where Congress faced a formidable rival in the National Conference, a predominantly but not exclusively Kashmiri Muslim organization, Mrs Gandhi appealed explicitly to communal sentiments among Hindu voters in Jammu, accusing the Conference, a party totally committed to Kashmir's otherwise disputed accession to India, of harbouring 'anti-national' and 'pro-Pakistan' inclinations.[48] The result was electrifying. The Congress campaign 'polarize[d] the electorate on communal lines,' and 'BJP, with a traditional base of support in the Hindu-majority Jammu area...lost every seat it contested,' because of a 'shift of Hindu BJP supporters to Congress.'[49] The pattern was repeated in elections to the legislature of Delhi, another long-standing 'Hindu nationalist' stronghold. Congress again won decisively as 'RSS cadre maintained a neutral stance...[indeed] more *swayamsevaks* were clearly voting Congress.'[50] At this time, BJP, led by the 'moderate' Atal Behari Vajpayee, was emphasizing social issues more than nationalism: clearly, its clientele was more attracted to Mrs Gandhi's forceful message of 'national unity' and the necessity of a strong centralized state.

The Congress campaign, however, could hardly have evoked the response it did had it not been for the rapidly worsening situation in the Punjab, where secessionist sentiment had appeared among a small minority of Sikh youth. The role of the Congress regime in nurturing and exacerbating the violence that overwhelmed the Punjab in the

[48] The cooperation of Sheikh Abdullah, the National Conference founder, was instrumental in securing Kashmir's accession to India in the face of Pakistani hostility in 1947.

[49] Andersen and Damle, *The Brotherhood in Saffron*, p. 231.

[50] Ibid., pp. 231–2.

eighties has been documented elsewhere.[51] As Brass writes, 'relentless centralization and ruthless, unprincipled intervention by the centre in state politics have been the primary cause of the troubles in Punjab and elsewhere in India since Mrs Gandhi's rise to power.'[52] Mrs. Gandhi's two-pronged policy of caricaturing the Sikh Akali Dal party's regional autonomy claims as unpatriotic and secessionist, and of promoting the charismatic but obscure Sikh preacher Jarnail Singh Bhindranwale in order to divide the Akali base, finally culminated in the Indian Army's massive assault at Amritsar's Golden Temple in June 1984. Some 1000 Sikhs, including Bhindranwale, hundreds of his fighters, and a large number of pilgrims, died in the attack. The battle severely damaged the shrine, Sikhism's holiest, and undermined or terminated the allegiance of countless Sikhs not just to the Delhi regime, but also to the 'secular' Indian state. Mere weeks before the assault, Rajiv Gandhi, then being

[51] The best succint account is in Paul Brass, 'The Punjab Crisis and the Unity of India'. See also Patwant Singh and Harji Malik (eds), *Punjab: The Fatal Miscalculation* (Delhi: 1985). For the historical development of Sikh society and culture, see Richard Fox, *Lions of the Punjab: Culture in the Making* (Berkeley: University of California Press, 1985).

[52] Brass, 'The Punjab Crisis and the Unity of India,' p. 210. Of course, this can hardly be regarded as the *only* factor in the causation of the Punjab tragedy. A more complete explanation would have to adopt a much longer time-frame and involve consideration of social-structural factors; most importantly, changing class relations in the Punjab since the 1960s and the rise and consolidation of a class of wealthy, advanced-capitalist farmers among the intermediate-caste Jat Sikhs in the Punjab countryside. Members of this class were among the earliest and most important beneficiaries of India's 'Green Revolution', and rural Jat Sikh youth formed the hard-core of the movement for a separate Sikh state, Khalistan. Their alienation stemmed in part from economic problems generated by the modernization process, especially unemployment. But what gave this alienation a militantly separatist character in the 1980s was a perception among this relatively compact and deeply religious community that their political demands, as well as economic and cultural rights, were being denied and disrespected by a 'Hindu' or 'Brahminical' state. The Indian military attack on the Golden Temple in 1984 effectively confirmed these suspicions. And a communal target and outlet for Jat Sikh anger was readily available: Punjab's Hindus, who are much more urbanized than the Sikhs, and unlike the latter, concentrated in trading and shopkeeping occupations. See for example, Sucha Singh Gill and K. C. Singhal, 'The Punjab Problem: Its Historical Roots', *Economic and Political Weekly*, 7 April, 1984, pp. 603–8.

groomed for the succession, 'referred to Bhindranwale as a "religious leader" and declared...that the latter was not responsible for the "terrorism" and "extremist politics" prevailing in Punjab.'[53]

The emergence of a small armed movement among Jat Sikh youth in Punjab and Bhindranwale's inflammatory declamations against 'Brahminical domination' however, endowed the regime's propaganda about 'national unity and integrity' being in grave danger, with a veneer of credibility. It is tempting to conclude that the 'Punjab problem' was encouraged to fester precisely because of the purpose it served for the Congress party and regime. The advantage sought to be derived from the 'threat' posed to 'national security' by Bhindranwale's motley following was transparent. After the military assault, 'Mrs Gandhi...said openly...that Hindu *dharma* [faith] was under attack' from the Sikhs: such charges were increasingly coupled with the accusation that Pakistan was abetting Sikh 'terrorism'.[54] Mrs Gandhi did not live to reap the fruits of the electoral strategy she was perfecting with such ruthlessness. Her son, instead, led Congress to the largest electoral triumph in Indian history. One 'issue' predominated—'national unity in danger'—as Rajiv Gandhi criss-crossed the country abusing Sikhs in general, and the Anandpur Sahib Resolution, the hapless Akali autonomy charter, in particular. Any talk of amending centre-state relations, and of rejuvenating Indian federalism, was immediately dubbed a mixture of treason and heresy in this environment.[55] Asked whether he regretted the orchestrated pogrom that killed thousands of Sikhs in Delhi and elsewhere following Indira Gandhi's assassination, the new leader responded: 'When a giant tree falls, the earth shakes.'[56] Many electors proved enormously receptive to this logic: 'the Punjab crisis, and its communal overtones, had reverberations across the North and South, especially among the middle-classes.'[57] The magic-wand of majoritarian nationalism had again worked

---

[53] Ibid., p. 191.

[54] Kothari, *State Against Democracy*, p. 247.

[55] During 1983–84, Mrs Gandhi used the pretext of having to strengthen the central state to cope with 'separatism' to engineer dismissals of the democratically-elected opposition governments of Andhra Pradesh and Jammu and Kashmir. These coups were given a coating of legality through the invocation of Article 356 of the Indian Constitution, which empowers India's titular President to dismiss provincial governments at the behest of the centre.

[56] The worst carnage was in Delhi, and was widely reported to have been organized and instigated by leading Congress politicians.

[57] Kothari, *State Against Democracy*, p. 248.

wonders for a party and regime that was not only manifestly incapable of offering solutions to India's long-term structural problems, but was constantly creating new crisis-areas through its policies. The politics of majoritarian nationalism had proved, for the moment, a potent substitute for not just a lack of improvement but a constant decline in the regime's efficacy and effectiveness.

Ironically, this unprecedented majoritarian-nationalist assertion had disastrous consequences for the one party that had consistently claimed to represent India's integral majority. BJP was reduced to two seats in the 540-member Parliament, as Congress appropriated 'both the old Jan Sangh slogan of One United India and more than half the old Jan Sangh voting base in northern and central India.'[58] In fact, BJP was 'totally decimated in Hindi-speaking states', amidst 'widespread speculation that many RSS cadre had backed Congress.' Indeed, Nanaji Deshmukh, a top RSS stalwart, publicly endorsed Rajiv Gandhi. It seemed that the 'view that a solid victory for Rajiv Gandhi was necessary to keep the forces of disintegration in check... had a compelling appeal for many RSS members... [and] for a large part of BJP's traditional constituency.'[59]

Given the proven value of majoritarian politics, it was little surprise that the beleaguered regime of Rajiv Gandhi would resort to the same artifice to try and cling on to power in the elections of November 1989. Thus, the Congress leader inaugurated his campaign at Ayodhya with a rousing call to the people to re-elect him and thereby help establish 'Ram Rajya' (the mythical 'Kingdom of Ram', embodying all that is good and noble) on Indian soil. This time, though, the formula failed to yield dividends, at least for Congress. Not that the majoritarian-nationalist impulse so evident in 1984 was absent. If anything, it had spread and deepened very considerably in the years since 1984, not least because of the policies of the regime. But this time, the prime beneficiary was the BJP, which increased its parliamentary representation from 2 to 85 seats, almost entirely because of a precipitous Congress slump through-out northern India. Why and how did this happen?

Many of the factors conditioning the 1967 election reappeared in magnified contemporary form in 1989: a crisis of leadership credibility, an economic downturn, dissension within and desertion from Congress, Congress non-performance and misrule at the centre and the provinces, popular anger with corruption among senior officials, and a general

---

[58] Brass, 'The Punjab Crisis and the Unity of India', p. 208.
[59] Andersen and Damle, *The Brotherhood in Saffron*, p. 234.

desire for change. But there was one crucial difference. Congress lost decisively because unlike 1967, the issue was no longer one solely pertaining to the legitimacy of a particular regime. The 'crisis' was now an organic crisis of state authority as such. Electors chose various opposition groups not so much because they were inspired by what the latter had to offer, but rather because continuation in office of the Congress regime was now seen as being detrimental (from various angles and viewpoints) to the continuation of India as a unified, democratic and 'secular' state. As BJP's election manifesto observed with a measure of accuracy: 'India today is in the grip of a serious multidimensional crisis of unprecedented proportions. The national mood is not just of cynicism but of mounting disgust and rage...a critical moment of history has arrived for India.'[60] How did this crisis come about, and what were its basic features?

While Rajiv·Gandhi's term was 'in many ways a culmination of trends...already...in evidence for quite some time,' there was also some 'discontinuity in both policies and style'.[61] For the first time, even the *rhetoric* of development was largely dispensed with. The emphasis was switched instead to technological modernization, symbolized by the Rajiv clique's peculiar obsession with computer use as a benchmark of progress, and expressed by the catchy slogan, 'Moving Into the 21st Century'. This, obviously, was a 'vision' that appealed only to the urbanized upwardly mobile classes of Indian society. 'The phenomenon of two Indias' was being given the stamp of state policy. The other noticeable trend was the continuing centralization of decision making on key issues and problems in the hands of the Prime Minister's personal 'coterie'. The implications of such concentration of authority for the legitimacy of the regime (and the state) are serious, for 'just as loyalties and accountability are required to be directed to the centre, resentments and confrontations also get centrally directed.'[62] The result of this dialectic was precisely what Kohli detected in the late 1980s: a correlation between growing 'centralization' of power and an increasing 'powerlessness' of the centralizers.[63]

[60] In *Expanding Horizons: BJP's First Decade* (Bombay: 1990), pp. 17, 28.

[61] Kothari, *State Against Democracy*, p. 232.

[62] Ibid., p. 189.

[63] Atul Kohli, *Democracy and Discontent: India's Growing Crisis of Governability* (New York: Cambridge University Press, 1990).

The process of 'de-institutionalization' of the hegemonic party also accelerated. Congress had already become the captive party of a single family during Indira Gandhi's rule: no party elections had been held at *any* level since 1972. But the process climaxed during Rajiv Gandhi's tenure. Yet even the parasitic *apparatchiks* who had milled around Mrs Gandhi were largely sidelined under Rajiv. The new elite at the apex of the party and state-apparatus was instead largely based on 'secondary kinship . . . on [extended] filial ties drawing on school, club, professional and business' linkages, of persons from the 'media and film world, admen, corporate managers, [wealthy] Non-Resident [expatriate] Indians, experts from multinational companies and . . . relatives and chums from public schools.'[64] Mrs Gandhi's policies had already almost destroyed the Congress organization at the provincial level and below, but this process, too, attained its apogee under Rajiv Gandhi. All this was sought to be compensated by a hyper-projection of Rajiv's photogenic personality on state-controlled television, and by an incessant parading of the purported virtues of four generations of the Nehru dynasty. By 1989, several of the Prime Minister's closest advisers (as indeed, Rajiv himself) were also suspected of siphoning off huge sums of money, obtained as commissions on various dirty deals, to foreign bank-accounts.[65]

This was one side of the picture. The party's overall strategy was by now implicitly if not explicitly premised on 'Hindu' majoritarianism. But majoritarian-nationalist sentiment of this kind is volatile, it has highs and lows. This was evident even in elections to a number of important provincial assemblies held in March 1985, by which time the pro-Congress 'national unity and integrity' fervour of the December 1984 poll had somewhat dissipated. In these elections, Congress was able to win only 57 per cent of all assembly seats at stake, compared to 79 per cent of parliamentary seats secured three months earlier. Indeed, Congress lost in three provinces (Karnataka, Andhra and Sikkim) and narrowly escaped defeat in two others: Maharashtra and Rajasthan.[66] Clearly, the regime's base was still not a solid, durable one. The crisis of legitimacy was continuing to fester beneath the surface.

[64] Kothari, *State Against Democracy*, p. 233.

[65] The controversy over huge bribes paid in the Bofors gun deal was the most notorious of such scandals.

[66] *In Pursuit of Lakshmi*, p. 206. The Rudolphs call this 'the bifurcation of the state and national political systems.'

There were, broadly, two alternative paths of consolidating the regime. One was through a recovery of efficacy and effectiveness in the key areas of national integration, development and social equalization. This necessarily presupposed a democratization of the Congress party and state-structure, a vastly increased responsiveness and accountability to the people, and a decentralization of the institutional framework of governance. The other was to keep stoking the fires of majoritarian nationalism, of the kind that had paid rich dividends in 1983–4. The regime chose the latter option, a decision that eventually proved fatal to its own survival. But the damage that was done went considerably beyond that. Kothari prophesied in 1987 that while the regime's strategy 'may not succeed, it may well end up so disrupting the political process... that 'recovery' may not be easy... worse still, as the antidote to such a dispensation will come in convulsions and violence, it will leave behind a badly mauled nation with a lot of scars.'[67] That prediction proved prophetic.

In October 1984, during the high noon of Indira Gandhi's appeals to the 'Hindu' majority, the VHP, RSS' affiliate on 'religious' affairs, announced a campaign to 'liberate' the purported site of 'Ramjanambhoomi' in Ayodhya, allegedly usurped by the Babri Mosque. The demand was revived the following year. On 1 February, 1986, a judge at the district court under whose jurisdiction Ayodhya fell decreed, in response to a VHP appeal, that the site was indeed that of a temple. Significantly, a curious chain of events occurred before and immediately after this verdict. As an eyewitness observer recorded:

...the [Congress-I] Uttar Pradesh government... precipitated the confrontation. It deliberately stepped into the... controversy, and... actually took sides... the [Congress-I] chief minister visited Ayodhya a few days before the... judgment [and]... met VHP members... on 1 February, shortly before the order... was announced, a crowd... of VHP supporters... collected at the site... this was seen as an indication by persons living there that they had advance knowledge of the verdict. A Doordarshan [government television] team too was present at the site, as if the government wished to publicize the entire event. The 'victory' celebrations were filmed and telecast on the national network [all-India news] the same evening.[68]

[67] Kothari, *State Against Democracy*, p. 238.
[68] Seema Mustafa, 'Uttar Pradesh Government Took Sides in Ayodhya Dispute', in Asghar Ali Engineer (ed.), *Babri Masjid–Ram Janambhoomi Controversy* (Delhi: Ajanta Books, 1990), p. 117.

This action, however, also precipitated massive protests from Muslim communities and organizations throughout India. And while Sikhs, a mere 2 per cent of India's population, and mostly concentrated in one province, Punjab, could be simply bypassed in the 'numbers game' to which Congress had reduced India's democratic process, the 12 per cent Muslim minority, much more spatially dispersed, was a different proposition altogether. They comprised more than 10 per cent of the electorate in 207 parliamentary constituencies, and over 20 per cent in 81 constituencies.[69] More importantly, Muslims have, in many ways, received a rather raw deal in 'secular' India. Their share of urban ghettoization and rural pauperization is proportionately greater than that of 'Hindus.' Muslims remain deplorably under-represented in the Indian Administrative Service, Indian Police Service, among officers of nationalized banks, in central and provincial government employment, in the judiciary, and in leading private-sector firms.[70] The Babri Mosque verdict thus merely added insult to injury. To many Muslims, it was also evidence that the 'secular' state was now abdicating even its responsibility to protect the dignity and collective identity of Muslims as a community.[71]

Indeed, the regime did make 'a desperate bid to regain the Muslim constituency.'[72] The way it went about it conformed to a pattern of behaviour by successive Congress regimes since 1947, which have tended to 'ignore the difficult business of economic needs [of Muslims] and concentrate on the protection of identity and religious rights.'[73] A Muslim woman named Shah Bano had filed years earlier for alimony from her husband, who had divorced her. The husband argued that alimony was impermissible under the *sharia*. The case went to India's Supreme Court, which ruled that a secular state's civil laws overrode any religious code. The dispute was poised thus, when the regime stepped in. Rajiv Gandhi

[69] Rudolph and Rudolph, *In Pursuit of Lakshmi*, pp. 194–7.

[70] See the statistics provided by Syed Shahabuddin in his journal *Muslim India*, and cited in M. J. Akbar, *India, The Siege Within: Challenges To a Nation's Unity* (Harmondsworth: Penguin, 1985), p. 310.

[71] The Hindutva movement claims that Indian Muslims have been used as a 'vote-bank' by Congress, which has 'appeased' them in return. The Rudolphs, however, have concluded on the basis of rigorous statistical analyses that 'Congress did not benefit from a "special relationship" with Muslims [in 1977, 1980 and 1984], *and may never have.*' *In Pursuit of Lakshmi*, p. 193. Emphasis added.

[72] Hasan, 'Changing Orientation of the State', p. 147.

[73] Akbar, *The Siege Within*, p. 311.

used his huge majority to pass a special law in parliament that made the *sharia* superior to the country's civil code in matters pertaining to maintenance of divorced Muslim women. Even so, the overwhelmingly Congress-dominated parliament passed the legislation only after a terse whip was issued commanding all Congress members to vote for the controversial Bill, and many prominent Muslim citizens deplored the manner in which the authority of the country's supreme judiciary had been violated.

This episode had far-reaching political repercussions. Most important, it provided a readymade propaganda weapon to the growing Hindutva movement's claim that the Indian state was 'pseudo-secular' (read: 'pro-Muslim'), and that it 'appeased' minorities at the expense of the interests of the organic 'majority.' Of course, if the Indian state was indeed 'pseudo-secular', it was not because it was 'appeasing' Muslims (after all, it was actively promoting discrimination against Muslim women), but because it had reduced the concept of secularism to mean an accommodation of the sum total of 'Hindu' and 'Muslim' obscurantisms. Nonetheless, the 'Hindu nationalist' contention that while the regime had seen fit to pass legislation 'appeasing' the Enemy, it was failing to respect the judicial verdict on Ayodhya, began to find a receptive audience among elements of the 'integral majority', especially in north India.

As the 1989 elections approached, the regime capitulated to the 'Hindu nationalist' current rising across northern India, by allowing VHP to lay the foundation-stone of the proposed Ram Temple at the mosque-site two weeks before the elections. Congress then claimed that 'the interests of the majority and minority communities had been successfully harmonized,' and Rajiv's Home Minister is reported to have suggested to the VHP that 'the Prime Minister... be allowed to lay the foundation stone.'[74] But the party's electoral prospects nonetheless fell victim to the fatal contradiction in its strategy. The committed Hindutva vote went overwhelmingly to BJP, which had unambiguously backed the temple-construction movement from the outset. Muslims, on the other hand, were decisively alienated from Congress, not least because of a devastating wave of anti-Muslim pogroms that swept northern India between September and November 1989.[75] Muslims in northern India

---

[74] A. G. Noorani, 'Congress Agreed to Ram Shilanyas', in Engineer (ed.), *Babri Masjid–Ram Janambhoomi Controversy*, p. 151.

[75] The worst violence occurred in Bhagalpur district of (then) Congress-ruled Bihar province. At least 2000 (mostly poor) Muslims were massacred there, and dozens of predominantly Muslim villages razed to the ground.

Congress attempts to have its cake & eat it too — appease but pursuing still major natl

voted overwhelmingly for Janata Dal, the new 'centrist' alternative to Congress in that region, and in other parts of the country, they opted for other non-Congress formations, such as the left-of-centre coalition ruling West Bengal. The regime had fallen between the cracks.

Of course, the rejection of Congress in the 1989 election was the result of *cumulative* failure of the regime on practically all fronts, not just because of the communal polarization it had helped bring about. Regime efficacy and effectiveness had indeed reached rock-bottom levels by the end of the decade. By 1989, India was in the throes of a serious economic recession and foreign-exchange shortage, the avoidable result of gross mismanagement by the regimes of Indira and especially Rajiv Gandhi. In the Punjab, the conflict between the Indian state and armed Sikh groups had deteriorated to a situation resembling civil war, despite massive police and military repression (or perhaps because of it), while in Assam, a strong separatist movement resurfaced in the end-eighties, spearheaded by the United Liberation Front of Assam (ULFA).[76] The regime's major foreign-policy venture, the attempt to impose peace through coercion in Sri Lanka, also ended in a fiasco, with the huge Indian military force there stymied by the resistance of Tamil nationalist guerrillas.[77] All this fostered widespread anxiety among influential social groups, the rapidly expanding urban middle-classes in particular, that the regime, while ceaselessly asserting the 'oneness' of the Indian 'nation' and the inviolability of the Indian state, was actually, through its policies, gradually bringing about the disintegration of that nation and the collapse of that state. As the BJP put it:

The Bharatiya Janata Party is wedded to the Unity and Integrity of India. It stands for Law and Order, for Justice, Social and Economic, and for Security, Internal

---

[76] Rajiv Gandhi did attempt, in 1985, to reach compromise agreements with elements of the opposition movements in Punjab and Assam. These agreements, however, failed to mitigate the conflicts in the longer-term. One reason was that the accords were not given a *chance* to work—the promises and concessions, limited as they were, were simply not implemented by the Delhi regime. But there were also deeper causes—the Punjab and Assam accords represented, at best, piecemeal and adhoc 'quick-fixes' to one of the most serious structural problems of the Indian state. It is no accident that the agreements were not implemented—even in their limited nature, they contradicted the centralizing drive that accelerated and deepened under Rajiv.

[77] See Sumantra Bose, *States, Nations, Sovereignty: Sri Lanka, India and the Tamil Eelam Movement* (New Delhi, Thousand Oaks and London: Sage Publications, 1994), Ch. 4.

and External ... the Rajiv Government has disappointed the country on all these counts ... in an atmosphere replete with vagueness and generality ... BJP's clear-cut commitments are an assurance to the people that they have a no-nonsense party on which they can rely ... on such nationally important matters as unity, integrity, defence, social justice and so on ...[78]

Since 1989–90, the organic crisis of the state has intensified, and certain factors have contributed to an expansion of the appeal of Hindutva ideology. This was reflected in the gains made by BJP in some parts of the country in the mid-term parliamentary poll of May-June 1991.[79] Two conjunctural developments, both reflections of unresolved structural maladies (caste conflict and centralization of state power, respectively) were especially important.

The decision, in mid-1990, of Janata Dal prime minister Vishwanath Pratap Singh to finally implement the recommendations of a government commission on reserving a substantial proportion of central government jobs for members of intermediate-caste groups is extremely relevant to explaining the salience of Hindutva reaction among certain upper-caste groups in northern and western India in the early 1990s. The eruption of a mass uprising for independence from Indian rule that began in early 1990 in Jammu and Kashmir, India's only 'Muslim-majority province', is similarly significant in accounting for the spread of 'Hindu nationalism', with its ultra-unitarist, anti-Muslim thrust, among urbanized middle and upper classes.

But before I move on to discuss the importance of these two key conjunctural factors, it is essential to supplement the theoretical emphasis on the historical development of India's state-structure, and the subversion of democratic values and institutions by Congress regimes, with an analysis of changing trends and patterns in India's political economy,

[78] In *Expanding Horizons*, p. 17.

[79] BJP increased its parliamentary representation from 85 to 119. This was an impressive performance, despite the fact that the party contested twice as many seats in 1991 compared to 1989. However, the gains were disproportionately in one province, Uttar Pradesh, where BJP wins rose from 8 in 1989 to 51 in 1991 (of a total of 85). Thus, apart from U. P., BJP relatively *lost ground* in terms of *seats* in the rest of the country. Very significantly, however, the BJP *vote* countrywide almost doubled, from 11.4 per cent in 1989 to 21 per cent in 1991. Gains were particularly impressive in provinces where BJP had hitherto been almost non-existent: the party won 12 per cent in West Bengal (from 2 per cent in 1989), and 29 per cent in Karnataka (3 per cent in 1989). See Hardgrave and Kochanek, *India: Government and Politics in a Developing Nation* (5th edition: 1993).

especially its caste-class structure. Such a discussion of social processes and forces enables us to better understand the following: how the Hindutva movement was able to capitalize on the crisis of state authority to expand its popular support; why certain social groups (and not others) in some regions of the country (but not others) are disproportionately drawn to 'Hindu nationalism'; and why the future prospects of this movement may be rather less promising than apocalyptic images of an unstoppable 'fundamentalist' tide looming over India are liable to suggest.

The Socio-economic Setting for the Expansion of 'Hindu Nationalism'

It has been said that 'Indian politics, until...independence, was an exercise in the accommodation of the middle classes, the overwhelming majority of whom were...Brahmin and other Forward [upper] castes.'[80] These forward castes consist of two major groupings. There are the Brahmins, Rajputs, Kayasthas, Khatris etc., whose power, in rural areas, originated from control of land, and in the towns and cities, from the benefit of early English education and employment in the colonial administration. The upper-caste category also includes a second group, the somewhat lower-ranking and highly urbanized castes of merchants, moneylenders, shopkeepers and small-scale entrepreneurs (the 'Vaishyas' or colloquially, 'banias'), who specialize in trading, petty manufacturing and banking, and other forms of urban (both big-city and small-town) commerce. The former group, who in urban areas tend to occupy the middle and upper levels of the class-hierarchy, came to dominate government, bureaucracy and the professions after independence. The second group, which can be described as mostly lower-middle class, has constituted the traditional support-base of 'Hindu nationalism' in northern India; hence the well-known 'bania party' appellation of the Jan Sangh.[81]

These groups were also the prime beneficiaries of India's post-colonial political economy, which some scholars of India, following Michael Kalecki, have characterized as an 'intermediate regime'. An intermediate regime, unlike both capitalist and socialist regimes, has, as part of the legacy of colonial rule, neither a dominant industrial bourgeoisie nor a

[80] Frankel, 'Middle Classes and Castes in India's Politics,' p. 226.

[81] In Christopher Bayly Rulers, Townsmen and Bazaars (Cambridge: Cambridge University Press, 1983), the author argues that the forward-caste population consolidated its identity and organizational networks during and even before the colonial period, and that significant elements thereof were attracted to 'Hindu nationalist' politics almost from the onset of the Indian nationalist movement.

well-developed proletariat, but is dominated by the middle and lower-middle classes.[82] This regime preserved the interests of the above groups by strictly limiting the penetration of foreign capital, and carefully regulating the growth of domestic capital. The regime also generated a vast and interlocking patronage-system (a polite term for institutionalized corruption and nepotism), involving bureaucrats, politicians, traders, manufacturers, lawyers and other professionals in complex but mutually profitable alliances of interest, a fact noted by scholars of Indian politics and the 'Congress system' even in the sixties.[83] By the eighties, according to Pranab Bardhan, this peculiar system resembled 'a patron-client regime fostered by a flabby and heterogeneous [class] coalition preoccupied in a spree of anarchical grabbing of public resources.'[84]

But this intermediate regime enjoyed its heyday in the 1950s and 1960s, and since then has been gradually but steadily undermined by changing class relations, frequently reflected, in the Indian context, through the prism of changing *caste* relations and attendant socio-political conflict. The roots of this process lie in the abolition of large landed estates in the 1950s, which killed 'the system of parasitic landlordism' but, thanks to the absence of wide-ranging land reform, helped 'facilitate the growth of a powerful class of rich capitalist farmers comprising former landlords, rich peasants and ex-tenants.' Most importantly, it also laid the basis for shifting the locus of economic affluence and eventually, political power in the countryside from 'a small layer of upper castes to a much larger stratum of intermediate castes.'[85]

The rise of this class of intermediate-caste cultivators, variously described as 'kulaks,' 'bullock-capitalists', 'agrarian bourgeoisie', 'capitalist

---

[82] Michael Kalecki, *Selected Essays on the Economic Growth of the Socialist and the Mixed Economy* (Cambridge: Cambridge University Press, 1972); K. N. Raj, 'The Politics and Economics of "Intermediate Regimes"', *Economic and Political Weekly*, 7 July, 1973, pp. 1189–98; Ashok Mitra, *Terms of Trade and Class Relations* (London: Frank Cass, 1977); Richard Fox, 'Urban Class and Communal Consciousness in Colonial Punjab: The Genesis of India's Intermediate Regime', *Modern Asian Studies* 18 (1984), pp. 459–89.

[83] For example, Rajni Kothari, *Politics in India* (Boston: Little Brown, 1970).

[84] Bardhan, *The Political Economy of Development in India* (Oxford: Basil Blackwell, 1984), p. 70. According to Bardhan, the coalition of dominant prorietary classes comprised, by the 1980s, industrial capitalists, rich farmers and urban professionals, including white-collar workers. See also Achin Vanaik, 'The Rajiv Congress in Search of Stability', *New Left Review*, 154 (1985), pp. 55–82.

[85] Vanaik, *The Painful Transition*, p. 78.

farmers' etc., received an enormous boost from the advent of the so-
called 'Green Revolution' in Indian agriculture, first in the wheat-growing
regions of Punjab and western U. P., and subsequently in the rice-growing
regions of Bihar, as well as in eastern and western India.[86] Intermediate-
caste groups ('Other Backward Classes' or OBCs in the official classification[87]), have a lengthy history of political cohesion and activism in
western and especially southern India.[88] But they came into their own
in the north only from the 1960s onwards, where their gradual emergence
as powerful social and political actors has had a tremendous impact on
the traditional caste-class structure, and on local, regional and national
politics. Their first independent political formations were already emerging in the late sixties (in U. P., the Bharatiya Kranti Dal of Chaudhary
Charan Singh, later rechristened Bharatiya Lok Dal), and by 1989-90,
the (non-Congress, non-BJP) chief ministers of both Bihar and Uttar
Pradesh were Yadavs, the single-most influential and assertive group in
this caste-category (other constituent caste-groups include Jats, Ahirs,
Kurmis, Koeris and Patidars).[89]

How has this long-term, structural change in India's social structure and
political economy affected the Indian state, and the fortunes of the
Hindutva movement? First, it has greatly heightened both rural-urban
social contradictions and those within the agrarian political economy. This
has been most marked in northern and western India, which, not at all

[86] On the Green Revolution, see Francine Frankel, *India's Green Revolution:
Economic Gains and Political Costs* (Princeton: Princeton University Press, 1971),
and *India's Political Economy, 1947-77: The Gradual Revolution* (Princeton:
Princeton University Press, 1978).

[87] Marc Galanter, *Competing Equalities: Law and the Backward Classes in India*
(Delhi: Oxford University Press, 1984), esp. pp. 179-87. See also note 28.

[88] The first example, 'anti-Brahmin' mobilization among Tamils in south
India, dates to the late colonial period. Its post-colonial political incarnation, the
Dravidian movement, won provincial power in 1967 and has exerted hegemony
in Tamil Nadu politics ever since.

[89] See Harry Blair, 'Rising Kulaks and Backward Classes in Bihar: Social
Change in the Late 1970s', *Economic and Political Weekly*, 12 January, 1980,
pp. 64-74; 'Structural Change, the Agricultural Sector and Politics in Bihar', in
John Wood (ed.), *State Politics in Contemporary India: Crisis or Continuity?*
(Boulder and London: Westview Press, 1984), pp. 197-228; Paul Brass, *Caste,
Faction and Party in Indian Politics* (Vol. 1) (Delhi: Chanakya Publications, 1983),
p. 331; Jan Breman, *Of Peasants, Migrants and Paupers* (Delhi: Oxford University
Press, 1985), p. 433; Bardhan, *The Political Economy of Development in India*, p. 54;
Richard Fox, 'Hindu Nationalism in the Making, or the Rise of the Hindian,'
pp. 72-6 and *Gandhian Utopia*, pp. 249-58.

coincidentally, are also the regions that have experienced the greatest surge of Hindutva support in recent years. Traditional upper-caste landed elites naturally feel threatened by the growing political clout of the intermediate-caste peasantry, whom they regard as *nouveau-riche* upstarts. Tensions between Harijan landless labour and the new 'kulaks' have also led to violent conflict, recent partially successful efforts at political coalition-building between the two sides notwithstanding. The agrarian capitalist class also makes demands that are directly at odds with the established interests of the urban middle and lower-middle classes, who in northern and western India, are disproportionately upper-castes. For example, they agitate vociferously for water, electricity and fertilizer subsidies and for higher procurement-prices for their produce. These necessarily have to be financed through government measures that hit the urban lower-middle class (the traditional Hindutva constituency) hardest; eg. higher prices for essential foodstuffs in urban areas, and higher wages and lower profits in the urban commercial sector. But the most direct and explosive clash of material interest ensues when the OBC younger generation campaigns for greater access to higher education and state-sector employment opportunities, which can only be actualized through government-sponsored reservations (affirmative-action) policies. This affects not only the lower-middle class *bania* groups, but more importantly, the upper-caste middle classes who have cornered the lion's share of bureaucratic and professional employment since independence.[90]

---

[90] There appears to be some scholarly disagreement as to whether friction between the upper and intermediate castes amounts to intra- or inter-class conflict. Fox holds that 'this confrontation is...not a class struggle but competition within a class', since both groups belong to different segments (urban and rural) of the lower-middle class, broadly defined 'Hindu Nationalism in the Making', p. 74. Frankel, on the other hand, seems to discern strong echoes of class conflict in this caste-competition, and sees the rise of the OBCs as 'the first round of a direct assault on the entire structure of privilege put in place during the colonial period'. 'Middle Classes and Castes,' pp. 225–61. The disagreement seems attributable partly to differences in the way these authors delineate the boundaries of 'class', a difficult task given the high (and growing) degree of social differentiation in India. In this essay, I am principally concerned with explaining how such overlapping caste/class conflicts have affected the Indian state and led to an expansion of support, in some provinces and regions, for the Hindutva movement. For this purpose, I do make a distinction between the lower-middle *bania* class of urbanized north India, which has traditionally supported Jan Sangh and BJP, and the landed upper-castes and urban middle-class professionals and bureaucrats, who by and large are more recent converts.

As for the Indian state, this political-economic development has strained the capacities of the 'intermediate regime' and its patronage-dispensing mechanisms to the point of breakdown. In order to accommodate the aspirations of even a fraction of the 52 per cent of the Indian population which is, according to one official calculation, OBC, state-sector employment and other forms of patronage would have to increase at a rate which is clearly not feasible. Moreover, this would have to be accomplished without alienating the urban and rural upper-castes who have traditionally formed critical components of Congress electoral coalitions in volatile northern provinces like Bihar and U. P. This was a virtually impossible task, given that upper-castes comprised the bulk of Congress leadership elites in these provinces. These dominants simply could not be expected to give up what they regarded as their inheritance without a fight. The long-standing response of the democratic regime to this dilemma was to ignore the issue, and pretend against all odds that it did not exist. This worked for a while; for instance, the recommendations of a government commission in 1955 on instituting substantial reservations for OBCs in senior bureaucratic posts and professional higher education were not taken up for discussion in the Congress-dominated parliament till 1964. A similar report, submitted by the government-appointed Mandal Commission in 1980, remained in cold storage till Congress was ousted from central power in end-1989.

Unsuccessful efforts to introduce limited reservations at the provincial level for OBCs were made by short-lived non-Congress (and intermediate caste-led) provincial governments in Bihar and U. P. in 1978, after having been blocked by Congress governments (elected primarily on the support of a curious upper caste-Harijan-Muslim axis)[91] for years. This

---

[91] Harijans have for long predominantly supported Congress, which has advertised itself as their 'protector', a rather ironic claim given that much of the worst anti-Harijan violence and discrimination has been practised by upper-caste Congress backers, especially in the north Indian countryside. One reason for the Harijan-Congress nexus is the elaborate reservations system for scheduled castes and tribes, introduced by Nehru's regime in the fifties and since then identified with Congress: other Congress-sponsored palliatives for Harijan poverty have also played a role in particular provinces and regions. In recent years, however, an independent political formation of the scheduled castes, the Bahujan Samaj Party (BSP) has appeared on the political scene and cut deeply into Congress' scheduled-caste base. BSP draws its committed cadre disproportionately from among Harijans who have benefited from reservations and now seek greater political power. Muslim support for 'secular' Congress in return for

precipitated caste polarization, social turmoil and violent conflict on an unprecedented scale. A similar attempt made in 1985 by the Congress government of the western province of Gujarat was also stymied by fierce upper-caste resistance. The latter rioted viciously not just against government property but with police complicity, also murdered and terrorized the hapless Muslim minority, for the most part a soft target confined to urban ghettoes (the Muslims being an important but in many ways most vulnerable element of the Congress electoral coalition in this province). The most significant political outcome of the Gujarat fiasco was upper-caste consolidation behind the BJP, a party rhetorically committed not only to the indivisible, organic unity of the 'Hindu nation' (an ideological scheme which obviously rendered the very notion of caste contradictions superfluous, if not illegitimate), but also the political affiliate of an organization, RSS, which has consistently displayed unflinching hostility to the idea of 'reservations'.[92]

The events in Bihar and U. P. in the late seventies, and in Gujarat in the mid-eighties, were replicated in magnified form throughout north India following V. P. Singh's announcement about implementing the Mandal Commission recommendations in 1990. In the changed circumstances of organic crisis and Congress decline, this led to a consolidation of the upper-caste, middle/lower middle class vote behind BJP, especially in urban and semi-urban but also in rural areas. This was most pronounced in Uttar Pradesh, where large-scale defection of upper-caste Congress supporters to 'Hindu nationalism', and its fortuitous conjunction with a splintering of the OBC, Muslim and Harijan electorate among several contenders, enabled impressive BJP victories, thanks to the first-past-the post electoral system,[93] in both provincial and parliamentary elections in 1991 (this is discussed in greater detail in the next sub-section).

---

security and protection has been eroding since the 1970s, as alternative choices became available. But the most dramatic erosion has occurred since the mid-1980s, as Muslims gradually recognized the self-serving hypocrisy of Congress 'secularism' as well as the inability and/or unwillingness of Congress governments to protect them from communal violence.

[92] See, for example, an issue of an RSS journal *Manthan*, 4 (1982), devoted entirely to the reservation question.

[93] This system tends to translate relatively slender voting pluralities into substantial majorities in terms of seats obtained. It long assured Congress hegemony, but is now a major factor aggravating the instability of the multi-party system at both central and provincial levels.

In northern and western Indian provinces, where large upper-caste populations live (U. P. has the highest concentration of Brahmins and other 'forwards' of any province in India, 20 per cent), and where a symbiotic relationship has historically existed between ritual upper-caste status, socioeconomic dominance and political power,

as a result of the...complex of changes that simultaneously undermined the ideological legitimacy, social prestige, economic strength and monopoly political power of the Forward Castes, the demand for reservations in educational institutions and government posts raised by the Backward Classes was...a signal for all-out struggle...what is at issue...is the age-old privileged position of the upper castes on all fronts: social status, economic strength, educational advantages, high-prestige occupations and political power.[94]

Unlike southern India, where a different constellation of historical and social-structural circumstances made it possible to accommodate the demands of intermediate-caste groups within the broad framework of the 'intermediate regime' and the political economy of the Indian state through a mixture of reformism, co-optation and adaptation, this conflict has so far proved much more problematic and intractable in western and especially northern India.[95] And as upper-caste urban and rural dominants in these regions decided that a weakened, indecisive Congress (which failed to take an unequivocal stand on the Mandal issue) could no longer be relied on to ensure the social status quo and their privilege, the appeal of 'Hindu nationalism' became irresistible for many in these groups. For the simple reason that 'Hindu nationalism', much like radical Islamist consciousness, offers, in Addi's words,

a total conception of life in society...[based on] the community's mythic unity... [it] does not acknowledge the division of society into divergent interests, whether economic, ideological [etc.]...religion can become a means to hide these divisions. Thus religion is mobilized to avoid the creation of institutions that can express social and ideological differences within the community...this rests upon the view that religion can make social divergences disappear...[96]

---

[94] Frankel, 'Middle Classes and Castes in India's Politics', pp. 255, 259.

[95] For an explanation of the divergent outcomes in Andhra and Tamil Nadu on the one hand, and U. P. and Bihar on the other, see Frankel, Ibid. For studies of inter-and intra-regional variations in the evolution of caste-class relationships, see Frankel and M. S. A. Rao (eds), *Dominance and State Power in Modern India* (Delhi: Oxford University Press, 1989).

[96] Lahouari Addi, 'The Islamist Challenge: Religion and Modernity in Algeria', *Journal of Democracy* 3, 4 (Oct. 1992), pp. 75–83.

Thus, while Hindutva ideologues claim that theirs is a 'catch-all' term encompassing a pan-Indian identity, it is in reality more of a 'cover-up' construct for various types of social conflict and cleavage, based on caste, class, regional and ethnic differences, that have become especially salient in the 1980s and 1990s. Much of the 'Hindian' base is not only regionally specific but also particular to upper-caste, middle and lower-middle class groups, especially in urban and semi-urban areas. Because of long-term changes in India's political economy and social-structural configuration, these groups have developed serious misgivings about the capacity of Congress, hitherto the party of choice for most dominant and vested interests, to assure the preservation or even survival of those interests. The state they have long identified with and regarded as their own is now reeling from a legitimacy crisis, brought on by institutional torpidity and ideological bankruptcy. As competing social groups become ever more politically articulate, organized and effective, especially at the levels of local and provincial politics, the incapacity of this 'distressed political regime' and 'omnipresent but feeble' state[97] to accommodate and reconcile conflicting interests, and effectively and efficaciously address multiplying challenges, is increasingly laid bare. In this context, the BJP's promise of building a 'resurgent, resolute and modern India' by revitalizing a universally shared Hindu identity (which constitutes the 'essential personality of the Indian nation')[98] becomes, with its implicit denial of the relevance or even existence of social contradictions and conflicts, an increasingly appealing political alternative for these disillusioned and apprehensive elements. And for those privileged groups that have expanded BJP's hitherto *bania*-dominated clientele by abandoning Congress, the change has really been more of a switch than a metamorphosis, for what in any case 'distinguished Congress from... [political] groups with an explicitly Hindu communal outlook was the moderated, controlled and implicit character of its Hindu nationalist appeal',[99] rather than any mythical, ideal-typical 'secularist' commitment. Little wonder, then, that an opinion poll conducted in the immediate aftermath of the Babri Mosque's destruction (and amidst raging communal violence), which predicted an increase in BJP's parliamentary representation from 119 to 170 seats, also found that 'the major gains for

[97] Kohli, *Democracy and Discontent*, pp. 6, 8.
[98] L. K. Advani, 'Agony and Opportunity', *The Telegraph* (Calcutta), 4 January, 1993.
[99] Vanaik, *The Painful Transition*, p. 143.

BJP are in the Hindi [speaking] belt [of north India], particularly Uttar
Pradesh and...Bihar,' and that 'in the Hindu versus Hindu divide,
political differences are now based on caste.' More specifically, the survey
discovered that Brahmins were solidly backing the BJP, and the party also
received very substantial support from the other upper (Kshatriya and
Vaishya) castes. But its base among OBC, Harijan and tribal voters
remained weak, and of course, Muslims shunned it like the plague.[100]

This, then, constituted the socio-economic setting for the emergence of
'Hindu nationalism' as a dynamic force in Indian politics. This context
helps explain why BJP has benefited thus far from the organic crisis of the
Indian state, but it also suggests that the Hindutva movement will have to
contest and overcome countervailing social forces and political currents
that are no less dynamic in order to translate its vision of a glorious Hindu

[100] 'A Nation Divided', *India Today*, 15 January, 1993, pp. 14–20. Of course,
the BJP did increase its votes very substantially in eastern and southern provinces
like Bengal and Karnataka in the 1991 elections. But in Bengal, most of its support
came from the highly urbanized Greater Calcutta area and provincial towns,
and, I suspect, from upper-caste, middle and lower-middle class Hindus, not the
vast and politically crucial countryside. Also, the increase was largely because
of popular disillusionment with both the province's major political formations,
the longstanding and increasingly listless leftist ruling coalition and the hopelessly
inept and factionalized Congress opposition. In Karnataka, the BJP surge was
even more spectacular, but based almost entirely on forward-caste support
(backing from OBCs and Harijans remained marginal) and popular alienation
from the corruption and ineptitude of the 'established' parties. On Karnataka
and BJP's limited prospects in the south generally, see 'Southern Scepticism',
India Today, 31 March, 1993, pp. 42–5. Thus, patterns of BJP expansion in
Karnataka and Bengal are by-and-large consistent with my general argument.
BJP's 'war-of-position' strategy in the south and east relies on raising 'local issues',
usually involving corruption and incompetence on the part of established parties
and provincial governments, while stoking latent communal issues, such as the
alleged mass migrations of Bangladeshi Muslims into West Bengal. This has so
far been a very partial success, at best.

I also do not suggest that *all* BJP supporters are upper-castes or urbanites.
In certain rural areas of Madhya Pradesh, southern Bihar and Maharashtra, for
example, BJP has reaped limited support from Harijans and Adivasis as a result
of assiduous welfare work over many years at the grassroots level by the RSS.
RSS has operated schools, clinics, vocational training centres and orphanages
in many impoverished communities (and exploited them blithely to propagate
its own world-view), providing essential services where the state has failed to meet
its responsibilities. In this sense, RSS methods of political base-building are
similar to those of certain Islamist movements in the modern Middle East.

nation into reality. Riven as the 'Hindu' formation is by internal divisions, this is precisely where the Muslim as full-time villain and scapegoat can serve a most useful purpose. It has been noted that caste and communal violence have a 'symbiotic relationship.'[101] Gujarat's anti-reservation agitation soon turned into anti-Muslim violence, and upper-caste protests against Mandal in 1990, with a little egging on by BJP, soon generated lethal attacks on Muslims throughout northern India. This displacement of hatred, and the conjunction of caste/class interest with communal sentiment and indoctrination, arguably reached its peak in Bombay after the mosque-demolition. There, an especially vicious group, Shiv Sena, which declares rhetorical allegiance to 'Hindu nationalism' (and is electorally allied with BJP), but whose membership consists almost entirely of upper-caste, lower-middle class petty-bourgeois and lumpen youth, organized massive pogroms against Muslims in end-1992 and early 1993. A year later, the same group was on the rampage again, this time systematically targeting low-caste Hindus in 'revenge' for the renaming of a major university in the province after the Harijan leader B. R. Ambedkar.

It is true that direct social contradictions between Hindus and Muslims, such as those between lower-middle class Hindu employers and consumers and Muslim artisans and skilled labour (some of whom have prospered by working in the Middle East), exist in some urban locales. But for the most part, the Hindutva movement's inordinate emphasis on the Mughal Babar's desecration of Lord Ram's birthplace,[102] and on the Kashmiri Muslims' attempt to inflict a 'second partition' on Mother India in connivance with Pakistan, have to be understood in terms of the desperate imperative to unite a hopelessly divided and fractured 'nation' by invoking the common threat allegedly posed by the pan-Islamic fundamentalist conspiracy. Communal animosity towards Muslims is

---

[101] Fox, *Gandhian Utopia*, p. 257.

[102] It is possible that the Ramjanambhoomi campaign struck a resonant chord among many intermediate and even low-caste Hindus, especially in north India. But there are historical precedents which suggest that such solidarity may be temporary and tenuous. As Gyanendra Pandey has shown, a cow-protection movement in a Bihar district in the late colonial era succeeded in constructing a working communal coalition between intermediate-caste cultivators and upper-caste landowners. Yet the latter were still "far from willing to accept the former as anything but a pretty lowly and barely touchable group." And when in the 1920s and 1930s the intermediate castes became more organized and assertive, the landed elite actually joined hands with Muslim *zamindars* to keep the upstarts in their place. *The Construction of Communalism in Colonial North India* (Delhi: Oxford University Press, 1990), Ch. 5.

further inflamed by Muslim participation in informal blocs or alliances with political groupings representing intermediate and low castes. Creating communal polarization, it is hoped, will help negate those other, troublesome cleavages: those of caste, class, region and ethnicity.

Creating the Conjuncture for the 'Hindu Nationalist' Surge: Kashmir and Mandal

As mentioned already, Janata Dal Prime Minister V. P Singh decided in mid-1990 to implement the recommendations of the Mandal Commission Report. The impact that the implementation would have was mostly symbolic,[103] and the announcement was almost certainly motivated by Singh's partisan electoral calculations.[104] However, the announcement provoked a violent anti-Mandal agitation by upper-caste youth and students among the middle and lower-middle classes of urbanized north India. By bringing caste divisions (the Achilles heel of Hindu society) and explosive caste conflict to the forefront of national politics, the Mandal controversy bore potentially grave implications for the long-term project of the Hindutva movement. This was because the 'Mandal Commission, despite the limited and token nature of its recommendations... cleave[d] the monolithic facade of [mythical] Hindu unity right down the middle.'[105]

However, BJP was confronted with a dilemma as to how to respond to this challenge. An outright condemnation of the Commission's recommendations would risk alienating countless 'Hindu' voters. The

---

[103] The government-appointed Mandal Commission had recommended more than ten years previously that 27 per cent of jobs in the central government and of places in government-supported institutions of higher education be reserved for the approximately 52 per cent of 'Hindus' it classified as 'Other Backward Classes' or OBCs, i.e. those who were neither Harijans/tribals nor Brahmins/other 'forward' castes. There are certainly problems with the idea of 'reservations' as a panacea to social inequity, as well as with the classification scheme employed by the Commission. However, the practical impact of the implementation would have been minor—only some 40,000 jobs would be affected annually in a country where aspiring workforce entrants every year number in the millions.

[104] Himself an upper-caste (Thakur), Singh was at the time trying to strengthen his personal base by projecting himself as the saviour of the 'backwards' and the harbinger of 'social justice'. This strategy was somewhat reminiscent of Mrs Gandhi's 'Garibi Hatao' rhetoric.

[105] Sukumar Muralidharan, 'Mandal, Mandir aur Masjid: 'Hindu' Communalism and the Crisis of the State', in Panikkar (ed.), *Communalism in India*, p. 217.

party resolved this dilemma by reviving that symbol of Hindu/national 'unity', 'pride' and 'honour', the demand that a temple dedicated to Ram be installed on the site of the Babri Mosque. The top party leader, L. K. Advani, personally led a 'march to Ayodhya' across a broad swathe of western, central and northern India, stirring serious communal violence along the route. Advani was arrested before he could reach Ayodhya, but thousands of Hindutva activists attempted to storm the mosque in end-October 1990. The Uttar Pradesh government of Janata Dal Chief Minister Mulayam Singh Yadav thereupon ordered police to open fire to disperse the mob, and several dozen persons were killed. This incident brought down the V.P. Singh government, as it lost its working majority in parliament after BJP withdrew its support in protest. It also enabled BJP to win the majority of both parliamentary and provincial assembly seats in Uttar Pradesh in 1991. This, however, was not because of any massive or uniform pro-Hindutva upsurge among a broad cross-section of Hindus. The BJP, in fact, won its majorities in U.P. with only a slender plurality, 32 per cent, of the popular vote. What *had* happened was that the first-past-the-post electoral system (which has favoured Congress for decades) benefited BJP this time,[106] and this was reinforced by the fact that the anti-BJP vote was badly split among three contenders: two Janata Dal factions and Congress. But even so, it is undeniable that BJP had sharply increased its support in U. P. Where did this increase (8 per cent to 32 per cent between 1989 and 1991) come from? It is instructive to note that this increase was mainly at the expense of a massive desertion of upper-caste voters (in urban *and* rural areas) from Congress, which had failed to take an unambiguous stand on the Mandal issue. The Congress vote in the province halved between 1989 and 1991, from 32 per cent to just 16 per cent.[107]

---

[106] The BJP benefited yet again from the first-past-the post system when, in March 1995, the BJP–Shiv Sena combine won the majority of seats in Maharashtra's legislative assembly with barely 30 per cent of the popular vote.

[107] For a historical account of the evolution of the very complex caste-class dynamic in Uttar Pradesh politics, see Zoya Hasan, 'Power and Mobilization: Patterns of Resilience and Change in Uttar Pradesh Politics,' in Frankel and Rao (eds), *Dominance and State Power in Modern India* (Vol. 1), pp. 133–203. Two themes stand out: the gradual but steady rise to economic affluence and political influence of the intermediate castes, and the continuing stranglehold on the U. P. Congress organization of the upper castes, which prevented Congress from reaching out to the former. Thus, when the latter ditched Congress for BJP, and Muslims and a section of the Harijans grew alienated as well, the Congress voting base simply crumbled. A rather similar process has taken place in Bihar.

The other key conjunctural development was the popular uprising against Indian rule that began in Indian-administered Jammu and Kashmir at the beginning of 1990. The timing itself was largely coincidental, and was the culmination of a long process of alienation of Kashmiri Muslims from the Indian state. I will not go into an explanation of the Kashmir tragedy here, except to note that the insurrection currently raging there is the direct result of a consistent policy of oppression and manipulation of the Kashmiri people, and denial and subversion of their basic democratic and human rights, by the Indian state; starting with Nehru, and continued by the Indira and Rajiv regimes.[108] It is thoroughly misleading, therefore, to depict the Kashmir conflict as the revolt of a 'Muslim-majority province' against 'predominantly Hindu' India. The battle is more accurately characterized as one between the brutally coercive power of a big state (staffed mainly by 'Hindus') and the resistance of a people who *happen* to be mostly Muslim. The Kashmir uprising has however supplied the Hindutva movement with an unrivalled propaganda weapon. For here was 'evidence' of the diabolical designs of a group of Muslims living in India to destroy India's unity in conjunction with the historical enemy, Pakistan. The 'enemy within, enemy without' (where the Indian Muslim is the fifth-columnist for Pakistan) conspiracy theory, a longstanding staple of the 'Hindu nationalist' world-view, was ostensibly finding some vindication. The BJP therefore consistently gives the Kashmir issue absolute centrality in its program and strategy.[109] And the BJP's ultra-hawkish stand on Kashmir, as well as its in itself correct accusation that the Congress regime is proving incapable of containing what it calls a covert war against India's territorial integrity being waged there by Pakistan and its agents, has found a receptive audience among many Indians. Most prominent

[108] The many grievous wrongs perpetrated on the Kashmiri people by the Indian state include: reduction of electoral democracy to a travesty through political repression and blatant doctoring of elections (consistently since the 1950s); an almost complete denial in practice of the regional autonomy promised to Kashmiris under Article 370 of the Indian Constitution; and, since 1990, a reign of military terror against the population in general. For recent research and writing on Kashmir, see Balraj Puri, *Kashmir: Towards Insurgency* (Delhi: Orient Longman, 1993), and Sumantra Bose, *The Challenge in Kashmir: Democracy, Self-Determination and a Just Peace* (Delhi: Sage India; London and New Jersey: Zed Books, 1996).

[109] In January 1992, for example, BJP president Joshi led a 'March to Kashmir' to draw attention to what the BJP regards as Pakistan-sponsored fundamentalist

among these are the vastly expanded (and disproportionately upper caste) urbanized lower-middle and middle classes, including the groups Baxter once called 'the all but de-Hinduized rationalists among the more Westernized elite,'[110] especially in larger cities, who were once thought to be immune to the 'fundamentalist' Hindutva virus. The Kashmir question starkly illustrates my principal argument in the next section, which is devoted to Hindutva ideology: that Hindutva politics is far more an *explicitly modern political interpretation of pan-Indian nationalism* than a manifestation of atavistic 'religious fundamentalism'.

Theoretical Implications: A Dialectic of Semi-loyal and Disloyal Oppositions, and of State-Led and State-Seeking Nationalisms

There seems to be a dialectical relationship between the emergence of powerful 'disloyal oppositions' to the Indian state in Kashmir, Punjab and Assam, and the growth of the 'semi-loyal opposition' represented by BJP as a reaction to the 'disloyal oppositions', and to the incapacity of the regime to destroy the latter. Caught in the middle, it was the regime's legitimacy that got undermined, providing a fertile context for further advances by the semi-loyal opposition. However, it was the Indian state's failure to constructively address the demands, aspirations and grievances of Kashmiris, Sikhs and Assamese, as well as its cynical policies of manipulation and repression, that gave rise to the disloyal oppositions in the first place. Thus, the *roots* of the organic crisis of the Indian state may well lie in unresolved structural problems: such as, in the case of the problem of multi-ethnicity, a rigid and historically deeply rooted ideological conception of a unitary Indian 'nation' and its indivisible, inalienable 'integrity' and 'sovereignty', as well as its institutional manifestation, an entrenched state-apparatus resistant to democratization and devolution of power. But the more *immediate* factors that have

---

terrorism plaguing that land. After the demolition of the Babri Mosque, top BJP leaders repeatedly complained that while everyone seemed greatly concerned about the fate of a disputed 'structure', none paid any attention to the destruction of Hindu temples by 'Muslim terrorists' in Kashmir. However, in February 1993, an investigative team sent to Kashmir by India's largest English-language newsmagazine found that of 25 temples alleged by the BJP to have been destroyed, 23 were in perfect condition. See Harinder Baweja, 'Kashmir Temples: Damaging Lies,' *India Today*, 28 February, 1993, pp. 22–5.

[110] Baxter, *The Jana Sangh*, p. 314.

precipitated and exacerbated the crisis are to some extent problems that became, in Linz's words, 'unsolvable because of the way in which the democratic leadership...formulated them and its [in]ability to implement certain solutions or overcome certain constraints that should not [otherwise have been] insuperable...a regime's unsolvable problems are often the work of its elites.'[111] In particular, Congress elites seem to have (deliberately?) 'misperceive[d]...opposition to a particular constitution [of the state]...as anti-democratic, when there would be room for such opposition in a democratic constitutional framework,' for 'full democracy must allow the expression of the nationalism of the periphery.'[112] In particular, 'decentralization, or local and regional self-government... [could have] reduce[d] the feeling of those not participating in the... regime that they have been excluded.'[113] Such a 'process of incorporation,' Linz rightly comments, 'can be very important in the legitimation of an open, competitive democratic system.'[114] The failure of Congress regimes to conduct this process of incorporation, through a democratization of the state-structure and a reformulation of its institutional and ideological bases in response to new societal demands and challenges, not only undermined its own legitimacy, and eventually led to an organic crisis of state authority itself. It also also paved the way for 'ultranationalistic and voluntaristic responses'[115] to the crisis, as epitomized by the Hindutva movement.

But this dialectic of political regimes and political oppositions, and of various types of oppositions, is equally a dialectic between types of nationalism, and specifically what Charles Tilly has termed 'state-led' and 'state-seeking' nationalisms.[116] State-led nationalism is defined by Comaroff and Stern as 'the authoritative claim of a nation-state to expressions of common sentiment and exclusive commitment, of loyal attachment and joint responsibility, on the part of its citizens,' and by Tilly as rulers speaking 'in a nation's name successfully demand[ing] that citizens identify themselves with that nation and subordinate other interests to those of the state' (note the congruence of nation and state in this

---

[111] Linz, *The Breakdown of Democratic Regimes*, p. 51.

[112] Ibid., pp. 34, 46.

[113] Ibid., p. 34.

[114] Ibid., p. 45.

[115] Ibid., p. 51.

[116] Charles Tilly, 'States and Nationalism in Europe 1492–1992', *Theory and Society* 23, 1 (February 1994), p. 133.

formulation).[117] State-seeking nationalism alludes to 'representatives of some population that currently did not have collective control of a state' making an 'assertion of a right to sovereignty, autonomy and territory . . . by virtue of an affective connection to a shared history and culture.'[118]

In contemporary India, regimes of the Congress party, which have largely controlled the post-colonial state, have obviously been the principal advocates and implementers of state-led nationalism. But the semi-loyal opposition represented by the Hindutva movement is also an example of state-led nationalism (I argue this point in greater detail in the next section). Hindu nationalists merely seek to impose their own *variant* of state-led nationalism on India's peoples, in the belief that this will succeed in papering over problems and socio-political conflicts where the Congress variant has failed. But the Hindutva brand of state-led nationalism is simply a more explicit and extreme version (and, in some ways, a logical culmination) of the officially-sanctioned, 'secular' Congress ideology and practice. It is thus inherently detrimental to prospects of democratic stability in a country which not only does not approximate the 'homogeneity and commitment conjured up by the label "nation-state",'[119] but is a virtually unparalleled mosaic of diverse ethnic, linguistic, religious and cultural communities.

Tilly argues that the state-led nationalist project in Europe, which gathered coherence and momentum only from the end-18th century onwards, entailed centralization of political power, concentration of the means and resources of extraction and coercion, and cultural standardization and homogenization, the latter frequently evoking an 'other', the alien enemy within or without. But the very spread of 'this vast top-down process' greatly 'increased the incentives and opportunities for state-seeking nationalism. State-led nationalism activated the formation, mobilization and claim-making of ethnic groups . . . throughout Europe . . . as those groups that controlled the state-apparatus pursued campaigns of homogenization and assimmilation, they faced not just widespread resistance but newly mobilized demands for political autonomy, even independence.'[120] In other words, a dialectical correspondence could be discerned between the salience and intensity of state-led and state-seeking

---

[117] John Comaroff and Paul Stern, 'New Perspectives on Nationalism and War', *Theory and Society* 23, 1 (Feb. 1994), p. 37; Tilly, ibid., p. 133.

[118] Tilly, ibid., p. 133; Comaroff and Stern, ibid., p. 37.

[119] Tilly, 'States and Nationalism in Europe 1492–1992', p. 137.

[120] Ibid., pp. 142–3.

nationalisms. This was particularly so because in some countries and upto a certain point, at least, the strongly centralist state-led nationalist impulse went hand in hand with an expansion in definitions of citizenship, ideas of popular sovereignty and strengthening of institutions of representative democracy. A strikingly similar process is noticeable in late twentieth-century India, where the state-led nationalism of the post-colonial regime has combined with a democratic political context to set off mobilization and claim-making by ethnic groups, and led to demands for political autonomy (Jharkhand, Gorkhaland, Bodoland) or even independence (Kashmir, Punjab, Assam, Nagaland). Unable, by and large, to either reconcile or repress such claims, the 'secular' regime has grown increasingly discredited, opening up the space for 'Hindu nationalism' to present itself as the definitive solution to the crisis. The risk is that this pseudo-alternative vision, being an even more exclusivist and intolerant variant of the state-led nationalism that is a major source of the problem, might do irreparable damage to a beleaguered democratic state and its fragile social fabric. In particular, 'a rampant Hindu nationalism would dramatically catalyse the latent unhappiness of the south and east with the [perceived] political domination of the Hindi belt and the north Indian Hindi-speaking Hindu. It would be intolerable to a [100 million-strong] Muslim community... and would exacerbate caste conflict beyond safety.'[121]

'Hindu Nationalism': The Highest Stage of Anti-Democratic State-Centralism

Indeed, it is difficult to exaggerate the culpability of the 'secular' state and democratic regime in this matter. As Muralidharan argues, Congress has been

the other face of the ideology of indivisible *Hindutva*. With its highly personalized politics centred around a particular dynasty, its denial of the principles of Indian federalism, and its rigidly centralized, unipolar character, the Congress-I [party and regime] embodies the monolithic nationalism... [ex]plicit in the idea of *Hindu Rashtra*...the Indira-Rajiv *raj* patented and propagated a notion of national unity that is in conflict with the liberty and well-being of the nation's citizens, and the autonomy and integrity of its political institutions[122]...

[121] Vanaik, *The Painful Transition*, p. 146.

[122] The 'threats' to 'national unity and integrity' have been exploited by Congress regimes to enact and harshly implement a whole range of repressive,

Congress-I is by nature averse to all forms of political mobilization, except those with a majoritarian orientation.[123]

As Hasan notes, 'the centralizing tendency of the Indian state,' that unique contribution of Congress regimes, *'requires* a [homogenizing, monolithic] ideology of unity.'[124] Unlike among others Bipan Chandra, I believe that the 'majoritarian orientation' of Congress politics, an overt and repeated electoral resort after 1983, is no mere 'opportunist' expedient of a 'basically secular' party and regime. To the contrary, the logic of and impulse towards this form of political mobilization is *embedded* in Congress' unitary, zero-sum conception of the structure of the Indian state and of state power, as well as in the failure of post-1947 regimes to 'solve the basic problems facing [the] ... system, and those that become salient in any historical moment', leave alone any will or capacity to 'actually ... implement the policies formulated, with the desired results.' In this sense, 'communalism ... is not an aberration but something that is part of the system ... it is a direct outcome of its inherent logic, and one in which its key actors play a [central, defining] role.'[125]

The correlation between the crisis of hegemony of the Congress party and the rise of BJP is equally striking. The parts of India where BJP has made its greatest gains to date (Uttar Pradesh, Madhya Pradesh, Rajasthan, Himachal Pradesh, Gujarat, Maharashtra: all in northern, central and western India) are those where the Congress base has been seriously eroded over the years, but where a viable, unified non-BJP alternative to Congress has either failed to materialize, as yet, or not proved sufficiently durable thus far. By contrast, the Hindutva forces find it difficult to make decisive inroads precisely in those provinces and regions where the decline in Congress hegemony has seen the rise of a relatively coherent and resilient alternative formation to replace

---

anti-democratic legislation. These include the Disturbed Areas, Public Safety and Armed Forces (Special Powers) Acts, the National Security Act (*NSA*), and, most notorious of all, the Terrorism and Disruptive Activities (Prevention) Act (*TADA*). Many of the hapless victims, far from being 'terrorists', are not even political dissidents of a peaceful kind. See for example *Lawless Roads: A Report on TADA, 1985–93* (Delhi: People's Union for Democratic Rights, 1993).

[123] Muralidharan, 'Mandal, Mandir aur Masjid', p. 211.

[124] Hasan, 'Changing Orientation of the State', p. 152. Emphasis added.

[125] Kothari, *State Against Democracy*, p. 240.

Congress: Tamil nationalist parties in Tamil Nadu,[126] Telugu Desam in Andhra Pradesh, left-of-centre groupings in Kerala and West Bengal, or even the fragile intermediate caste-Harijan-Muslim coalitions constructed by Mulayam Yadav in U. P. and Laloo Yadav in Bihar.[127] It is also significant that the one southern province where BJP *has* emerged as a major factor is Karnataka, where the decline of Congress has been only impermanently and partially substituted by R. K. Hegde's Janata Party government, and subsequently by H. D. Deve Gowda's Janata Dal.[128] Gramsci's 'Observations on Certain Aspects of the Structure of Political

[126] BJP support continues to be almost non-existent in Tamil Nadu, where a mere 2.5 per cent of voters (mostly Tamil Brahmins affiliated with RSS) were backing the party, according to an opinion poll published in April 1993: see *India Today*, 15 April, 1993. This is no accident, but a consequence of the trajectory of political development in Tamil Nadu, where a political tendency, institutionalized in the major Dravidian parties, and built on regional (i.e. not pan-Indian but anti-north Indian), 'backward' caste-specific (anti-'Brahminical') and linguistic (i.e. anti-Hindi) Tamil nationalism, has come to exert hegemonic power. The small upper-caste layer has been marginalized from political life (though not business, commercial and professional occupations), and Tamil nationalist governments have consolidated popularity through wide-ranging reservations and social welfare programmes for intermediate and lower castes. However, these governments have consciously avoided structural reforms: Tamil Nadu is one of India's poorest provinces, and hardly any redistribution of wealth or alteration of the class structure has occurred. If Frankel is at all correct in claiming that just as the Dravidian movement 'brought the low castes and lower middle classes to power in Tamil Nadu, a similar experiment is being tried [in the 1980s and 1990s] in the northern states,' especially Bihar and U.P. ('Middle Classes and Castes in India's Politics', p. 260), the achievements and limitations of the Tamil experiment deserve close attention. For an erudite analysis, see David Washbrook, 'Caste, Class and Dominance in Modern Tamil Nadu: Neo-Brahminism, Dravidianism and Tamil Nationalism', in *Dominance and State Power in Modern India*, pp.204–64.

[127] The socio-economic contradiction between Harijan landless labour and intermediate-caste landholding peasants seems the most serious of several underlying dilemmas plaguing these coalitions, especially in U. P.

[128] The relatively low levels of BJP support among even the professional middle classes in the urban south can be partly explained by their caste-composition. In comparison to their counterparts in the north, who are disproportionately upper-caste, these classes are much more differentiated in terms of caste composition. This is at least partly attributable to the vigorous affirmative-action programmes that have been in place in southern India for many years.

Parties in Periods of Organic Crisis' is thus extremely pertinent to the fluid situation in Indian party-politics in the wake of the decline of its hegemony:

At a certain point in their historical lives, social groups become detached from their traditional parties...the traditional parties in that particular organizational form...are no longer recognized [by these groups] as [their] expression. When such crises occur, the immediate situation becomes delicate and dangerous, because the field is open for violent solutions, for the activities of unknown forces, represented by charismatic 'men [or movements] of destiny'... these situations of conflict between 'represented and representatives' reverberate out from the terrain of parties...throughout the state organism... how are they created in the first place? In every country the process is different, though the content is the same. And the content is the crisis of...hegemony...a 'crisis of authority' is spoken of: this is precisely the crisis of hegemony, or the crisis of the state as a whole.[129]

This, then, is the organic crisis of state power which has provided the historical conjuncture for the rise of the 'Hindu nationalist' alternative. The crises of regime legitimacy and Congress hegemony have found reflection in multiple fractures and cleavages in India's social fabric. The country seems polarized on lines of region (only 5 of BJP's 119 parliamentary seats in 1991 came from southern India, and the party failed to win any seats at all in several eastern provinces like Bengal and Orissa), ethnicity (Kashmir, Assam, Punjab), caste (and class), especially in northern and western India, and religion ('Hindu versus Muslim'). As Gramsci wrote of Italy immediately after World War I, it was as if 'all the conflicts...all the contradictions...inherent in the country's social structure' had come to 'the surface with explosive force.'[130]

The *Sangh Parivar* took the crisis very seriously. By 1988, RSS had diagnosed the essence of the problem, and postulated its own solution:

The Sangh has viewed the problems of various centrifugal forces raising their heads with slogans of various types of separate interests and identities as being due to the...drying up of the unifying life-sap of our society. *The best solution therefore to these internal stresses and strains lies in strengthening and nurturing the basic roots of the Hindu ethos,* out of which all the various sects and creeds, languages and dialects, customs and traditions [and] philosophical doctrines and theories have emerged.[131]

[129] Forgacs, *An Antonio Gramsci Reader*, pp. 217–9.
[130] Ibid., pp. 144–6.
[131] See H. V. Seshadri (ed.), *RSS: A Vision in Action* (Bangalore: Jagarana Prakashana, 1988), p. 9. Emphasis added.

As Linz remarks, 'fascist appeal is based on the need to affirm national solidarity against a system that allowed [and was subsequently unable to control or reconcile] cleavage and conflict...within society.'[132] And like European fascisms, the Hindutva movement long symbolized 'the idiot-fringe of defeated conservatism.' But 'history teaches us that even the most tenuous phantoms can come to life if objective circumstances change. The fantasies of one generation can provide the mental furniture, even the life-blood, of another.' This happens 'not because these ideas themselves have any validity, but because objective circumstances... change.'[133]

Like three decades of FLN rule in Algeria, four decades of Congress hegemony in India generated these changed objective circumstances. Or perhaps they were not so changed after all. Addi's description of the central facets of the FLN regime seem as applicable to Congress: '...the egalitarianism they promised, the aspirations and...liberties they suppressed, the critical sensibility they fought, the cult of leader-for-life, the confiscation of public space: these were so many elements that perpetuated the colonial social model.'[134] But most significantly, like Algeria's Islamist opposition, Hindu nationalists do 'not reject this model'. They merely 'accuse the [incumbent] leadership of being incapable of *realizing* it.'[135] The BJP conception of monolithic nation and indivisible state-sovereignty is a straightforward derivative of the conception 'patented and propagated' by Congress, with the 'Hindutva' ethic added on. The declaratory BJP stand on current economic policy does not appear very substantively different from the Congress position.[136] On regional policy for South Asia, and on policy towards Indian nationalities, BJP merely subscribes to a more explicitly extreme version of the 'secular' Congress

[132] Linz, *The Breakdown of Democratic Regimes*, p. 47.
[133] Hugh Trevor-Roper, 'The Phenomenon of Fascism', in S. J. Woolf (ed.), *European Fascism* (London: Weidenfeld and Nicholson, 1968), pp. 22–3.
[134] Addi,'Algeria's Democracy Between the Islamists and the Elite', p. 36.
[135] Ibid., p. 36. Emphasis added.
[136] There appears to be some confusion in the Hindutva ranks on what stance to adopt towards the Indian government's current 'economic liberalization' program, being conducted in accordance with the tenets of IMF 'structural adjustment' doctrine. Some industrialists and big businessmen who are recent converts to the Hindutva cause view the reforms favourably. They are among the domestic industrial capitalist class that eventually emerged in India precisely because of the intermediate regime's success in keeping foreign capital at bay,

view, and practice.[137] The BJP claim, rather, is that 'Hindutva' will succeed where the regime's formula of 'national unity and integrity' has failed. Gramsci's analysis of fascist Italy, in his celebrated 'Lyons Thesis', has some relevance to the crisis in contemporary India:

In substance, fascism merely modifies the program of conservation and reaction which has always dominated Italian politics, through a different way of conceiving the unification of the reactionary forces. It replaces the tactic of agreements and compromises by the project of achieving the organic unity of all the [reactionary] forces in a single political organism under the control of a single centre... fascism... fitted into the framework of traditional Italian [state] policies... it was therefore favoured... by... the old ruling groups... socially... fascism found its base in the urban petty-bourgeoisie and in a new rural bourgeoisie... [but] this project... also allowe[d] fascism to win the support of the most decisively reactionary part of the industrial bourgeoisie and of the landowners.[138]

It is thus possible, in a historicist and structural framework, to interpret the rise of 'Hindu nationalism' as a rearguard defence of the Indian state as presently constituted. It remains to explain why Hindutva *ideology* is so well-tailored to this classic project of 'passive revolution'.

THE IDEOLOGICAL 'ALTERNATIVE' OF 'HINDU NATIONALISM'

'Hindutva', the core concept of 'Hindu nationalist' doctrine, is an explicitly modern political formulation of Indian nationalism. Vinayak

---

and now seek new opportunities in deregulation and collaboration with foreign and multinational capital. But the RSS leadership, perhaps reflecting the agenda and apprehension of its core constituency, the lower-middle class, is intensely suspicious of liberalization. It has encouraged its affiliates to organize protests against IMF conditionalities and GATT strictures. BJP leaders tend to be somewhat ambivalent: Advani, for example, has stated that BJP welcomes foreign investment, but in high-technology rather than consumer goods industries. Interview in *India Abroad*, 23 April, 1993, p. 6. More recently, however, leaders like Vajpayee have expressed stronger reservations about the liberalization process, and during 1994, the RSS launched a 'Swadeshi Jagaran Manch' (Nationalist Consciousness Forum) to agitate against consumption of imported goods.

[137] See L.K. Advani's interview in *India Abroad* (New York), 23 April, 1993, p. 6.

[138] Forgacs, *An Antonio Gramsci Reader*, pp. 147–8.

Savarkar, a convinced atheist who invented the idea in the 1920s, was emphatic that his was a comprehensive, totalizing concept, of which religious identity formed merely one component:

the concept of...'Hindutva'...is more comprehensive than...'Hinduism.' It is to draw pointed attention to this distinction that I coined the word...Hinduism concerns the religious systems of the Hindus, their theology and dogma. But this is precisely a matter that...[Hindu nationalists] leave entirely to individual or group conscience and faith... 'Hindutva'...refers not only to the religious aspect [of the Hindu nation]...but comprehends...their cultural, linguistic, social and political aspects as well...[139]

Hindutva is thus the conceptual expression of

common affinities, cultural, religious, historical, linguistic and racial, which through the process of countless centuries of association and assimilation moulded us into a homogeneous and organic Nation and...induced a will to lead a corporate and common National Life. The Hindus...are an organic National Being.[140]

It logically followed that the 'Hindustan of tomorrow must be indivisible... a unitarian nation from Kashmir to Rameshwar[am], from Sindh to Assam', and that the organic nation must find consummation in 'an internal[ly] centralized state.'[141] The Hindutva programme, past and present, thus seems to fit Ashis Nandy's category of 'religion-as-ideology', as distinguished from 'religion-as-faith'. While the latter is 'definitionally non-monolithic and operationally plural', the former denotes 'religion as a sub-national, national or cross-national identifier of populations contesting for...non-religious, usually political or socio-economic interests.'[142] To

[139] *Hindu-Rashtra Darshan* (Veer Savarkar Prakashan: Bombay, 1984), pp. 10, 78.

[140] Ibid., p. 79.

[141] Ibid., pp. 7, 196.

[142] Nandy, 'The Politics of Secularism', p. 70. Nandy's scathing critique of state-secularism, as well as of the Hindutva 'alternative', is acute and insightful. The problem with his work, to my mind, is that it greatly exaggerates the power and importance of religion, and consequently advocates a solution to India's problems that is both extremely idealistic and extremely limited. He prescribes a renewed 'religious tolerance', which, he claims, is 'inherent in everyday Hinduism, Islam, Buddhism and Sikhism.' Ibid., p. 86. To him, the trouble with Indian politics is that while 'the ills of religion have found expression...the strengths have not been available for checking the corruption and violence of public life' ('An Anti-Secularist Manifesto', pp. 14–24). This good religion/bad religion dichotomy is questionable in itself, though one certainly cannot find fault

proponents of 'religion-as-ideology', mobilization based on 'religious' identity and issues serves a purpose. It is an 'ideological principle useful for *political* mobilization', for it helps 'homogenize... co-believers into proper *political* formations'.[143] Religion is then simultaneously an instrument of and subordinate to a *political project*, which, in this case, is the capture of the Indian state via a protracted war of position. 'Hindu nationalism', far from representing 'a retrogression into primitivism and... a pathology of traditions', is therefore a 'by-product and a pathology of modernity... [for] whatever the revivalist Hindu may seek to revive, it is not Hinduism'.[144]

As Bhattacharya has succinctly expressed it:

The discourse of [Hindutva] communalism criticizes other religions for being monolithic, but aspires to build a monolithic unity. It glorifies diversity within Hinduism as a mark of its superiority over Semitic religions, but seeks to repress this diversity. It identifies aggressiveness as an evil intrinsic to other religions, but attempts to instil the same quality in all Hindus. It talks of patience and tolerance as innate virtues of Hindus, yet sees these traits as the basis of Hindu weakness. It condemns other religions for their politics of religious repression and temple destruction, but organizes itself around the same politics... it demeans both religion and 'tradition'.[145]

Far from representing 'religious fundamentalism', it seems then that Hindutva has precious little to do with the doctrinal inheritances and historical legacies of Hinduism. If anything, it bases itself on a *negation* and *rejection* of much of that inheritance and tradition, the profusion of 'religious' rhetoric and emotive appeals to 'religious' symbols notwithstanding. But if the Hindutva movement is not a manifestation of

---

with the notion of being tolerant to one's neighbours. But the real weakness of Nandy's argument is that it neglects to consider that a recovery of religious tolerance, while certainly desirable, is neither possible nor an adequate prescription for democratic renewal of a state and society which is gripped by complex and multidimensional crises rooted in the political and socio-economic domains.

[143] Ibid., p. 78, 83. Emphases added.

[144] Ibid., p. 83. Indeed, some of the most famously devout Hindu populations are located in south India, the region where the appeal of Hindutva politics is still rather slight.

[145] Bhattacharya, 'Myth, History and the Politics of Ramjanambhoomi', p. 131. Vanaik, too, has effectively refuted the claim frequently made by Hindutva apologists that none need fear anything from the 'Hindu nationalist' movement because of the 'innate tolerance' of the Hindu faith and tradition. As he says,

'fundamentalism', then what *is* it? It is essential to answer this question
to understand the nature of the role, and the salience of the appeal, of
this particular 'religion-as-ideology' in India of the 1990s.

I argue that 'Hindutva' represents an understanding of Indian nationalism that strips the concept of all nuance, historicity and complexity, and
reduces it to a brute (and utterly mythical) 'Hindu' majoritarianism. *But
it is quite similar, in its basic emphasis and content, to the monolithic, unitary
conception of Indian nationalism that has increasingly served as the official
ideology of the post-colonial Indian state.*[146] This helps explain why 'Hindu
nationalism' as a *political* creed has assumed salience and potency in the
context of the organic crisis of state power in India. A more explicitly
extreme and exclusive version of the same world-view as that propagated
and practised by Congress regimes will, or so Hindu nationalists claim,
solve India's problems and conflicts and foster a renewal of that organic
entity, the 'Hindu nation'. Where Hindu nationalism *does* differ from its
post-colonial Congress counterpart is in its explicitly 'communal' (anti-
Muslim) focus: indeed, the Hindutva concept was originally concocted
with the specific purpose of excluding Muslims from membership in the
Indian nation, and from citizenship in the independent Indian state.[147] But
as we have seen, even this divergence has been, in recent years, more
at the level of *rhetoric* than of *praxis*.

'in the past, Hinduism's renowned 'tolerance' was the result of its *lack* of self-
consciousness and the very *absence* of a 'Hindu' coherence and the notion of
a 'Hindu community'. Caste (an expression of social intolerance) was the
organizing principle . . . today's self-consciously avowed 'tolerance' masks an . . .
arrogance and dismissal of other . . . religions [read: Islam] which by contrast are
'intolerant' and therefore 'inferior'.' *The Painful Transition*, pp. 150–1, and
'Reflections on Nationalism and Communalism in India,' p. 55. Emphases mine.

[146] As Partha Chatterjee has put it, following the transfer of power in 1947,
Indian nationalism became a single 'discourse of order' and of 'the . . .
organization of power'. *Nationalist Thought and the Colonial World*, pp. 49–51.

[147] Savarkar had formulated the 'two-nation theory' (of mutually antagonistic
and incompatible Hindu and Muslim 'nations') almost two decades before it was
formally adopted by the All-India Muslim League as the rationale of its demand
for Pakistan. See *Hindu Rashtra Darshan*, pp. 15, 23–4, 44. The view that Hindus
and Muslims are inherently incompatible has been forcefully reiterated in the
post-colonial phase by Madhav Sadashiv Golwalkar, RSS supremo between 1940
and 1973. See his *magnum opus* (otherwise known as the RSS 'Bible'), *Bunch of
Thoughts* (Bangalore: Vikram Prakashan, 1968), pp. 147–8.

The similarities, on the other hand, are compelling. Hindu nationalists *do not at all reject* the Congress model of post-colonial 'nation-building.' They accuse it of impotence and ineffectiveness because it has *not gone far enough. The 'secular' state and 'communal' politics, far from being binary opposites, have in reality been interwoven and implicated in one another*: they are two sides of the coin of a monolithic and state-centralist conceptualization of Indian nationalism. As I argued at the outset of this essay, *their relationship is therefore dialectical, not adversarial.* As Vanaik notes, 'the most powerful collective identity of our times ... is nation and nationality.' The 'Hindu nationalist,' consequently, 'does not seek to *confront* nationalism in the name of a *greater* religious loyalty, but seeks to *co-opt* it.'[148] And as Ram-Prasad has persuasively argued, 'whereas the religious fundamentalist takes the scriptural source to provide the priorly determined essence of identity ... the Hindutva ideologue takes the [Hindu] nation to be that source,' and 'the special nature of Hindutva ideology lies in the way in which "Hinduism" can be conceived of as a culturally derived, nation-forming religious tradition.'[149] Hindutva ideology is above all an extreme form of state-led nationalism.

The dialectical relationship of 'secularism' and 'communalism' in post-colonial India has, moreover, deep roots in the decades of popular mobilization against colonial power. Fox has demonstrated how amenable many aspects of Gandhian thinking proved, from the mid-1970s onwards, to appropriation and reconstitution by 'Hindu nationalists'.[150] It is indeed undeniable that 'the Hindu nationalism of contemporary India has vital historical precedents and foundations' in the anti-colonial movement.[151] As Pandey puts it, far from being binary opposites,

---

[148] 'Reflections on Nationalism and Communalism in India', pp. 56–7. First and third emphases added.

[149] See C. Ram-Prasad, 'Hindutva Ideology: Extracting the Fundamentals', *Contemporary South Asia* 2, 3 (1993), pp. 285–309, for a very thoughtful discussion of this and related issues.

[150] Fox, *Gandhian Utopia*, Chs. 11 and 12. Of course, Gandhian and Hindutva thought are hardly perfectly congruent or synonymous. Fox stresses the many divergences (genuine universalism and humanism as opposed to sectarianism and intolerance) as well as the points of convergence; see especially, pp. 245–9. For an account that emphasizes the differences, see Ashis Nandy, *At the Edge of Psychology* (Delhi: Oxford University Press, 1980), esp. pp. 76–84.

[151] Vanaik, *The Painful Transition*, pp. 142–3. Vanaik points out that Gandhi 'made the [Indian] national movement a mass movement by substantially Hinduizing it.' The Mahatma envisioned that 'if appeal to ... religious loyalties

'communalism and nationalism, as we understand them today, arose together; the age of communalism was concurrent with the age of nationalism; they were part of the same discourse.'[152] A Congress document from the 1930s, for example, stated that 'from the beginning [of history] her [India's] *one mission* had been to weld her myriad children into *a harmonious people* by giving them a political, economic and *cultural* unity.'[153] This view found echoes in the writings of the arch-secularist Jawaharlal Nehru: 'Ancient India...was a world in itself, *a culture and a civilization* which gave shape to all things...some kind of a dream of unity has occupied the mind of India since the dawn of civilization.'[154]

Hindu nationalists (the 'communalists' of the post-colonial dispensation) did not, and do not, disagree with this Nehruvian 'vision'. For instance, Savarkar writes in the late 1930s that 'ever since the Vaidic ages, for some 5,000 years...our forefathers had been shaping the formation of our people into a religious, racial, cultural and political unit.'[155] Indeed, he claims that he is

the last man to ignore the benefits that...we...have reaped from the Indian National Congress...[for] it had...contributed immensely to the consolidation of Hindudom.. by rubbing off...provincial, linguistic and secional angularities, divisions and diversities...[156]

And in 1951, Jan Sangh's founding document asserted that 'the whole of Bharatavarsha, from the Himalayas to Kanyakumari...has been through the ages a living organic whole, geographically, culturally and historically.'[157]

---

constituted the first stage whereby the masses could be drawn into the national movement, the second stage.. would strip away the inessentials of religion, the artificial barriers [for all faiths were essentially one in the Gandhian universalist paradigm] and consolidate an overarching national identity all the stronger from being based on 'true' religious belief and commitment. The first part of his strategic perspective was a resounding success; the second a tragic miscalculation. Communal cleavages came to dominate the National Movement era and communalism has come to dominate much of contemporary Indian politics.'

[152] Pandey, *The Construction of Communalism*, p. 236.

[153] Cited in Ibid., p. 252. Emphases mine.

[154] Nehru, *The Discovery of India* (Delhi: Oxford University Press, 1989), p. 62. Emphasis added.

[155] *Hindu Rashtra Darshan*, p. 36.

[156] Ibid., p. 43.

[157] *Manifesto of the All-India Bharatiya Jana Sangh* (Delhi: 1951), p. 2.

The *one* factor that made Congress 'pseudo-nationalists' and Hindutva-ites 'the only real Indian Nationalists' was, according to Savarkar, 'the Congressite pursuit of the silly fad of...Hindu-Muslim unity.'[158] Otherwise, Hindu nationalists found nothing amiss with notions of *a* culture and *a* civilization. Indeed, they vigorously asserted that 'Bharatiya culture' was 'one and indivisible', and that 'any talk of composite culture' was 'unrealistic, illogical and dangerous, for it tends to weaken national unity and encourage fissiparous tendencies.'[159] The difference lay in that Hindu nationalists also equate 'national culture' with what they call 'Hindu culture',[160] a 'concept' not necessarily any more dubious than Nehru's dream of a unified, uniform (and 'secular') culture. Thus, in 1969, the Jan Sangh, proclaiming 'Indianization' its ultimate goal, defined it as 'the subordination of all narrow loyalties like...religion, caste, region, language or dogma to the overriding loyalty to the nation.'[161] As to what was constitutive of this nation, a leading Hindutva ideologue was unambiguous: 'It is the Hinduness of a man that makes him a national of India.'[162] And RSS did not disagree at all with the goal of 'harmonizing' the people. They only claimed, in a letter to Nehru in 1948, that 'Rashtriya Swayamsevak Sangh's...is the only ideology that can harmonize and integrate the interests of different groups and classes.'[163]

But what seems missing from *both* the 'Hindu nationalist' and 'secular-nationalist' constructions is

any sense of the...peoples and classes of the subcontinent struggling to realize their *many* versions of truth, honour and a just life. There was no room here for.. the class-divided and regionally diverse perceptions of the 'imagined community', out of the struggle for which Indian nationalism and the Indian national movement arose...[164]

[158] Savarkar, *Hindu-Rashtra Darshan*, pp. 31, 50, 54.

[159] *Manifesto of the...Jan Sangh*, p. 2.

[160] *RSS: A Vision in Action*, p. 14.

[161] Appendix in Balraj Madhok, *Indianization? What, Why and How* (Delhi: S. Chand, 1978).

[162] Madhok, *Indian Nationalism* (Delhi: Bharati Sahitya Sadan, 1969), p. 95.

[163] Reproduced in the RSS paper *Organiser*, 23 October, 1948, p. 15.

[164] Pandey, *The Construction of Communalism*, p. 253, emphasis added. Of course, Indian nationalism is hardly axiomatically coterminous with 'Hindu nationalism', despite the strong element of ideological ambiguity on this question in the freedom movement. I have elsewhere sharply refuted the exaggerated and self-serving claims on this subject of BJP leader L. K. Advani, who has asserted that 'India's freedom struggle was rooted...in a Hindu ethos,' and

Little wonder, then, that after independence, Nehru's 'secular' regime almost reneged on the longstanding Congress promise concerning linguistic reorganization of India's provinces, attempting to perpetuate, instead, the 'administrative zones' of the British. At that time, RSS and Jan Sangh too resolutely opposed linguistic provinces, citing their 'disintegrative' potential, and similarly upheld the merits of regional administrative zones under a centralized system. Or that the first post-independence cabinet of secular India prominently featured the top 'Hindu nationalist' (communal?) politician of that era, Shyama Prasad Mukherjee: he was Nehru's Industries Minister from 1947 to 1950. Or that a post-Nehru Congress regime tried to impose Hindi as the sole national and official language, and almost precipitated the secession of Tamil Nadu from the Union in the process (Hindu nationalists have always been diehard Hindi chauvinists[165]). Or, indeed, that Congress-I and BJP are engaged, in the 1990s, in a demagogic contest of competitive chauvinism, with assorted external villains (led by Pakistan) and their agents being scapegoated by both for India's ills.

CONCLUSION

So what solutions does 'Hindu nationalism' have to offer to the crisis confronting India's state and society? The short answer is that as the highest stage of the anti-democratic politics that has caused this crisis, it has none, at least none capable of bringing about lasting peace, justice and stability. Indeed, its entire platform is reducible to two complementary core ideas: repudiation, denial, suppression or neutralization of the manifold forms of diversity, conflict, cleavage and oppression in Indian society, on the one hand; and a glorification of the monolithic, organic unity of the 'nation' (preferably in its 'natural' hierarchy, though this is sometimes oblique and qualified), and a concomitant deification of

---

reduced nationalist leaders from Gandhi to Jayaprakash Narayan to the lowest common denominator of 'Hindu nationalist'. The legacy of the Indian independence struggle is far too rich and complex to be appropriated in this crass manner. See Advani's article in *The Telegraph*, 4 Jan., 1993, and my op-ed rejoinder on 7 Jan., 1993. See also Vanaik, *The Painful Transition*, pp. 139–43.

[165] See Savarkar, *Hindu Rashtra Darshan*, 84–7; Golwalkar, *Bunch of Thoughts*, (Bangalore: Vikram Prakashan, 1968) pp. 112–3; and K. R. Malkani, *Principles for a New Political Party* (Delhi: Vijay Pustak Bhandar, 1951), p. ii.

indivisible and unitary state power, on the other. This is true of 'Hindu nationalist' declaratory positions, and of the *praxis* of various functional groups of the *Sangh Parivar*, such as the labour, peasant, youth, student, teachers' and women's affiliates, on practically all substantive issues. These include Indian nationalities, federalism and regional autonomy; caste contradictions and oppression; poverty and class conflicts in the agrarian and industrial sectors; and women's subordination.[166]

[166] See, for example, Golwalkar, *Bunch of Thoughts*, K. R. Malkani; *Principles for a New Political Party* (Delhi: 1951); Seshadri (ed.), *RSS: A Vision in Action*; Savarkar; *Hindu Rashtra Darshan*; and Andersen and Damle, *The Brotherhood in Saffron*.

On the national question, currently an exceptionally urgent issue in the subcontinent, Golwalkar, the revered 'Shri Guruji' of the present generation of BJP leaders (the vast majority of BJP officials, at *all* levels of the organization, have had their political socialization in the RSS), has this to say: 'The most important and effective step will be to bury...for good all talk of a federal structure...to sweep away the existence of all autonomous and semi-autonomous states within.. Bharat and proclaim "One Country, One State, One Legislature, One Executive", with no trace of fragmentational, regional, sectarian, linguistic or other types of pride being given scope for playing havoc with our integrated harmony. Let the Constitution be...redrafted, so as to establish this Unitary form of Government'. *Bunch of Thoughts*, pp. 437–8.

On the question of caste, Golwalkar exemplifies the Hindu nationalist tendency to trivialize centuries of caste oppression, even while paying lip-service to the iniquities of the caste-system. He writes that while in the twentieth century 'the caste-system has degenerated beyond all recognition,' the hierarchy has 'in fact served as a great bond of social cohesion...for thousands of years of our glorious national life.' On class inequality, he claims that such 'disparity is an indivisible part of nature and we have to live with it.' *Bunch of Thoughts*, pp. 18, 108–10.

On the topic of socio-economic inequalities and class conflict, Savarkar advocates an organic-statist system where 'the interests of both capital and labour will be subordinated to the interests of the Nation as a whole,' with the 'same principle' applying to peasant and landlord in the agrarian economy. *Hindu Rashtra Darshan*, pp. 109–11. In *RSS: A Vision in Action* (pp. 242–8), RSS speaks glowingly of how its labour affiliate, Bharatiya Mazdoor Sangh (BMS), works in accordance with the 'Bharatiya' concept of the 'industrial family', with 'the capitalist, the labourers and managerial staff' forming 'harmonious' parts of this fraternal brotherhood. It 'rejects the theory of class conflict', as well as the 'idea of collective bargaining by workers', for such notions 'ill-fit this integral concept' and encourage a 'separatist labour consciousness.' Instead, BMS gives priority to the 'welfare of the nation.' The 'concept of the agricultural family and

162   SUMANTRA BOSE

Yet the rise of 'Hindu nationalism' is no chance, arbitrary phenomenon. It is deeply rooted in the historical development of India's post-
colonial political and social structures, and it is an expression of the
organic crisis of the Indian state. So long as regime efficacy and
effectiveness remain grossly deficient, and the Congress' crisis of
hegemony (and the resulting instability and fragmentation of the party-
system) persists and deepens, its malignant symptom, 'Hindu nationalism', is likely to endure as a dynamic and disruptive political force. It
will not do to wish away the Hindutva movement simply on the grounds
that 'Hindus' have historically never constituted a unified, solidary
collectivity, but rather the opposite.[167] To the extent that all modes of
collective identity are social and political constructions, 'invented' or

---

concomitant spirit of harmony among the several limbs of agricultural production' similarly informs the activities of RSS' peasant affiliate, the Bharatiya Kisan
Sangh (BKS), thereby 'eliminating class conflict and other socially self-destructive
propaganda.' Identical ideas are to be found in Malkani, *Principles for a New
Political Party*, a founding document of Jan Sangh (Malkani is presently senior
vice-president of BJP). Indeed, the *Sangh Parivar* applies its concept of 'integral
harmony', a euphemism for organic-statism, even in the educational field, as
reflected in the guiding ideology of its student wing, the Akhil Bharatiya Vidyarthi
Parishad (ABVP). See Andersen and Damle, *The Brotherhood in Saffron*,
pp. 119–21.

As for the oppression of women, RSS, the engine of national resurgence, is
an exclusively male fraternity, with membership denied to women. The RSS
does claim, however, that its rather obscure women's affiliate, the Rashtra Sevika
Samiti, exemplifies 'organized *stree-shakti*' (woman-power). The manifestations
of organized woman-power, as listed in a recent RSS publication, include serving
food, looking after children, 'rendering her husband's work easier through her
spirit of adjustment and efficient management of daily chores,' and producing
sons who later also became fulltime RSS activists. See Seshadri (ed.), *RSS: A
Vision in Action*, pp. 151–3. The high-profile participation of female activists like
Uma Bharti and Sadhvi Rithambara in Hindutva agitations should, I believe,
be seen in this overall context of a completely male-dominated organizational
hierarchy and male-centric political ideology. Several articles on the relationship
of Hindutva politics to women's rights and activism appear in the *Bulletin of
Concerned Asian Scholars*, 25, 4 (Oct.–Dec. 1993).

[167] As for instance implied by the celebrated historian Romila Thapar in
'Communalism and the Historical Legacy: Some Facets', in Panikkar (ed.),
Communalism in India, pp. 17–33.

imagined' in some way,[168] there is nothing *ipso facto* illegitimate about he late twentieth-century political phenomenon of 'Hindu nationalism.'

In fact, in its role as rearguard defender of the present Indian state, his movement's otherwise impoverished programme *does* hold out the I think illusory) prospect of *suppressing* or *neutralizing* conflicts, cleavages and contradictions in the social structure that have become not just salient but explosive. Hence the inordinate appeal of its passive revolution project to those very sizeable and influential elements of the national-bourgeoisie, petty-bourgeoisie and rural dominants who identify strongly with the present constitution of the Indian state and/or the social *status quo* that has prevailed since independence, and feel threatened by the multidimensional strife visited upon India by and under Congress regimes. It is no accident that the Hindutva support base reflects, in addition to its regionally skewed nature (predominantly northern and western India), an upper-caste, urban/semi-urban bias.[169] From Uttar Pradesh to Karnataka, and Gujarat to West Bengal, it is the desertion of 'the most decisively reactionary part' of the traditional Congress constituency that has, to a large extent, made possible the expansion of Hindutva's social base.

Yet India's massively complex and diverse social-structural formation still represents a serious obstacle to the taking of state power by the Hindutva movement. The 'Hindu nationalist' world-view, deeply rooted in the outlook of its core base, the *banias* and upper-caste Hindi-speaking Hindus of north India (and to some extent Maratha Brahmins, the founders of RSS), continues to have rather little resonance with numerous

---

[168] See for example Benedict Anderson, *Imagined Communities: Reflections on the Origin and Spread of Nationalism* (London: Verso, 2nd edition 1991); Eric Hobsbawm and Terence Ranger (eds.), *The Invention of Tradition* (Cambridge: Cambridge University Press, 1983).

[169] This seems confirmed by patterns of BJP support in elections held in November 1993 to the provincial legislatures of Uttar Pradesh, Madhya Pradesh, Rajasthan, Himachal Pradesh and Delhi appears that the BJP is encountering serious problems in its strenuous attempts to decisively diversify its social base to encompass intermediate castes and Harijans, and rural as well as urban areas. The party *has* had limited success in this endeavour, but it still has a long way to go. And, of course, the challenge of making decisive inroads in southern and eastern India still remains a daunting one for BJP. For analysis and psephological findings, see 'Saffron Setback', *India Today*, 15 December, 1993, and 'Election Analysis', *Frontline*, 28 January, 1994, pp. 96–109.

caste, ethnic, linguistic and regional groups throughout India, even in
the present situation of anomie and confusion in civil society. The
Hindutva movement's war of position will doubtless continue; yet it
remains uncertain that this mobilizational effort, beset with internal
contradictions and external challenges, will be able to translate the
movement's agenda into reality. Ironically, but appropriately, it is the
enormous heterogeneity of a country which is in its essence a panorama
of minorities that stands as the most formidable barrier to the triumphant
consummation of the majoritarian myth.*

---

* This essay was completed in 1995. Since it is a broad empirical-theory
perspective on the rise of 'Hindu nationalism' in the context of major 'structural'
changes in patterns of exercise of state authority and modification of social forces
in Indian politics, I have decided against further 'updating' to incorporate the
most recent developments in India's politics. Instead, I leave it to the reader
to judge the arguement in light of the most recent developments (notably the
general elections of May 1996, in which the BJP and its allies emerged as the
single largest parliamentary bloc, albeit with only 23 per cent of the popular
vote—compared to 21 per cent in 1991—mostly drawn from northern and western
India).

7

Development Strategy in India:
A Political Economy Perspective

Jayati Ghosh

The debate on development strategy in India has mirrored and provided a synoptic outline of the worldwide debate. This has been true throughout this century, from the controversy between 'nationalist' and 'imperialist' positions on the causes for the lack of development of the colonial Indian economy, to the elaboration of a state-led planning strategy in a mixed economy during the Nehru era, to the later moves towards 'liberalization' and greater market orientation that have marked the past decade. As elsewhere, the debate has been characterized by sharply drawn theoretical and ideological positions, which have found expression in a much more muddy, confused and complex reality. And as in other parts of the world which have, in the second half of the century, been obsessed with the necessity for rapid industrialization, the actual workings of any strategy have been fundamentally affected by the political economy context and the dynamics of class relations which have determined its functioning.

In this paper, a brief (and necessarily sketchy) attempt is made to situate the broad strategies of development and their effects in India, in such a socio-political context. To begin with, the general experience of growth and development in India is briefly outlined, and then I consider some of the alternative explanations that have been advanced within a political economy framework. These provide the background for an attempt to capture some of the important forces behind the particular pattern of development (or lack of it) that the post-independence Indian economy has experienced.

STRATEGIES OF DEVELOPMENT

The Nehru-Mahalanobis strategy of development which marked the first few decades of post-Independence Indian economic growth was not simply the brainchild of a few leaders, but actually had its roots in the nationalist struggle for independence. In India as elsewhere among newly-independent nations in the middle of the twentieth century, it seemed evident that the need to free the economy from domination by metropolitan capital and provide for a measure of economic autonomy required the active intervention of the state in a planning framework. So widespread was this perception among ruling elites as well as in mass consciousness, that it achieved the status of national consensus. Thus, the group of industrialists representing large capital who were responsible for the 'Bombay Plan' of 1944 were insistent upon the need for a mixed economy in which the state would take responsibility for the provision of infrastructure as well as large and heavy industrial investment. The more radical approaches also emphasized the crucial role of government, not only in redistribution and reduction of poverty, but in providing a pattern of growth which would provide for a diversified industrial economy catering to mass consumption needs as well as mitigate the usual market failures.

The mixed economy that developed subsequently had a mixed record. There were some definite, albeit relatively modest, successes: these include the pushing up of the rate of growth in both agriculture and industry from the earlier stagnant colonial levels, some degree of industrial diversification and the achievement of national self-reliance in certain important sectors, notably food. However, the strategy has also been much criticized on many fronts, from both Right and Left perspectives.

To consider the achievements first, there has been from the 1950s a dramatic step-up in rates of both industrial and agricultural growth as compared to the near-stagnation of the colonial period. Thus, compared to the estimates of per capita national income for the period 1880 to 1947 of between 0 and 0.4 per cent per capita at a compound annual rate, the corresponding rate for the period 1950–1 to 1990–1 has been 1.7 per cent. The decade of the eighties actually witnessed an acceleration of the overall growth rate, although this was less evident in the material-producing sectors and much more marked for services. Agricultural growth over the entire period has been roughly stable at a rate of around 3 per cent per annum, while manufacturing industry has shown distinct phases: an acceleration in the period 1950–64 during the first period of systematic planning, followed by a deceleration until the late 1970s, and a renewed spurt thereafter led primarily by an expansion of state expenditure.

This overall growth has also involved a considerable diversification of industrial production, essentially following from the import-substituting industrialization strategy which allowed various capital goods sectors and other infant industries to come up and achieve some level of production. This itself was a sharp break from the colonial period when only very specific manufacturing industries could come up: at first those with special transport advantages such as cotton and jute textiles, and later those which benefitted from the inter-war system of tariff protection, such as sugar and certain light consumer goods. The pattern of planned investment by the state engendered the development of a significant capital goods sector in both public and private hands, as well as related intermediate production. The diversification was reflected in the changed structure of exports: from being primarily an exporter of primary commodities in the colonial period, exports were now dominated by manufactured goods, and during the seventies one of the fastest growing elements of these exports was actually engineering goods.

The other chief success of the overall growth strategy has been the achievement of domestic self-sufficiency in food production, in particular from the crisis period of the mid-1960s when India had to import foodgrain on an urgent basis to tide over domestic shortage. It must be pointed out that this self-sufficiency has been achieved at a rather low level of per capita consumption, which has increased only marginally from the early 1970s.[1] What it means is that this increase has occurred along with an elimination of dependence on imports, which amounted to as much as 12 per cent of domestic availability of foodgrain in the period 1964–6. In recent years there has also been a marked increase in domestic production of oilseeds, which had become a major item of imports during the 1980s.

These achievements may appear rather modest, especially when seen in relation to the growth performance of the rapidly-growing economies of East and Southeast Asia during the same period. But they do represent a marked break from the colonial period, and it is also notable that until the 1980s, these had been attained without very sharp fluctuations in output growth or a build-up of external debt as in Latin America. Nonetheless, the overall record of post-Independence economic growth is clearly inadequate in many crucial respects and it was evident from

---

[1] Thus per capita availability in terms of grams per day has increased from an average of 463 in the triennium 1970–2 to 487 in the triennium 1990–2, and that too largely because of the record harvest of 1991. [CMIE, *Basic Statistics Relating to the Indian Economy*, 1993.]

at least two decades earlier that a drastic refashioning of the entire growth strategy was required. The subsequent policy revisions and reforms of the late 1980s and early 1990s have been identified as reactions to the perceived inadequacies of this growth pattern, although in effect they represent only one alternative path of 'reform' which is not necessarily the most effective for addressing the primary economic ills of the country.

The major criticisms of the past growth experience which are currently in vogue have actually been part of a right-wing critique for some decades now.[2] These relate to the export pessimism which underlay the import substituting pattern of industrialization and contributed to price incentives against agriculture as well as a 'high-cost' industrial economy, and the emphasis on state control and regulation of economic life which created a complex and wasteful system involving corruption, delays and numerous micro-level inefficiencies. Such perceptions have also informed the official moves towards deregulation and liberalization which become explicitly a part of the government's economic strategy.

These were undoubtedly significant problems and the critique which emphasizes them bears an essential descriptive validity. But it can plausibly be argued that the real failures of Indian development lay elsewhere. The most prominent deficiencies reflect the fact that such growth as did occur was fundamentally unbalanced and in crucial respects unsustainable, even as it failed to provide minimum basic needs to the bulk of the population and allowed for the persistence of absolute poverty among a fairly large section of the population. The pattern of growth has been unbalanced on various levels: in terms of the relative development of the different material and non-material sectors, the rates of urban and rural per capita income generation, the spatial spread of growth which has actually been highly regionally concentrated, and the accentuated income inequalities associated with the growth process. Agricultural growth has been focussed on a pattern of commercialized farming based on 'Green Revolution' techniques which are energy-intensive, high in material input use, very dependent upon assured water

[2] Among the critiques are Jagdish Bhagwati and Padma Desai, *India: Planning for Industrialisation* (London: Oxford University Press, 1970) Jagdish Bhagwati and T. N. Srinivasan, *Foreign Trade Regimes and Economic Development: India,* (National Bureau of Economic Research, New York, 1975) Isher Ahluwahlia, *Industrial Stagnation in India* (Delhi: Oxford University Press, 1985) and, very recently, Jagdish Bhagwati, *India in Transition: Freeing the Economy* (Oxford: Clarendon Press, 1993). Curiously, these arguments are now echoed also in government documents, such as the Ministry of Finance, GOI, *Aspects of the Black Economy in India* (New Delhi, 1993).

supply, and increasingly subject to problems of diminishing returns and increasing per unit costs. The whole domain of dryland farming has been generally neglected, and with it the development of sustainable agricultural packages which are less ecologically damaging and cater more directly to the needs of diverse local populations.

Related to this is the unfortunate reality that four decades of planned development have not created a situation in which state and market operations combine to provide basic needs to the bulk of the population. This inadequate provision to the masses of essential items of survival including both goods such as food, clothing and minimally acceptable housing, and services such as universal primary education, adequate health care and sanitation, must be counted as the singlemost damaging aspect of the development process. Not only is the availability deficient in aggregate terms, but access to such basic minimum goods and services is very unequally distributed, and is determined not only by wealth and asset positions, but by a complex system of patronage and clientelism in both rural and urban India. Women face particular difficulties in male-dominated society, not only in terms of access to goods and services such as health and education but also as regards employment and intra-household distribution of resources. The developmental process thus far has, if anything, further marginalised women, other than a minority in the upper income groups.

The persistence of large pockets of absolute poverty, defined in the strictest sense of the lack of an income sufficient to ensure the minimum calorific consumption of members of the household, is another major failure. Although all the different estimates of the extent and severity of poverty indicate that poverty in both absolute and relative terms has declined since the mid-1970s, it remains significant in aggregate terms, with around one-third of the rural population and one-fifth of the urban population falling below the poverty line towards the end of the 1980s.[3] Further, since the rate of decline of poverty has not been uniform across regions, it has become increasingly concentrated in the central and eastern regions of the country, and still remains primarily a rural phenomenon, indicating the lack of adequate rural development in large parts of the country.

These tendencies are related to a broader pattern which is that of the low level of labour productivity across the economy as a whole. Productivity growth has been confined to a few isolated sectors, and these

---

[3] See ILO and UNDP, *India: Employment, Poverty and Economic Policies* (Delhi, 1993) for a review of recent estimates of poverty and their implications.

have had few linkages with the rest of the economy so that the high-growth enclaves have not generated a virtuous cycle of economy-wide productivity enhancement. Most wastefully of all, there has been an inability to make productive use of the large reserves of trained and untrained labour. The consequent slack in resource use in the form of continued open and disguised unemployment must count among the crucial areas of failure of the economic strategy.

These long-run inadequacies combined in the recent past with short-run mismanagement, particularly over the decade of the eighties, to create a situation of economic crisis by the beginning of this decade. To a large extent the changes in economic strategy in the 1980s stemmed from the limitations of the earlier strategy as well as the nature of the state and the ruling elites, which allowed only one type of response to the perceived economic problems of the country.

The 1980s were marked by a dramatic increase in overall fiscal deficits, and for the first time in the post-Independence era, deficits in the current revenue account of the government. The substantial growth of government expenditure that this was associated with (even though some significant proportion leaked out in the form of defence imports) led to a Keynesian-type spending boom in the economy, in which growth rates averaged around 5 per cent per annum over the decade, above the 'Hindu' rate of growth of 3 per cent which had been the norm in earlier decades. The multiplier effects of this process meant that employment even in the rural areas appears to have registered growth, although employment elasticities in all the important sectors are estimated to have fallen. Inflationary pressures were limited by the gradual moves towards import liberalization, which allowed for a substantial growth of non-oil imports over the decade and the increasing import-intensity of domestic manufacturing production. Such expansion was obviously not sustainable, driven as it was by fiscal deficits financed by increasing public debt and associated with continuous balance of payments deficits and growing external debt. These internal and external imbalances pushed the economy towards a situation in which a crisis of payments was more or less inevitable; the only question was the precise timing.

The response of the government to the external payments crisis of 1990–1 was to approach the multilateral lending institutions (and in particular the IMF) for special financial assistance, and embark on a programme of stabilization-cum-adjustment which essentially involved continuing the moves towards liberalization which had been instituted in the earlier decade. The chief point of interest about the current package is that the 'liberalizing' structural adjustment measures are being implemented in a context in which stabilization policies have been at best partial and in crucial senses unsuccessful. Thus, although the balance of payments appears to be far more stable, this was due first to enhanced official borrowing (which has meant that the external debt of the country continues to increase) and subsequently due to the inflow of portfolio finance in Indian securities which reflects a worldwide phenomenon of investor interest in 'emerging markets'. Meanwhile, internal balance in the sense of a balance on the revenue account of the government was never achieved, the revenue deficit has grown to historic proportions, and consequently the overall fiscal deficit also has increased once again. At the same time, the cuts in capital expenditure of the government have involved a recession in manufacturing industry and declines in employment generation even compared to the earlier sluggish levels.

THEORIES OF THE STATE AND INDIA'S MACRO-ECONOMY

It would be simplistic in the extreme to attribute either the failures or the successes to government policy in itself or to the merits or demerits of any particular strategy. Clearly, the past experience can only be understood with reference to the nature of the society and the historical evolution of both markets and other social institutions, the relative power configurations across classes and groups and the interaction between politics and economics that expresses itself as the outcome of various forms of government intervention. There is a tradition in the Indian economic literature which has explicitly concerned itself with assessing the nature of government intervention in the economy with reference to its political economy. Some of these arguments are briefly considered in this section.

It was true that the immediately post-colonial literature on the Indian macro-economy assumed a broad consensus in favour of industrialization, a mixed economy and certain obvious developmental goals. It thus ignored the possibilities of internal conflicts and competing claims for resources in the mechanics of state action, and concentrated instead on the technicalities of the matter of rapidly increasing production and incomes. The macro-economic literature of the fifties, for example, was completely 'technocratic' in its discussion of state involvement. Not only was the necessity for state intervention taken for granted (along the lines of development literature of that period throughout the world), but it was also assumed that the state was (unlike its colonial predecessor) inherently benevolent in its desire for the material betterment of the people, and essentially oriented to the development of the whole economy rather than favouring particular classes or groups. The issues that dominated the discussion were those relating to the type of trade and industrial strategy (import-substituting versus export-oriented), the investment allocation in the plans, etc. The Nehru–Mahalanobis strategy that became the hallmark of the fifties and sixties assumed a 'developmental state', so much so that even in the framing of the five-year plans themselves it was taken for granted that successful land reforms and other state-directed institutional changes relating to agriculture would increase output in that sector without additional expenditure by the government.

A similar idea has imbued other recent considerations of the macro-economy in which the interaction of the state with the economy is largely seen as a problem of correct formulation of policy and design of intervention, as well as subsequent implementation. Thus, Chakravarty in what is otherwise an excellent account of the experience of development planning in India, concentrated essentially on the economic and technical constraints facing state policy, with an implicit assumption that the state itself essentially pursued its stated developmental goals, only coming up against difficulties posed by the political and economic structures *outside* it.[4] While this is useful in highlighting the precise economic difficulties associated with the planning process, it does leave the picture incomplete, since many of the constraints which appear to be 'external' to the state are actually related to the nature of the state itself.

In a similar vein, Jalan has spoken of redefining the role of government in India, arguing that 'the primary failure in several developing countries, including India, has been in implementation and in the tacit assumption that the state had an unlimited capacity to intervene.'[5] This tends to ignore the point that it was the nature of the state itself and the other political, social and institutional realities which created a certain role for government in the first place, and meant that this role had very definite implications for growth and distribution quite separate from its stated designs.

The subsequent evolution of the economy as well as both the successes and failures of state intervention, have tempered the idealistic vision of the developmental state untainted by the dominance of class interests and above the fray of social antagonism. Indeed, the reaction

[4] Sukhamoy Chakravarty, *Development Planning: The Indian Experience* (Delhi: Oxford University Press, 1987).

[5] Bimal Jalan, *India's Economic Crisis: The Way Ahead* (Delhi: Oxford University Press, 1991), p. 87.

to the simpler version of this position, from the mainstream neo-classical perspective, came fairly swiftly. Early critiques of the strategy of development were provided by Bhagwati and Srinivasan among others until these actually came to dominate economic policy discussion in the late eighties. The early works essentially identified 'government failure' as the root cause of all the major developmental problems of post-independence India. Thus the combination of the strategy of planning with import-substituting industrialization and regulation of private industry was seen to have resulted in a 'high-cost economy' replete with inefficiencies, corruption, delays, distortions due to perverted market signals, stifling of entrepreneurial zeal through bureaucratic control, etc. In addition the specific strategy based on export pessimism along with substantial dependence on public sector industrial investment came under fire not only for discriminating against agriculture and labour-intensive production but also because it created a gargantuan state sector whose performance was seen to be well below desired levels.

The basic premise in this approach has been that all state intervention (other than in the most basic functions of law and order and protection of private property which are essential for markets to function) is undesirable and leads to inefficiency-creating distortions. Not only is this rather simplistic and absolutist in position, but it also does little to explain why the actual functioning of state policies occurred in this particular manner in India, nor why the state policies themselves have altered over time. Other than describe the negative fallout in terms of the propagation of rent-seeking activities, therefore, this approach does little to advance a political economy understanding of Indian macro-economic processes.

Another type of reaction to the 'developmental state' perception in India has come from the view that the state is not autonomous at all but rather is completely subordinated to the pressures and pulls of interest groups. This view is best expressed by Bardhan: 'Indian public economy has thus become an elaborate network of patronage and subsidies. The heterogeneous interest groups fight and bargain for their share in the spoils of the system and often strike compromises in the form of "log-rolling" in the usual fashion of pressure-group politics.'[6] Since none of the classes or interest groups has been individually strong enough to dominate the state's resource allocation process, the result is a proliferation of subsidies and transfers to placate all of them. This in turn involves

[6] Pranab Bardhan, 'A Political Economy Perspective on Development', in B. Jalan (ed.), *The Indian Economy: Problems and Prospects* (New Delhi: Penguin, 1992), p. 325.

a government that is quantitatively enormous and has a large body of
regulatory practice, but is nonetheless rather weak in shaping the
economy. This argument is really only a post facto explanation of
observed failure rather than a theory of state and macro-economic
interaction. Indeed, similar evidence of clientelism and corruption can
be found not only in fast-growing economies like those of Japan and
South Korea, but also less successful economies such as Pakistan, the
Philippines and Turkey. This argument is essentially an application of
the theory of coalitions to the macro-economy; there is no insight into
why particular groups have been dominant or are able to influence the
Indian state, why and how the relations between these groups, the rest
of society and the state have changed over time, and what has determined
ideological and policy regime changes such as the shift in emphasis from
'planning' to 'liberalization'.

In contrast to this conception, there is a view of the relative autonomy
of the Indian state that comes from its sheer size in the economy as well
as its ideological position in the society. 'The state's dominance is related
to its material condition, to its overwhelming control of investment and
employment in the organized sector, and to its ideological advantage
as the presumed defender of the collective interest and socialist purposes
and as the enemy of private and partial gains.'[7] Thus, 'the resources it
controls and the state's strategic and bargaining advantage make it
possible for the state in India to be not only relatively autonomous and
self-determined but also self-interested.'[8] This autonomy of the state as
a 'third actor' in Indian politics is in turn seen to have contributed to
a centrist-oriented social pluralism in which class politics has been
marginal and subordinate to other social formations such as caste,
religious and language communities and regional nationalisms. Here too,
the macro-economic processes are not really explained. Thus, as this
powerful 'third actor', what has prevented the state in India from
achieving its stated developmental and distributional goals? And why,
over time, have both the rate and pattern of growth as well as its sectoral
regional and class-wise distribution varied?

In Marxist and other radical assessments of the Indian economy, there
has been explicit consideration of the nature of the Indian state and its
dynamics in relation to the stated goals of modernization within a
'socialistic pattern of society'. Doubts were expressed about the ability

---

[7] Lloyd Rudolph and Susanne Rudolph, *In Pursuit of Lakshmi* (Chicago:
University of Chicago Press, 1987), p. 13.

[8] Ibid., p. 399.

of a 'mixed economy' to function efficiently, since official plan targets depended crucially on private sector responses, and the pattern of income distribution dictated a likely pattern of private resource allocation behaviour completely at variance with the official goals. The limits to (and problems with) regulation and control over the private sector were clearly recognised.[9] This literature gave great emphasis to the importance of institutional change *prior* to the planning process, since asset redistribution, in particular land reform, was seen as essential in altering initial endowments in a way so as to ensure balanced growth. The inability to achieve land reform, or any other asset redistribution of significance, or indeed to control the acquisitive tendencies of the elites, was seen to reflect the nature of the state itself.

Some early writings described the nature of the state as one of an (uneasy) alliance between the rural landed classes and the big industrial bourgeoisie, influenced also by the interaction with metropolitan capital.[10] However, since the relationship between state and society was seen as a dialectical one, the nature of the state was not viewed as immutable, but constantly changing along with the shifting configuration of class forces.

Mitra used the idea that the different dominant classes had divergent economic interests to point out how shifts in the intersectoral terms of trade could be instigated by state action.[11] The rich farmer lobby was able to ensure high farm output prices through influencing the government procurement price which operated as a floor, and this meant that terms of trade shifted in favour of agriculture. This not only worsened the material condition of both industrial workers and the rural workers and small peasants who were net purchasers of food, it also contributed to industrial stagnation in various ways. While numerous difficulties exist with this argument, most notably that in a context of oligopolistic industry such political manipulation of farm prices would affect the level of agricultural prices but not the terms of trade (since industrialists could choose to raise their prices in order to maintain profit margins), the political economy perception of the state implicit in this argument is a useful one. Thus this analysis highlighted not only the ability of particular classes to affect specific sectoral policies (such as in this case, the farm procurement price, which was also seen to differ according to region and crop depending on the political strength of the concerned farmers) but

[9] See, for example, the papers in K.M. Kurien (ed.), *State and Society in India* (Bombay: Orient Longman, 1974).

[10] Thus Prabhat Patnaik 'On the Political Economy of Under-Development' in *Economic and Political Weekly* (Annual Number, Feb. 1973), pp. 197–212.

[11] Ashok Mitra, *Terms of Trade and Class Relations* (London: Cass, 1977).

also the impact that this has had on the macro-economy, and in turn how the behaviour of the economy affected the government's decisions in the next round.

Other writers have explored this interaction also with the specific aim of explaining macro-economic trends.[12] Thus Patnaik modelled the growth process in terms of the state interacting with capital and labour, in a context of an inflation barrier posed by the political sensitivity of the state to the impact of inflation on the more vocal social groups. This inflationary barrier forces the state to cut back on its own real spending since it is also politically constrained from raising more tax revenues. In turn this contributes to the decline in overall growth given the close association between public and private investments. The fiscal crisis of the state—brought on by political economy reasons relating to its very nature—thus leads to a more general economic stagnation. In later works, Patnaik has explained the expansion of the 1980s in terms of a resurgence of government expenditure, this time based on the accrual of internal and external debt.[13] This has also rendered the economy as well as the polity more vulnerable to external pressures and more dependent upon acceptability by international capital. Chandra has analysed official regulatory practice with reference to the external sector and multinational corporations, and has discussed both capital inflow and technology transfer in the context of a state which has a contradictory relationship with external capital, simultaneously dependent and striving for some autonomous space.[14] Bagchi has considered the various facets of intermeshing of government decisions relating to the economy and the configuration of class forces and social institutions, to try and explain why the Indian case differs in significant ways from both the Latin American and East Asian stereotypes.[15]

[12] Prabhat Patnaik, *Time, Inflation and Growth: Some Macro-Economic Themes in an Indian Perspective* (Calcutta: Orient Longman, 1988).

[13] Prabhat Patnaik, 'International Capital and National Economic Policy: A Critique of India's Economic Reforms', in *Economic and Political Weekly*, 19 March, Vol. XXIX, no. 12.

[14] Nirmal Chandra, *The Retarded Economies: Foreign Domination and Class Relations in India and Other Emerging Nations* (Bombay: Oxford University Press, 1988).

[15] Amiya Kumar Bagchi, *Public Intervention and Industrial Restructuring in China, India and the Republic of Korea* (International Labour Office, New Delhi, 1986), and 'From a Fractured Compromise to a Democratic Consensus? Planning and Political Economy in Post-Colonial India', in *Economic and Political Weekly*, (Annual Number, 1993).

STATE AUTHORITARIANISM AND ECONOMIC LIBERALIZATION

It is obvious from all this that the more critical political economy question relates not merely to why particular macro-economic strategies have been adopted by the Indian government, but rather why the actual workings of the strategy were so much at variance with the planned processes and desired results. In the post-Independence period, three major factors contributed to the disparity between the stated objectives of government economic policies and the observed outcomes.

First of all, the official strategy was predicated on no major institutional change—such as land reforms or other types of asset or income redistribution that were important pre-conditions for sustained growth, for instance, in the more successful Asian countries. The absence of such change, given the prevailing inequalities in income distribution as well as unequal access to social and political power, meant that the base for economic growth and industrialization continued to be a relatively narrow one, and that the gains from this limited growth were also appropriated to a disproportionate extent by a relatively small segment of the population.

This was especially important because of the nature of those dominant classes which were the beneficiaries of the growth process. In the rural areas, the landed proprietors and rich farmers who largely garnered whatever gains emanated from development, and in particular from the 'Green Revolution', were typically concerned with maximizing short-term gains. This meant that in some contexts trading and moneylending became more attractive and significant as sources of rural surplus appropriation. Further, where agriculture remained or became the primary source of profit and rent, unsustainable patterns of cultivation became widespread. This reflected the greater commercialization of agricultural production, the more intensive use of monetized inputs, and the concentration of crop expansion efforts into 'Green Revolution' techniques involving reliance on a package of high-yielding standardized seeds, chemical fertilizer and pesticides and assured water supply through irrigation. The problems of diminishing returns and rising per unit costs of cultivation that plague large parts of Indian farming today, as well as the widespread degradation of land, water and forest resources, can be associated with this general tendency.

In industry, the dominant business class was one in which the spirit of independent and autonomous entrepreneurship was not fully developed. The very history of the formation of the industrial bourgeoisie from the colonial period onwards determined this deficiency: dependent upon the nationalist state for providing both infrastructure and large heavy investments and protection, and upon international capital for technology, it presumed state assistance for its own expansion and had a contradictory relationship with international capital. Thus industrial investment was typically directed into 'safe' areas which either met demands generated by the public sector through its own investment and expenditure, or produced consumer goods largely for the better off sections, in a protected domestic environment; and both more efficient production of mass consumer goods and export markets were relatively neglected. The other politically significant category of urban middle classes, which grew in number throughout the post-independence period, was also notable for its direct or indirect dependence upon state expenditure both for its existence and for its sources of income.

The nature of these dominant classes gave a greater force to the third factor that operated in determining the lopsided pattern of development—the sheer inability of the state to restrain the acquisitive tendencies of these richer groups. Of course the interaction between state and society is a complex process and cannot be captured by any simple unidimensional description, but it is clear that this factor was at the heart of many of the imbalances and distortions that emerged over time in the economy. The inability to control the acquisitiveness and aggrandizement of a (shifting) minority in the society had several manifestations and results. In a mixed economy with the private sector investment and production decisions determined by the unequal distribution of purchasing power, it meant that government allocations were often out of line with flows generated by private agents. This made the planning process more difficult to implement according to intention, and also increasingly irrelevant as private sector allocations actually determined the course of the economy. The substantial growth of the parallel or 'black' economy, which has been variously estimated at between one-fifth and one-third the value of recorded national income, was a further indication of this general tendency.

The incapacity of the government to tax the rich meant not only that direct taxes as a proportion of total income decreased continuously over the entire period, but also that taxes themselves declined in importance as sources of government income. From the mid-seventies onwards, state expenditures also became increasingly oriented towards subsidies to favoured groups (whether in industry or agriculture) and to providing largely middle class employment in the government and public sector.[16] The combination of constrained taxation and increased expenditure, particularly in the eighties, implied growing fiscal problems of the state and culminated in the fiscal crises of recent times. It is important to remember that the fiscal profligacy of the eighties was not simply a sign of macro-economic mismanagement; more significantly, it reflected the longer term tendencies of political economy within the system. Finally, the proclivity to private enrichment at social expense permeated the ranks of bureaucratic functionaries as well, and made corruption a systemic feature which further added to inefficiencies.

This perspective allows us to analyse the shifts in government policy as reflecting the interaction between state and political, economic and social processes. The recent trend towards 'liberalization', just as much as the earlier explicitly 'dirigiste' and protectionist strategy, primarily serves the interests of dominant groups within the society. In a sense the shift can be dated from the early or mid-eighties, although pressures for the change were evident even within government for as much as a decade earlier. The recent shifts represent not so much a change in policy as an intensification of the earlier tendency, although they have been designated as part of an economic 'reform' process that was required precisely because of the crisis at the end of the decade of the eighties.

One important social change which arguably has been influential in causing pressures for a shift in macro-economic strategy is the growing globalization of Indian society. The 'NRI phenomenon', by means of which a qualitatively significant number of people from the Indian elites and middle classes actually became resident abroad, contributed in no small measure to the consumerist demands which fuelled the drive for import liberalization and other forms of opening up of the economy. The political and economic importance of Non Resident Indians stems not only from the fact that they are viewed as potentially important sources of capital inflow, but also because of their close links with (and in some instances, the fact that they are virtually indistinguishable from) politically

---

[16] While such public sector employment generation was primarily directed towards middle class white collar workers, it also had some 'trickle-down' effect on less privileged groups. Thus the declines in employment rates noted in both rural and urban areas observed over the 1980s has been found to be strongly related to the role of government as employment generator. See Abhijit Sen and Jayati Ghosh, *Trends in Rural Employment and the Poverty-Employment Linkage*, ILO-ARTEP Working Paper (New Delhi, 1993).

dominant groups within the domestic society. In addition, in the very recent past, the media revolution and the growing importance of television which have imparted a significant impetus to the international demonstration effect, have added to liberalizing and consumerist demands.

The consequences of these tendencies in terms of overall economic growth and development indicators have already been described above. But there are further implications which have a bearing on the material conditions and social and political functioning of citizens. The first important point in this regard relates to the changed nature of government interaction with the economy and polity. Contrary to the standard representations of the process of 'economic liberalization', the recent transformations in economic strategy do not really represent a 'withdrawal of the state' in the economic arena in India, but rather a transformation of the character of the association. Government and bureaucracy are still critical in economic functioning, whether explicitly or implicitly, and this is in a context in which economic and financial powers are being further centralised, both vis-à-vis the state governments and within the various agencies of the central government. In turn, this means that the 'rent-seeking' activities which are often seen as the negative result of government intervention are equally, if not more, significant in this context when the range of active government involvement is supposedly declining, as in privatization of state assets. This reflects a political economy wherein not only is the primary economic role of the state that of protecting private property, but the state itself is seen to be effectively the private property of the elite, albeit contested and in need of periodic popular legitimization.

The centralized, centralizing and increasingly authoritarian state is in fact a necessary requirement for this type of liberalizing structural adjustment, as experience around the world makes evident. Interestingly, this greater degree of centralization and reduced devolution of power to people at more local levels, is part of an overall process in which the state is simultaneously weaker institutionally and the civil society is more cynical even about the state's basic functions regarding law and order and protection of the minimum rights of citizens. In such a setting, the proclivity of the state is essentially to seek forms of external legitimization, whether through the approbation of foreign financiers or the perceived discipline of international markets.

The lack of genuine popular internal legitimization for the process of structural change reflects an essential aspect of such change—the substantially increased income inequalities associated with these policies and the processes they unleash. Commercialization and the greater play of market forces typically operate to increase economic inequalities, and the reduction of 'welfare' activities of the developmental state which could, to some extent, have mitigated the harsher aspects of such a process are inhibited by the stabilization and structural adjustment which are part of this paradigm. Thus, even the so-called 'success stories' of this overall strategy are those where a recovery has finally been achieved at far more unequal distributions of assets and income than prevailed earlier, while elsewhere the strategy has involved greater inequality at stagnant or lower levels of per capita income. This tends to reinforce the natural political-economic tendencies in a country like India whereby the more privileged groups seek to perpetuate and increase their control over the limited resources and channels of income generation in the economy.

The growing inequality that is already becoming evident in India is reflected not so much in the narrowing of the category of the 'rich' or upper-income groups; indeed, these may possibly increase in absolute numbers due to the proliferation of service sector and other white collar activities that tend to expand in such periods. Of course, there is a concomitant centralization of private resources as much as public, and this centralization also involves the greater access and control of non-nationals and non-residents. However, the more important aspect is that of the effective economic disenfranchisement of important groups of people—sometimes those occupying whole physical spaces in rural areas, or urban slum dwellers who constitute both the reserve army of labour for industrialization and the most fertile source of labour supply for extra-legal activities. Within economic classes, particular categories are more disadvantaged, in particular women who may become even more marginal in terms of market economies even though their role in material production and reproduction obviously remains crucial. Related to this is the declining access of poorer groups to public goods and services as well as public-generated employment such as rural employment schemes, which not only reduce their real material living standards but also further reduce their bargaining power vis-à-vis employers and richer groups generally.

These simultaneous trends of greater centralization and greater income inequality have contributed significantly to the various regional, separatist and fissiparous tendencies that have become so prominent a part of the Indian society and polity. While it would be crude economic determinism to suggest that the prime motive force behind such tendencies is economic, there is no doubt that economic processes, and in particular the patterns of public and private centralization noted above, have played an important role in creating frustration and encouraging divisive forces. The lack of any genuine devolution of power from the central government to the states and from the states to locally elected and accountable authorities has been one source of frustration; the very spread of media and the advertising/distribution of large (often multinational) companies in a situation where access remains restricted is another notable source.

Finally, another consequence of the patterns identified earlier is the general breakdown of the rule of law that has become characteristic of economic (and also of much social and political) functioning. This is not a recent change so much as the culmination of a process that has been at work for nearly half a century, since a prominent feature of the Indian government was its inability to impose the acceptance of rules necessary for efficient capitalism rather than promote short-term private enrichment. The extent and spread of government regulations and controls had spawned a huge parallel economy which ultimately reflected the state's powerlessness rather than its actual reach. The current government strategy is one of regularizing such incomes and bringing them under the 'white' economy simply by doing away with the regulation or providing incentives for declaring such incomes (rather than punishments for not declaring them). This has the effect of actually giving official sanctity and recognition to this parallel 'black' economy, allowing lawlessness to become a regular feature which pervades all aspects of civil society and allowing everything, including the fundamental rights of citizens, to become marketable and negotiable. The dramatic increase in public cynicism about and mistrust of those institutions which are essential for a healthy democracy and for a smoothly functioning democracy can be traced to this process.

While this sounds extremely pessimistic and gloomy, it need not be so. Indeed, it has been argued that the strengths of the Indian economy and polity come from the same source as its weaknesses—in the very vastness and diversity of its population and geographical spread, which restrains both absolutist tendencies and extreme strategies, and makes generalizations misleading. Further, there is no doubt that there have been major changes in public consciousness and in awareness of rights and duties amongst the people as a whole, largely stemming from the electoral process and the nature of political democracy in independent India. And equally, there is no doubt about the tremendous potential for rapid economic development and human creativity which exists in the country. It is possible that national and international configurations can change in such a way that this potential can be realized, in the context of a more decentralized and democratic state which is geared to providing infrastructure and basic needs of the people. Such a configuration can result, in turn, from the very political and economic processes that have been outlined above.

8

The State Against Society: The Great Divide in Indian Social Science Discourse*

Pranab Bardhan

Readers of the Indian economic development literature have long been familiar with the contrary views on the role of the state. These have, of course, been duly reflected in the continuous policy debates in India, on issues of trade and industrial policy, on nationalization and the priority of public investment, and the size of the public sector, right from the early days of planning, when, after the death of Patel, the 'leftists' in the Congress Party under the leadership of Nehru gradually emerged victorious in formulating the development strategy, and these debates have continued down to the dramatic announcements of 'liberalization' first in the early days of his grandson's rule and again more recently since 1991–2. But in this paper we shall deal with a more fundamental attack on the attempted developmental role of the nation-state in India, that has come in recent years from a diverse group of writers, mostly social historians, cultural anthropologists and political sociologists.[1] They have questioned the agenda-setting presumptions and the legitimizing myths of state-directed development led by a 'rational', 'modern' elite. The development economists, preoccupied with the much narrower debates on liberalization, have by and large failed to address the serious issues

---

* I have had helpful discussion on the theme of the paper with Dipesh Chakrabarty, Partha Chatterjee, Sudipta Kaviraj, Vijay Joshi and James Scott.

[1] For a sample of their writings, see P. Chatterjee, *National Thought and the Colonial World: A Derivative Discourse?* (London: Zed Books, 1986); A Nandy, 'The Political Culture of the Indian State', *Daedalus*, (Fall, 1989); R. Kothari, *The State against Democracy: In Search of Humane Governance* (New Delhi: Ajanta Publications, 1988); R. Guha (ed.), *Subaltern Studies: Writings on South Asian History and Society*, Vols. 1–5 (Delhi: Oxford University Press, 1982–8).

raised by this group of writers, whom, in the absence of a better unifying name, I shall call the *anarcho-communitarians*.

Let us start by tracing some steps back in history on the tortuous relationship between the state and society in India. Pre-colonial India never had a strong civil society in the European sense of a dense network of social structures. But recent evidence has rendered largely untenable the description in colonial sociology of an Asiatic society with an Oriental despotic state ruling the roost over inert self-sufficient timeless village communities organized on unchanging principles of caste and *jajmani*. This Orientalist caricature particularly ignores not merely a high degree of mobility in large sections of the peasantry but also a whole set of vibrant community institutions (temple sects, lineage groups, caste clusters, assemblies of landholders or local headmen, mercantile and other organizations of a vigorous exchange economy, etc.) which served complex social, economic and political functions in medieval India and enjoyed a high degree of autonomy with their own claim to resources and their own system of rights.[2] The imperial state had a great deal of ceremonial eminence, but its systems of bureaucracy were weakly articulated and difficult to control, and it had limited powers of interfering with the social groups' internal organization or their structure of claims and obligations. To use the metaphor of Kaviraj, the state occupied only a kind of high ground in the middle of 'a circle of circles', each circle formed by a relatively unenumerated, multilayered, active, and rather fluid community.[3]

From the seventeenth century onward, however, the pressure from the military-fiscal state to tighten the loose tributary arrangements and to extend its extractive revenue and monopoly rights increased. The process of breaking down the authority of community institutions and stripping them of their economic and political functions culminated under the colonial administration. Washbrook (1988) suggests, with obvious irony, that more than anytime before in Indian history, the Oriental despotic state really came into existence in the middle of the nineteenth century under the British, claiming rights to all resources and

---

[2] For a useful survey, on which I have drawn, of the new literature see D. Washbrook 'Progress and Problems: South Asian, Economic and Social History (1720 to 1860)', *Modern Asian Studies*, 1988. Unlike the Cambridge historians, I am, however, somewhat hesitant in describing the exchange or mercantile economy as capitalist.

[3] S. Kaviraj, 'On State, Society and Discourse in India', mimeograph (1989).

delegitimizing all counter-claims from society to authority against it: the colonial state distorted an Indian ('Sultanist') tradition to suit its own pre-emptive purpose.[4]

In 1947 the national government inherited (and chose to retain) this apparatus of the colonial state largely unaltered, including that of the police, army, judiciary, legal system as well as the much vaunted civil service (which, at least at the points of its everyday encounter with the natives, was neither particularly service-oriented nor very 'civil'). It was especially this bureaucracy that was harnessed by the new leadership to the tasks of promoting economic development. The anarcho-communitarian writers claim that a small modernist elite arrogated to itself the title to speak on behalf of the society in general and deliberately went about a state-directed programme of heavy industrialization and modernization, with a grandiose vision of progress borrowed from the Western ideas of Enlightenment and the nation-state, a vision unshared by the people at large and ungrounded in the vernacular everyday discourse of the local communities in the sprawling villages and small towns of India. In this view, the elite's 'discovery of India' was in some sense really an 'invention', their 'universalistic' principle of development and nation-building was essentially a particular project for fostering the 'modern' sector and the metropolitan culture catering largely to themselves. In this process they have allowed the nation-state to appropriate the social space, to stifle, distort, and marginalize the diverse local solidarities and traditions, to organize spectacular technological or military extravaganzas to boost national confidence, and preside over mindless gigantic development programmes uprooting communities and disrupting the ecological balance. Among many such writers and activists, 'development' has almost become a dirty word (unbeknown to most development economists).

But then, it could be asked, weren't the masses actively involved in the vast popular mobilizations of the freedom movement, where national development was clearly a leading part of the agenda, and poverty and underdevelopment constituted a major nationalist indictment of the colonial rule? To this one may say that first of all, Gandhiji (I shall keep referring to Mohandas Gandhi in this name, in order to avoid unnec-essary confusion with the other Gandhis in more recent Indian politics) who provided the rhetoric as well as the leadership in those mobilizations,

---

[4] Washbrook, 'Progress and Problems'.

trying his utmost in bridging the ideological gulf between the elite and the masses, had a drastically different view about industrialization and centralized state power[5] compared to that of the leaders of the state around the time of Independence (not just Nehru, but also Patel and Ambedkar). The marginalization of Gandhian ideas (as opposed to their rhetorical shell), particularly on the nature of the state and the development process, in the reinterpretation of the national mandate in post-Independence India has been an important political phenomenon.[6] Secondly, even during the freedom movement the nationalist leaders mobilized the people in a common cause against the British, but did not succeed in a hegemonic reconstitution of their beliefs or consciousness. As the many examples cited in the recent writings on 'subaltern' Indian

[5] In an interview with Francis Hickman in September 1940 Gandhiji says:

'Pandit Nehru wants industrialization because he thinks that, if it is socialized, it would be free from the evils of capitalism. My own view is that evils are inherent in industrialism, and no amount of socialization can eradicate them.'

In a letter to Rajkumari Amrit Kaur in June 1939 he writes about the work of the National Planning Committee:

'The whole of Jawaharlal's planning is a waste of effort.'

On 'enlightened anarchy' Gandhiji writes in January 1939 in *Sarvodaya*:

The power to control national life through national representatives is called political power. Representatives will become unnecessary if national life becomes so perfect as to be self-controlled. It will then be a state of enlightened anarchy in which each person will become his own ruler. He will conduct himself in such a way that his behaviour will not hamper the well-being of his neighbours. In an ideal State there will be no political institution and therefore no political power.

[6] Chatterjee (1986) draws attention to an interesting passage in Nehru's *Autobiography*, published in 1936:

Even some of Gandhiji's phrases sometimes jarred upon me—thus his frequent reference to *Rama Raj* as a golden age which was to return. But I was powerless to intervene, and I consoled myself with the thought that Gandhiji used the words because they were well known and understood by the masses. He had an amazing knack of reaching the heart of the people ...

He was a very difficult person to understand, sometimes his language was almost incomprehensible to an average modern. But we felt that we knew him well enough to realize he was a great and unique man and a glorious leader, and having put our faith in him we gave him an almost blank cheque, for the time being at least. Often we discussed his fads and peculiarities among ourselves and said, half-humorously, that *when Swaraj came these fads must not be encouraged*. (Italics mine).

history suggest, the masses usually put their own interpretations on the aims of the movement and proceeded to act them out, often in complete contradiction with the stated goals and methods of the nationalist leadership.

But again, haven't the goals of national development of the post-Independence state been repeatedly ratified by a democratic electorate? In response one can say that the first few elections, based as they were on pre-existing local structures of power, political 'bosses' and captive 'vote-banks', were not representative enough. Over the last two decades or so the manufactured consensus has come apart as the masses became more articulate, and the increasing self-affirmation of hitherto marginalized groups and communities has put the homogenizing centralizing goals of the nation-state under severe strain.

II

Even this encapsulated description of some commonalities in the anarcho-communitarians' position should make it clear that their anti-statism is radically different from that of the liberal neo-classical economists. Not merely are the former opposed to the latter's nationalist-modernist discourse and their preoccupation with economic efficiency based on supposedly universalistic postulates of human behavior in total insensitivity to localized contexts of cultural legitimation process, but they also deeply suspect the latters' frequent call for depoliticization of development policy. They look upon such attempts at sanitization of economic policy from the unclean processes of politics as part of the elite's strategy of keeping the masses at bay and subverting processes of political accountability. They are also usually against the liberal prescriptions of privatization, if it involves the onslaught of large-scale capitalism against small producers and local communities.

The great divide in the Indian social science discourse today is on the fundamental issues relating to a strong nation-state and its projects of modernization and industrialization. On this question the traditional Left-Right distinction is largely irrelevant, and there are strange bedfel-lows, their continuing differences on other issues notwithstanding.[7] On

---

[7] Even on the issue under discussion there are, of course, clearly divergent views. For example, among anarcho-communitarians one can distinguish the post-modernists from the anti-modernists, or the activists with clear positive goals from those who do not proceed beyond negative critiques of modernity. In this paper I am concentrating on the intersection of these sets.

one side of this divide are the anarcho-communitarians, which include, among others, Gandhian anarchists, anti-industrial 'small-is-beautiful' 'back-to-village' utopians, cultural-relativist anthropologists, intellectuals involved in grassroots movements for preservation of the environment and tribal autonomy as well as the radical historians of 'subalternity' (drawing upon Gramsci, Foucault and Habermas) deconstructing nationalist historiography. On the other side are the usually positivist economists (neo-classical liberals in the uncomfortable company of state socialists), die-hard Stalinists and leftover Fabians, mandarin administrators and technocrats, ideologues of the military-industrial complex, nationalist anti-imperialist historians, as well as the right-wing intellectuals espousing a combination of *Hindutva* and Chanakyaian statecraft. In some sense this intellectual divide was in part already inherent in the substantive differences in the vision of Independent India between Gandhiji and Nehru during the freedom movement, but these differences had been patched up from time to time for the sake of short-run political expediency, lost in the overwhelming turmoil of the decade in which India won Independence and overshadowed by the personal chemistry between the two leaders (with Gandhiji ultimately anointing Nehru as his chosen successor). But the denouement of the particular strategy of development followed in the first few decades after Independence has now reopened this deep division of discourse with new fissures arising from the accumulated tension in newly activated groups or the new flashpoints in society. (In recent years this has been reflected, for example, in the ideological gulf between the followers of Nehru and those of Lohia, with the latters' trenchant critique of the modernizing elite and the populist mobilization of backward caste groups).

I find in the anarcho-communitarian critique of modernization much that is persuasive and valuable. In particular, it highlights the arrogant ignorance on the part of development planners of the gaping ideological chasm that separates them from the masses for whom (and on whose behalf) they plan. State-directed technocratic development projects which do not involve the people but simply treat them as objects of the development process often end up primarily as conduits of largesse for elite groups—middlemen, contractors, officials, politicians and favoured special interest groups—and very little reaches the intended beneficiaries. Even when a significant amount reaches the latter, the benefits are sometimes of the wrong kind, inappropriate technologically and environmentally, unsustainable, corrosive of local institutions of community bonding and self-help, and always leaving untapped the large reservoir of local potential, ingenuity and information. On these and other grounds the case for decentralized autonomous development is, of course, very strong. But I also see several problems and glaring inadequacies with the anarcho-communitarian case.

III

First, the all-pervasiveness of the state is not all the modernizing elite's doing. The community institutions have been in decay for quite some time, at least partly out of internal reasons. The high degree of social inequality and (caste, class or gender based) oppression within the local communities[8] made their continuous consolidation difficult, particularly as the expansion of the market-nexus increased opportunities for 'exit' and the democratic process slowly increased those for 'voice'. With the decline of hierarchical authority and with the moral and political environment of age-old deference to community norms changing, the local overlords reneged on some of their traditional patronage functions and appeals to supra-local authorities for conflict resolution, arbitration and protection became more common. The state's penetration was thus partly in response to invitation to fill an institutional vacuum. Popular demands, for example, of land reform legislation (for the abolition of revenue intermediaries, for rent control and security of tenure), however tardy and shallow it may have been in implementation, have brought in the state in the remotest corners of village society, eroding in the process the traditional functions of local landlords and institutions in maintenance of irrigation works and *taccavi* loans, while they are not quite being replaced by the local arm of what is after all an alien, large, and often corrupt bureaucracy.

At the lower rungs of the bureaucracy the petty officials and guardians of law and order, of course, interpret the modernizing nation-state's writ in their own way and get involved in local community or class conflicts as partisans. The top leadership of the state has limited control or effective authority over their actual operations. The local people on their part approach their encounters with the state at this level with appropriate caution but total malfeasance. Since it belongs outside their moral community, it is just an opportunity to milk the state cow; one has only to be wary that the cow sometimes kicks nasty. The disproportionate benefits, of course, go to those who have the resources, connections and

---

[8] Tolerance of local oppression in communities or families in the name of 'cultural relativism' is no less offensive than tolerance of state violence in the name of some 'universalistic' principle of modernist rationality or nation-building.

dexterity to manipulate the milking process. Faced with such acute agency problems in the lower bureaucracy and with the marauding instincts of the local people (or at least their indirect power of quiet sabotage and 'everyday forms of resistance'), the state in some sense is quite powerless, even though it is more powerful than any of the past imperial states in Indian history in terms of its general command over economic and military resources, technology and information networks, and even though it occasionally does lash out with a great deal of clumsy violence.

At the local community level there is not just an institutional vacuum, there is a certain hollowness or formlessness at the core of the cultural tradition that binds it. Some of the supposedly timeless traditional ideas turn out to be of quite recent origin; as in many other societies there is a great deal of 'invention of traditions' and of 'imagined communities' as Thapar has noted in some of the communal-religious formations.[9] Community identities have always been particularly fluid in India; caste identity, for example, has changed its meaning quite a few times in the recent past. This fluidity gives considerable scope for political entrepreneurs to reshape the boundary and the concerns of the identity of a community. In recent years the processes of modernization and participatory politics and the access to media and other technological devices have actually *increased* the mobilization potential and sharpened the self-image of splinter ethnic groups and sub-national identities, quite contrary to the homogenizing efforts and centripetal urges of the modernizing elite.

Some of the anarcho-communitarians interpret the rising tempo of ethnic and communal unrest as an indicator of the diminishing hold of the modernist vision. But it may have more to do with another kind of institutional vacuum, more a weakening of the medium than of the message itself. We refer here particularly to the erosion over the last couple of decades of the political party as a mediating institution between the state and society. With the decline of the 'Congress system', widely noted by political scientists, the old structures and methods of compromise and accommodation are in great disarray. With the organizational channels of demand articulation and conflict resolution largely clogged, societal tensions spill over into the streets with increasing frequency in agitational politics, anomic violence and intransigent extremism. Many political scientists have, of course, accused the state elite, particularly

[9] R. Thapar, 'Communal-Religious Formations in India', *Modern Asian Studies* (1989).

under Indira Gandhi and her sons, of wrecking the impressive political machine of the Congress Party that they inherited from their less short-sighted predecessors. Without minimizing their role in the deinstitutionalization and personalization of political power, one can, to be fair, point out that the inevitable logic of an open pluralist polity, with its ever-widening circle of democratic awareness and raised aspirations, has generated, in the prevailing politics of scarcity, pressures of an intensity not quite experienced in the earlier regimes. The demand overload that has short-circuited the Congress system is thus partly a consequence, possibly unforeseen, of the democratic project initiated by the modernizing elite. The masses seem to have taken to this Western Enlightenment-inspired project[10] with a great deal of energy and assertiveness, and in a way the tensions and frustrations in the political arena seem to be partly generated by the increasing rather than diminishing, hold of at least this part of the modernist vision.

Decentralized development is, of course, a worthy goal. But the easy enthusiasm for this cause is not usually matched by an appreciation of the intricate questions it leaves unanswered. First, in situations of severe social and economic inequality if the poor and the underprivileged are not organized, the local bullies and the powerful people find it easy to capture the local institutions and the devolution of authority to the local level really works out to their advantage. Appeals to supra-local political authorities by the subalterns in such situations for protection and relief are not uncommon.[11] Decentralized development is, for example, beginning to work in West Bengal villages, where the poor are to some extent organized by a relatively disciplined centralized party, but in the adjoining state of Bihar, without such organization, decentralization may leave the poor grievously exposed to the mercies of the local overlords and thugs.

Second, local groups in rural areas often find it difficult to bear the brunt of locally covariate risks, and intervention by outside agencies becomes frequently necessary. For example, local development on the

---

[10] Gandhiji, it should be remembered, did not have much faith in the institutions of representative government. The Parliament, for example, he calls in his *Hind Swaraj*, 'a sterile woman and a prostitute'.

[11] Partha Chatterjee has pointed out to me that even in such cases of invited state intervention, the mechanism as well as the principle of state control is quite different in the modern state compared with, say, the case of traditional kings. The centralization of the knowledge system and of the legal, accounting, and enumerative mechanisms make the modern intervention qualitatively different.

basis of locally raised resources and locally mobilized credit often becomes unviable because in a bad crop year everyone is badly off, and in the absence of a territorially diversified portfolio the local self-help credit institutions are likely to go bankrupt.

Third, if one looks at the historical processes of development in the world one always finds a certain trade-off between the informational efficiency and community bonding effects of small-scale localized development and the economies of large-scale production and specialization. The division of labour and specialization are severely limited by the extent of market defined by the personalized exchange process of a small community. One may not believe in a model of capital-intensive 'energy-guzzling' environment-poisoning industrialization, but at the same time one cannot deny that under the continued demographic pressure (brought about largely by the mortality-reducing effects of 'modern' medicine) on land, the escape from extremely low labour productivity and technological stagnation has to involve, after a point, expansion of the scale and complexity of production and exchange.[12] As the economy becomes more complex and the network of interdependence widens far beyond the domain of face-to-face local communities, the state necessarily gets involved in devising coordinating principles and institutional structures aimed at reducing the uncertainty of social impersonal interaction. With state involvement and the exigencies of large-scale organization, there come the inevitable impersonal bureaucracy often insensitive to the nuances of local needs, the law enforcement authority arbitrary in its exercise of the state monopoly of violence and the delegation of planning to a specialized technocracy of experts impervious to the contextual contents of popular consciousness and demands. A part of all this is, of course, avoidable and one cannot exaggerate the importance of exploring the extent of feasible decentralization and of devolution of power to the level of locally shared values and goals. But one may not be able to wish away some of the inevitable organizational costs of a more complex economy and society, although one needs to do more about reducing the unequal incidence of these costs on the weaker sections of the population. Similarly, one cannot wish away some of the externalities of the development process which the decentralized authority of local communities are unable and sometimes

[12] It is somewhat ironical to find some of the protagonists of decentralized development being vocal in demanding centralized state protection of small-scale enterprises when they are threatened by market competition from the large units.

even unwilling to cope with and state coordination again becomes necessary. One such example of externality and inadequacy of local control mechanisms is in the case of upstream deforestation causing flooding and soil erosion in the downstream communities. Another case is when the local community is not very sensitive to larger environmentalist concerns, or when issues of local livelihood compete with preservationist issues (as in the case, discussed by Herring of the Silent Valley hydro-electric project in South India, when the elitist state had to intervene to protect a rain forest in the face of local democratic pressures in favour of despoliation.[13] The usual cases of the centralized state in alliance with large commercial interests threatening local conservation and livelihoods should not blind us to these alternative possibilities.

Fourth, a complex economy necessarily becomes more involved in an interdependent international network of trade, investment and transactions in technology. In dealing with today's world of giant transnational companies and state involvement in predatory trade and technology policies in other countries, a weak or loosely functioning state is at a considerable bargaining disadvantage.

Autonomous local development also leads to a great deal of regional inequality, particularly because of differences in prior resource endowments and institutions. During the period of decentralized rural development under local communes in China (with serious restrictions on inter-area migration), regional inequality in incomes was quite high, and cases of poor villages trying, usually in vain, to join a more prosperous neighbouring commune was not uncommon. In India, a part of the economic demands in the Punjab agitations for autonomy against the Central government have been motivated by an unmistakable reluctance to share that region's relative prosperity with poorer regions elsewhere. In a large diverse multinational country like India, a very weak centre may work to the advantage of the more powerful regions and dominant communities and against the weaker regions and groups, even if we dismiss as unlikely the more extreme dangers of pre-Revolution Chinese-style warlordism or the African-style incessant inter-tribal warfare.

In this context it is interesting to note how, sometimes, intensely parochial and traditional cultural communities look to the modernizing elite at the centre as a protector and arbiter against other parochial cultural communities in the country. For example, over the years in Indian politics indigenous groups and (usually anti-Brahmin) cultural

[13] See R .J. Herring, 'Rethinking the Commons', unpublished, 1989.

solidarities in the South have often supported and looked up to the political leadership at the centre of the members of a highly westernized (North Indian Brahmin) family—the Nehru 'dynasty'—even when the latter lost support with the traditional communities in the Hindi heartland (or the 'cow-belt' in Indian journalist parlance). The extraordinary political durability of this family over several decades is a testimony to the usefulness of a westernized elite as a buffer amidst the clashing communities of regional chauvinism.

Finally, while the anarcho-communitarians' emphasis on humane people-sensitive cultural solidarity-sustaining development, decentralization of power and strengthening of popular resistance and involvement is widely shared, it is not always easy to go along with their moral postulates of human behaviour and the essential presumption of the ideal of the Gandhian man, self-controlled and of limited needs. The development process in this view is suspect since it removes the traditional checks on competition, individualism and consumerism. Not merely does this view underplay the elements of calculated pragmatism of peasants in their participation in the local community, there is also an underlying fear of the fragility of individual resistance to the lure of expanding wants and the competitive striving for their gratification. The young are particularly vulnerable to these temptations, as the threatened gerontocracy in control of traditional institutions are quick to point out. There is also a trace of patronizing elitism in questioning the projects of development that will supposedly spoil the habits and the moral fibre of the lower classes. This is not to deny the usefulness of campaigns to increase the popular awareness of the long-run costs, both economic and cultural, of some of the grandiose modernization projects the state undertakes in the name of the people.

Name Index

Subject Index